Contemporary Turkish
Foreign Policy

Contemporary Turkish Foreign Policy

Yasemin Çelik

PRAEGER

Westport, Connecticut
London

Library of Congress Cataloging-in-Publication Data

Çelik, Yasemin.
    Contemporary Turkish foreign policy / Yasemin Çelik.
        p.   cm.
    Includes bibliographical references (p.   ) and index.
    ISBN 0–275–96590–2 (alk. paper)
    1. Turkey—Foreign relations—1980–   I. Title.
DR477.C44   1999
327.561'009'049—dc21   99–21270

British Library Cataloguing in Publication Data is available.

Library of Congress Catalog Card Number: 99–21270
ISBN: 0–275–96590–2

First published in 1999

Praeger Publishers, 88 Post Road West, Westport, CT 06881
An imprint of Greenwood Publishing Group, Inc.
www.praeger.com

Printed in the United States of America

The paper used in this book complies with the
Permanent Paper Standard issued by the National
Information Standards Organization (Z39.48–1984).

10 9 8 7 6 5 4 3 2 1

For Douglas

Contents

Preface

This book was conceived at a time of great changes in the structure of the international system. As the cold war that had dominated world affairs for nearly fifty years ended, questions regarding how these tremendous alterations would affect individual countries rose to the forefront of international relations theory. Motivated by the desire to uncover such major, systematic changes in Turkey, especially in Turkish foreign policy, I embarked on this research endeavor. Throughout my journey, I learned to question commonly held views (including mine) and be prepared for findings that were unexpected. Despite a number of challenges along the way, producing *Contemporary Turkish Foreign Policy* has been infinitely rewarding.

This book would not have been possible without the invaluable advice and mentoring of Asher Arian and Howard Lentner who read many drafts and provided constructive criticism. I would also like to express my gratitude to W. Ofuatey-Kodjoe for his professional and personal guidance throughout the years. My thanks also go to my husband, Douglas Levine, for his relentless encouragement and devotion, and my parents, Aliye and Metin Çelik, for their continual support. This project was also supported in part by a grant from the Institute of Turkish Studies in Washington, D.C.

Introduction

Fundamental changes have taken place in the structure of the international system in the past decade. The disintegration of the Soviet Union brought to a close the era of bipolarity that had prevailed since the end of World War II. Consequently, the international system that had been defined by the hostile competition between the United States and the Soviet Union no longer exists. There is an intense debate in international relations theory regarding the type of international structure that is replacing bipolarity. While some scholars, such as John Mearsheimer, assert that the bipolar system is being replaced by a multipolar one, others, like Joseph Nye, argue that it is not yet clear what type of system is emerging.[1] Political scientists on opposing sides of this debate, however, agree that the significant changes in the international system have had tremendous repercussions for many countries, and that the transformation of the structure of the international system sheds a different light not only on international relations theory but also on foreign policy analysis. This book explores the contention that Turkish foreign policy has been greatly affected by the end of the cold war.

TURKISH FOREIGN POLICY DURING THE COLD WAR

In the aftermath of World War II and the formation of a bipolar international system, foreign policy decision-making in Turkey became largely defined by the role that Ankara played in the international system. The necessity of forging close ties with the West in order to protect national security became apparent for Turkey as early as 1945 when Joseph Stalin made demands for territorial concessions from Turkey. He asserted that the Soviet Union would not renew the Turkish-Soviet Treaty of Neutrality and Nonaggression of 1925 until Turkey surrendered the northeastern provinces of Kars and Ardahan and established joint control of the straits of Bosporus and Dardanelles with the Soviets. Although President Ismet Inönü declared that Turkey would not compromise its independence and territorial integrity by stating that it was "under no obligation to give up Turkish soil or Turkish rights to anyone," the Soviet demands led Turkish politicians to realize the seriousness of the threat emanating from their large and extremely powerful neighbor.[2] Still in the process of recovering from World War I and the War of Independence, Turkey did not have the means to deter this expansionist power that had advanced its ideological and physical penetration all the way to Berlin by the end of World War II. Turkish policymakers thus recognized that Turkey would only be able to avert Moscow's demands if it formed a close alliance with the only other superpower, the United States. Washington supported Ankara's efforts in resisting the Soviet claims, and with the Truman Doctrine of February 1947 it provided substantial amounts of financial and military assistance for this purpose. Ankara was convinced, however, that a bilateral relationship with Washington was not sufficient to protect its security; it needed to be included in a variety of Western institutions and be fully integrated into the Western alliance in order to prevent further encroachments from Moscow. As a result, its most important foreign policy goal in the late 1940s and early 1950s was gaining admission into the North Atlantic Treaty Organization (NATO). In order to prove its allegiance to the West (and facilitate its admission into this alliance), Ankara even contributed a brigade of 4,500 soldiers to the Allied coalition mission to protect the Republic of Korea from North Korea, which was being aided by the Soviets. This action prompted the United States to strengthen its support of Turkish membership in NATO and convince members with reservations about Turkish membership to lift their objections. Consequently, Turkey joined the organization when it signed the Protocol of Entry on February 18, 1952. In so doing, it set the stage for the foreign policy that would be in place for the next thirty-seven years.

Turkey's role in the alliance was rather well defined; it was to resist Soviet expansionism by serving as NATO's southern flank. In order to perform this role successfully, Turkey needed to maintain a strong military apparatus. As such, Turkey's most important foreign policy concern for the next four decades consisted of containing the Soviet threat. This single-minded foreign policy behavior was only interrupted twice: during the eruption of the first Cyprus crisis in 1963–1964 and the second, in 1973–1974. The first crisis broke out when Turkish leaders felt a pressing need to protect the Turkish Cypriot minority during the clashes that broke out with the Greek Cypriots in December 1963. The government decided to intervene physically in the island but operating under the assumption that the United States was its most important ally, Ankara informed Washington of its intentions. President Lyndon Johnson, however, responded in no uncertain terms that

"NATO allies have not had a chance to consider whether they have an obligation to protect Turkey against the Soviet Union if Turkey takes a step which results in Soviet intervention without the full consent and understanding of its NATO allies."[3] Turkey, in other words, would have to face the Soviets alone if its actions in Cyprus prompted Moscow's involvement in the conflict. The possibility of such a scenario prevented Turkish policymakers from intervening in Cyprus at this time but did not have the same effect ten years later. The second crisis occurred when the Cypriot national guard staged a coup d'état against the Cypriot president Archbishop Makarios III with the ultimate objective of forming a union with Greece. On this occasion, however, Ankara acted against the advice of the United States and deployed Turkish troops to occupy the northern part of the island in July 1974. This open defiance of American wishes led the U.S. Congress to impose an embargo on transfers of military equipment to Turkey.[4]

There were several reasons why Turkish foreign policy behavior strayed from its regular parameters during the Cyprus conflicts. The first crisis occurred at a time when the international environment was changing as a result of détente. As the hostilities between the superpowers somewhat abated during this time, Turkish policymakers felt more able to engage in foreign policy behavior that was independent from American interests. Meanwhile, the so-called Johnson letter led to the somewhat naive realization that the United States would not assist Turkey if its own security were not at stake. With this awareness, Ankara attempted to diversify Turkey's foreign policy relations. For example, Foreign Minister F. C. Erkin visited Moscow in October 1964 and announced, along with his Soviet counterpart, that the two countries had agreed to pursue good neighbor relations, respecting each other's sovereignty and territorial integrity while expanding trade and cultural exchanges.[5] In addition, Turkey became an associate member of the European Community in 1964 and established strong economic ties with member states. By the time that the second Cyprus crisis occurred, therefore, Ankara was reevaluating the United States's commitments to Turkey and attempting to pursue a more balanced foreign policy. Despite these brief shifts in foreign policy behavior, by the late 1970s, increased cold war hostilities (with the Soviet invasion of Afghanistan and the Iranian revolution) prompted Turkish foreign policy to be aligned once again with American interests. For most of the cold war period, therefore, Turkey remained staunchly Western in its foreign policy orientation.

Another major component of Turkish foreign policy that remained unwavering during the cold war period was the desire to stay out of the tumultuous politics of the Middle East. Once again, however, there was a brief period in which Turkish policymakers strayed from their established pattern. This occurred in the latter half of the 1950s when Turkey pursued an activist policy in the Middle East and aspired to a leadership position in the regional organizations of the Baghdad Pact and the succeeding Central Treaty Organization. During the rest of the cold war era, however, Turkey stayed out of the conflicts of the region.[6] It remained strictly neutral during the Iran-Iraq war and maintained diplomatic relations with both Israel and the Arab states. Turkey's foreign policy strategy of affiliation with the West and non-intervention in the regional politics of the Middle East was quite consistent throughout the cold war. In fact, the myth of Turkish foreign policy prior to 1989 was that Turkey's international commitments determined its economic policy as well as its foreign policy no matter which party or faction held office in government. Decision-making in Turkey had been defined by continuity and consensus: despite bitter partisan fights among politicians on domestic issues, there had been an implicit agreement that "international commitments extend beyond changes in party government or even constitutional regime."[7] Ferenc Vali, for example, said that "the fundamental goals of [Turkish] national policy, as determined under Atatürk, have not changed [and that] the official policy of the Turkish republic is frequently regarded as essentially unchanging, consistent, resolute, and popularly supported."[8] Similarly, Udo Steinbach asserted that, especially during the cold war, there were "few ruptures, emotional reactions, volte-faces in terms of changing alliances and military entanglements such as those that characterize the foreign policy of other states in the Middle East."[9] Agreeing with this nature of its foreign policy, the Turkish Ministry of Foreign Affairs states that:

Ever since its establishment in 1923, the Republic of Turkey has consistently pursued a foreign policy aimed at international peace based on the principle of "Peace at home and peace in the world," laid down by the Republic's founding father and first President, Mustafa Kemal Ataturk. The primary objectives of Turkish foreign policy have been to establish and maintain friendly and harmonious relations with all states, in particular with neighboring countries, to promote international cooperation in all fields, and participate actively in it; to resolve disputes through peaceful means, and to contribute to regional and global peace, stability, security and shared prosperity.[10]

TURKISH FOREIGN POLICY DURING THE POST–COLD WAR PERIOD

The continuity and consensus that characterized Turkish foreign policy were no longer its defining characteristics in the post–cold war period.

Rather, the foreign policy arena was dominated by uncertainty and disagreement among both politicians and the public regarding Turkey's foreign policy objectives as well as instruments. The end of the cold war, in other words, led to a search for a new "grand strategy."[11] Robert Art defines grand strategy as specifying the security and nonsecurity goals that a state should pursue and delineating how military power can serve those goals.[12] The changes in the international system opened up new opportunities and brought to the forefront new threats for Turkish foreign policy, making it necessary for Turkey to search for a new grand strategy that took these new parameters into account.

The end of the cold war has reduced threats to Turkey's national security and territorial integrity in such a way that, in the post–cold war era, Turkey's security environment was the safest it had been in the country's seventy-five-year history, mostly as a result of the collapse of the Soviet Union and the diminished threat from Russia.[13] The Russians, whom Turks feared for more than three hundred years, were no longer even Turkey's neighbors. The Russian Federation, the most powerful successor state of the former Soviet Union, was usually too immersed in its own political, economic, and security problems to pose a serious threat. In fact, despite some rivalry between Moscow and Ankara as to which one would wield greater influence in Central Asia and the Caucasus, Russia and Turkey grew to be close trading partners. The volume of trade between the two countries averaged $600 million per year during the cold war.[14] By 1995, however, Turkish exports to Russia had reached $1.2 billion and imports from Russia, $2 billion.[15] The Russian Federation had become Turkey's fourth largest trading partner (after Germany, the United States, and Italy). Both countries wanted to increase trade with each other further to achieve an annual volume of $15 billion by the year 2000.[16] In addition, Turkey developed relations with the other fourteen Soviet successor states. These ranged from very close bilateral ties to cooperation in multilateral settings to distant, and sometimes even hostile, relations. Even the most hostile of these relationships, however, did not pose the same level of threat to Turkish security that an antagonistic Soviet Union did for most of the cold war.

The ties Ankara developed with the three bordering Soviet successor states represent its different levels of involvement in the Commonwealth of Independent States. Turkey's relationship with Azerbaijan was perhaps its most important in the former Soviet republics because the two countries shared strong ethnic and linguistic ties. As a result, Ankara developed relations encompassing the cultural, diplomatic, military, and economic spheres. Scholarships were given to Azeri students, Turkish television stations broadcast to the region, and a small number of cadets even received military training in Turkey. Economic cooperation between the two countries was especially impressive with countless Turkish companies active in Azerbaijan's construction sector, a plethora of successful joint ventures, and the signing of agreements to transport Azeri oil through Turkey. Georgia, on the other hand, constituted a country with which Turkey formed a good relationship despite the lack of ethnic, religious, or linguistic similarities that existed with many of the other former Soviet republics. Once again, economic relations were strongest: Georgian purchases of goods bought privately in Turkey reached $15 million per year in the 1990s, Turkey exported electricity to Georgia, and both countries were members of the Black Sea Economic Cooperation zone (an organization to bring together the countries of the Black Sea region to expand economic relations, develop joint technical and scientific projects, monitor and control pollution, and encourage tourism). Meanwhile, relations with Armenia were among Turkey's most difficult in the region. The hostility with Armenia stemmed from the fact that the Armenians held Ankara responsible for the battles in 1915 during which, they claim, the Ottoman army carried out genocide on the Armenian population in eastern Turkey.[17] Despite historical animosities, however, Ankara and Yerevan succeeded in drafting a good-neighbor agreement as well as a protocol to initiate direct cross-border trade and to open a transnational highway. The conflict between Azerbaijan and Armenia in Nagorno-Karabakh and Turkey's subsequent ban on the transportation through Turkish territory of humanitarian and other goods bound for Armenia, however, strained relations between the two countries. In spite of such sporadic problems in Ankara's relations with the former Soviet republics, Turkey's northeastern border did not endanger Turkish security and territorial integrity in the same way that a consistently hostile, neighboring superpower did.

A bigger threat to security emanated from Turkey's traditionally unfriendly neighbors in the southeast: Iran, Iraq, and Syria. The danger from this area was also somewhat reduced in the post–cold war period, however, because Iraq and Syria were facing troubled economies and internal problems at this time. Iraq's military apparatus had been heavily damaged by the decade-long war with Iran and the subsequent Persian Gulf War, and its economy had been ravaged by the United Nations's sanctions imposed since 1991. Furthermore, both Iraq and Syria had lost the substantial amount of foreign aid they received from the Soviet Union. Although Iran and Turkey competed as to which could export its political and cultural system as a model for the former Soviet republics in Central Asia, they were not particularly hostile toward each other in their rivalry. In addition, except for Greece, Turkey's neighbors in Eastern Europe (such as Romania, Bulgaria, etc.) were no longer considered antagonistic after the East-West conflict no longer defined relations.

Despite these improvements in Turkey's security environment, it is important to note that not all threats to security had been lifted in the post–cold war era. Iran and Syria continued to interfere in Turkey by supporting (through financial contributions and military training) Islamist guerrillas and Kurdish separatist terrorists. A number of near-collisions with Greece exposed the fragility of the Aegean region's stability. In the spring of 1996, for example, the two countries nearly went to war in a heated debate as to who claimed sovereignty over a deserted, uninhabitable rock cluster in the Aegean Sea, and U.S. president Bill Clinton had to intervene in order to dissipate the situation. Furthermore, the conflict over Cyprus continued to present the potential for an international crisis because of the possibility that either the sporadic border skirmishes or the larger, unresolved issues would lead to something more threatening.

It is important to note that despite the decreased threats to security emanating from abroad, there was a considerable internal threat to Turkey's territorial integrity. The secessionist Kurdish Workers Party (*Partiya Karkaran Kurdistan*, PKK) had been waging a brutal terrorist war against the government since 1984 and the ongoing battles claimed more than ten thousand lives in the 1993–1995 period alone. The Kurdish insurgency aptly demonstrates the close link between the military and economic spheres in Turkish politics. The southeastern part of Turkey, in which Turkey's Kurdish population (who constitute about 10 percent of Turkey's sixty million people) was heavily concentrated, was the most underdeveloped part of the country. An extremely poor area, the southeast produced only 4 percent of the country's GDP and 2 percent of its industrial output.[18] The Turkish government was working to alleviate the Kurdish insurgency not only through military means but also by significantly increasing the level of economic development in the region. One proposed solution was the $32 billion Southeastern Anatolian Project (*Guneydogu Anadolu Projesi*, known by its Turkish acronym, GAP) that encompassed the building of twenty-two dams to generate electricity for industry, irrigate land for agriculture, and consequently, to bring badly needed services such as health care and education to the southeast. The reasoning behind GAP was that if the Kurdish inhabitants of the region gained social and economic benefits from the 3.5 million jobs that were expected to be created when the project is completed in the year 2005, they will have more incentives to resist joining the PKK and an interest in maintaining the status quo. No matter how valid this line of thinking is or how useful GAP will be in developing the southeast and abating the ongoing guerrilla war, this enormous project brings to the forefront the importance of integrating economic instruments when striving for political and military objectives.

International Political Economy

An important dilemma in international relations theory is concerned with how states decide whether to allocate scarce resources to pursue power or to pursue wealth. Each state has the formidable task of choosing between domestic, internal ends (intrinsically valued) and a military sector (instrumentally valued because of the strategic environment created by the international system)—between guns and butter.[19] During the cold war, Turkey's fragile security environment made it imperative for the state to focus on the pursuit of military power. Despite a few potential areas for conflict, however, Turkey's security environment improved significantly after the end of the cold war and the subsequent demise of the Soviet Union. One contention that arose in the aftermath of the cold war, therefore, was that diminishing international military concerns in the post–cold war period enabled and motivated Turkish policymakers to concentrate more on the economic arena.

Realizing the close interaction between the economic and political spheres, Kenneth Waltz argues that a decrease in military worries allows the state to focus on its technological and economic successes and failures, and replaces military competition with economic competition.[20] Waltz argues that the basic structure of international politics continues to be an anarchic system in which states fend for themselves, with or without the cooperation of other states. In such a system, leaders and their constituents are concerned with the relative international position of their state. Waltz asserts that nuclear weapons allow states to focus on economic and technological avenues of competition because they cannot be used to conquer or defend territory and thus limit the use of strategic power. Waltz's argument is that the only real purpose of nuclear weapons is to deter attacks on a country's vital interests. Accordingly, because states with nuclear weapons no longer use military force to gain a consequential advantage, they compete with one another in the technological and economic spheres in order to exert a greater influence on international outcomes. If the existence of nuclear weapons leads to diminishing military concerns and a subsequent concentration on economics and technology, a decrease in international security threats resulting from other reasons also leads the state to focus increasingly on the economic arena. Although Turkey was not a nuclear state, it was a state that experienced a decrease in international military threats resulting from the end of the cold war. As such, the expectation was that it could now direct its resources to concentrate on enhancing its economic well-being and on achieving such economic objectives as growth and development.

During the cold war, Turkish economic policy depended to a large extent on its foreign policy. The United States and the Soviet Union used foreign economic assistance as a major instrument of foreign policy and disbursed great sums to countries that were of strategic importance to them. Because of its strategic value to the United States and Europe, Turkey became a recipient of foreign aid with the Truman Doctrine (adopted to bolster Turkey and Greece against encroachments from the Soviets) and the Marshall Plan (established to provide American financial support for the economic recovery of Western Europe). In fact, during most of the cold war period, Turkey funded its development projects with the aid it received. As such, it became heavily dependent on the West, and especially the United States, for the financing of its economy. The United States and its allies were content to provide Turkey with substantial amounts of aid as long as Turkey fulfilled its duties as a loyal ally, aligning its foreign policy actions and decisions with their wishes and allowing American bases to operate from Turkish territory.[21] As a result, Turkish economic policy and Turkish foreign policy were inextricably intertwined. Turkey had to continue being a dependable ally of the West in order to keep on receiving foreign aid from the United States and Western Europe. The link between economic and foreign policy in Turkey was demonstrated during the aftermath of the second Cyprus crisis. When Ankara ignored American objections to a Turkish invasion of Cyprus and deployed Turkish troops to occupy the northern part of the island in July 1974, for example, Washington imposed an arms embargo on Turkey that remained in effect for the next three years.[22] Turkey also experienced a severe economic decline in the aftermath of the Cyprus crisis.

For most of Turkish history, including the period of the cold war, the economic objectives of growth and development were pursued not as goals in themselves but rather as means to an end, as a way of furthering Turkey's political and military objectives. The early leaders of the Republic, who very much wanted to westernize Turkey, believed that westernization could not be separated from economic and technological development. The purpose of such progress was to strengthen the Turkish state as a political and military entity. Social and humanitarian concerns were deemed to be secondary in importance.[23] The Ottoman state's philosophy that "there could be no power without an army, no army without adequate resources of revenue, no revenue without the prosperity of the subjects, and no prosperity without justice" remained the basic philosophy of Turkey's program of economic development.[24] In fact, during the cold war industrialization, higher agricultural yields, increased trade, better health care, and higher education standards were all seen as measures to bolster Turkey's military goals of preventing Soviet expansionism and maintaining national security. Meanwhile, Ankara pursued protectionist economic policies in order to isolate Turkey from the harmful cycles of the world economy. The state played a significant role in the economy, state economic enterprises (SEEs) were the major forces of production, and policymakers expected import-substitution to bring about economic growth and development.[25] It is puzzling that import-substituting industrialization, adopted to ensure Turkey's economic independence, was pursued at the same time as development funded by foreign economic assistance, which worked to increase its dependence on the West.

Despite Turkish policymakers' stated objectives of protecting the Turkish economy from the world economy, the 1974 American arms embargo and the subsequent reduction in foreign economic assistance from the West as well as the oil price shocks of 1973–1974 (which led to the quadrupling of crude oil prices) prompted Turkey to face its most severe economic crisis in the mid- to late-1970s. There was an extremely high inflation rate, severe unemployment, an expanding public sector deficit, unproductive SEEs, and foreign exchange problems.[26] The economic crisis was coupled with a high level of social and political unrest—extremist political violence, a high degree of factionalization, and a paralyzed state bureaucracy. In response to the growing problems in the country, the government of Prime Minister Süleyman Demirel adopted a package of drastic economic liberalization measures on January 24, 1980. These reforms consisted of strict structural adjustment measures directed toward opening up the Turkish economy to foreign competition, reducing the role of the state in economic affairs, stabilizing the economy, and restructuring it to achieve growth and development. It did not, however, yield immediate results because, in the face of the political crisis that plagued Turkey at the time, the government was not able to implement the necessary measures. It was only after the military establishment seized power in a coup d'état on September 12, 1980, that the January 24 reforms were implemented successfully because the armed forces succeeded in removing obstacles such as unions, strikes, and dissent by the opposition that had impeded the stabilization program. As such, import barriers were lowered, the Turkish lira was devalued, and restrictions on financial and monetary transactions were relaxed.

As a result of these comprehensive reforms, the Turkish economy stabilized rather quickly. The annual growth rate of the economy averaged 5.1 percent between 1981 and 1991, the highest in the Organization for Economic Co-operation and Development (OECD), and the economy expanded as a result of a vibrant tourist industry, the robust stock exchange, and increased trade.[27] The economic restructuring in Turkey also benefited from events that defined the international environment in the late 1970s.[28] The Soviet invasion of Afghanistan, the Iranian revolution, as well as the conflict in Lebanon increased cold war animosities, enhancing Turkey's strategic importance to United States's interests. As Turkish-American relations improved in the early 1980s, the World Bank and the International Monetary Fund (IMF) became more willing to lend funds to Turkey. These funds were instrumental in alleviating the economic problems discussed above.

The success of the January 24 reforms increased Turkish policymakers' awareness of the importance of the economic arena. They realized the need to alter the long-standing economic policy of pursuing growth and development as a means to reach inherently more important military and political goals. Turkish politicians were not the only ones to go through such a transformation. In earlier times, the predominant belief among political scientists was that military power was the ultimate type of power, and that states that possessed the greatest military strength controlled world affairs.[29] Furthermore, the traditional view declared that "enough national productivity to sustain a large military force, however much the people had to stint themselves, could make a state a great power."[30] The ultimate foreign policy objective—survival—was obtained by accruing military power. Leaders aspired to enhance their economic wealth to pay for weapons, increase their population to have more troops, and extend their territory to provide more secure borders.[31]

Military power, while still a central component of national power, does not play as dominant a role in the post–cold war era. In fact, identifying the resources that produce power capabilities has become much more difficult as a result of "radical transformations in the elements, the uses and the achievements of power."[32] Other types of power, especially economic power, are more important in the current world system than ever before. Robert Keohane and Joseph Nye construct a model of complex interdependence as an ideal type that sometimes reflects reality more adequately than another ideal type—realism. For realists, international politics is a struggle for power in which states are continuously involved in the activities of organized violence. In contrast to the realist assumption that there is a hierarchy of issues in world politics in which the high politics of military security dominates the low politics of economic and social affairs, complex interdependence theory assumes that the issues of international relations are not arranged in a hierarchy, and thus, that military security does not always dominate the agenda.[33] This is not to say that force is no longer important but that using or threatening force is not always the most effective way of wielding power. In most situations, the effects of military force are prohibitively costly and rather uncertain, and the instruments of military power are often not the best or most appropriate ones for achieving other objectives. The example of the Soviet Union demonstrates that a strong military base could not save an empire whose economy and polity were in disarray. As Mikhail Gorbachev told the Central Committee in May 1986, the Soviet Union was in a state of flux because it was "surrounded not by invincible armies but by superior economies."[34] As such, Ankara's priorities regarding economic objectives were expected to shift in the post–cold war era.

Search for New Foreign Policy Partners

Another expectation was that because Turkey's role in the international political system was such an important determinant of its foreign policy during the cold war, the change that occurred in the structure of the international system when the cold war ended would have a significant impact on Ankara's foreign policy orientation. As Hillal Dessouki and Bahgat Korany argue, a state's foreign policy orientation—its "general attitudes and commitments toward the external environment, its fundamental strategy for accomplishing its domestic and external objectives and aspirations and for coping with persistent threat"—may change as a result of a significant change in the global system.[35] Turkey pursued a foreign policy oriented toward the West during the cold war period. Its close alliance with the United States and Western Europe not only contributed to shaping its foreign policy behavior but was also an instrument for maintaining the country's territorial integrity and independence. The end of the cold war, therefore, had tremendous repercussions for Turkish foreign policy. In this new era, Turkish policymakers were no longer able to define their environment according to the role Turkey had played in the cold war, follow the same foreign policy strategies or even pursue the same goals. As a result, they questioned what role, if any, their country would play in the post–cold war international order.[36]

This book examines the argument that the end of the cold war and the removal of the Soviet threat diminished Turkey's strategic importance for the United States and Western Europe. Furthermore, because these areas were Ankara's most important foreign policy partners during the cold war, Turkish policymakers had to search for new foreign policy partners during the post–cold war period. Turkey's strategic value decreased at this time because the Western powers no longer needed to maintain a large coalition to contain Soviet expansionism. The Soviet Union no longer existed and the strongest successor state, the Russian Federation, wanted to establish avenues of cooperation with its former enemies. In the absence of common objectives (such as containing the Soviets), the social and political incompatibilities between Ankara and the Western powers were magnified, especially concerning human rights and the state of the democracy in Turkey. The European Community (EC, later known as the European Union), for example, rejected Turkey's application for full membership in 1989, sending a message to the Turkish public as well as to Turkish politicians that Turkey's future did not rest with Europe. There were numerous reasons cited for this rejection articulated in the "Opinion" published by the European Union's Commission on December 18, 1989. The Commission argued that Turkey's economic indicators, while significantly improved from the previous decade, were not at a level that was acceptable to the EC: its per capita GDP was about half that of the EC's poorest members; its annual population growth rate of 2.5 percent per year was ten times the EC average; Turkey's long-term foreign debt of $38 billion was the seventh highest in the world; and despite privatization, the state controlled 40 percent of manufacturing output.[37] Furthermore, at around 70 to 100 percent per year, Turkey's inflation rate was much higher than the EC average.

Turks, however, were more enraged by the Commission's observations about the deficiency of human rights and the unequal treatment of minorities in Turkey. Many policymakers as well as large sectors of the population believed that these were domestic matters that did not concern the European Community. Most Turks felt personally insulted by this rejection and fearful about what role their country would assume in the new world order if its future did not lie with Europe. One argument prevalent among the public and the politicians was that Turkey's rebuff was the result of growing prejudice and xenophobia in Western Europe; that Europeans did not want to include a country with a vastly different culture and religion in their exclusive club. In addition, several incidents of violence against Turkish "guest workers" in countries like Germany led to the perception that European governments were particularly lax in dealing with nationalistic neo-Nazi groups who committed crimes against Turks. Meanwhile, Ankara was also concerned that the Europeans were working on establishing post–cold war security alliances outside of NATO that would exclude Turkey. In the early 1990s, for example, it seemed that the West European Union (WEU) in which Turkey was only an observer would become an important regional alliance in the new international system. President Turgut Özal voiced his country's dissatisfaction with its limited role in the organization when he addressed the WEU in June 1991 by declaring that Turkey could not be expected to defend the continent if it could not "fully participate in the making of a new Europe."[38] It is important to note that despite this marginalization from Europe in the post–cold war era, Turkey continued to maintain a strong interest in Europe for political, economic, and security reasons, and a great majority of the Turkish elite remained committed to Western ideals. On a more "practical level, [however,] frustration with Turkey's limited role in Europe encouraged Turks to turn to alternative outlets for international activism in the republics of the former Soviet Union, the Balkans and the Middle East."[39]

Ankara's more regional approach to foreign policy became apparent in the early days of the post–cold war period when it assumed a central role in the Persian Gulf War. By becoming closely allied with the United States during the conflict, Turkish policymakers abandoned their long-standing policy of nonintervention in regional affairs. Soon after Iraq's occupation of Kuwait and the Security Council's subsequent imposition of comprehensive economic sanctions against Iraq in August 1990, Turkey interrupted the flow of petroleum from Iraq by shutting off the Iraqi pipelines on Turkish soil. As such, it contributed to the effective implementation of the United Nations's sanctions against Baghdad. Furthermore, American military aircraft were allowed to use the Incirlik Air Base for air strikes into Iraq, and nearly 100,000 Turkish troops were deployed along the Iraqi border. It was Ankara's desire to carve a new role for itself in the post–cold war international system that motivated its Gulf War actions. Realizing that the disintegration of the Soviet Union threatened to diminish Turkey's geostrategic value, Turkish policymakers were eager to find an alternative arena in which to assert their country's continued importance to its Western allies. As such, the Gulf War provided the perfect opportunity for Turkey to demonstrate that it was capable of playing roles other than the one it had perfected as a frontline state bordering a hostile Soviet Union.

The Middle East was not the only regional foreign policy arena Turkey explored in the early 1990s. As discussed above, the collapse of the Soviet Union allowed Turkey to establish close relations with the nearly fifty million Turkic-speaking people in Central Asia and the Caucasus with whom Turks shared strong ethnic, religious, cultural, and linguistic ties. One of the first countries to forge relations with these newly independent republics, Turkey became extensively involved in the region in a rather short period of time. The independence of the former Soviet republics was followed by many exchanges between Turkish and Turkic diplomats, during which numerous agreements and protocols calling for cooperation in such areas as banking, industry, agriculture, trade, and education were signed. Turkish policymakers as well as the leaders of the newly independent states hailed the importance of Turkish-Turkic relations, saying that the Turks of Turkey and the Turkic peoples in the former Soviet Union were "brothers" who had found each other after 150 years and that the Turkish people were no longer alone in the world. Meanwhile, Turkish leaders as well as the public believed that cooperation in a variety of fields with these newly independent states would lead to increased growth and economic development. Some even entertained the possibility that Ankara's close relations with the Turkic republics would lead to a rise in its international standing, perhaps even making it a regional leader in the post–cold war era.[40]

OUTLINE OF THE BOOK

Contemporary Turkish Foreign Policy thus examines Turkish foreign policy in a comparative perspective—during the cold war and post–cold war periods—to ascertain patterns of change as well as patterns of stability. The cold war era is defined as the period between 1945 and 1989, and the post–cold war era as the period between 1989 and March 1998. The year 1989 divides the two eras because of the events that took place in the Soviet Union and Eastern Europe during this year. The speech Mikhail Gorbachev made to the General Assembly of the United Nations on December 7, 1988, signaled that the end of the cold war was in sight. In this address, Gorbachev "expressed willingness to have the Soviet Union take a place in the forefront of international peace and cooperation" and that "further world progress is only possible through a consensus as we move toward a new world order."[41] In November 1989 the Berlin Wall—the concrete symbol of the division between the East and the West—crumbled; and in the following year Germany reunited. Soon afterward, almost all the communist governments in Eastern Europe either fell or underwent significant changes. The era of international relations characterized by the rivalry of the two superpowers, therefore, was effectively over by the time that the Soviet Union was formally disbanded on December 25, 1991.

Chapter 1 examines Turkey's domestic environment, its geography, social structure and population, economic capability, military capability, and political structure. Chapter 2 looks at foreign policy objectives and strategies as well as the decision-making process in the early years of the Turkish Republic: the period of neutrality (1923–1945) and alliance with the West (1945–1960). The same issues are discussed in the periods of the cooling off with the United States (1960–1980) and the third Turkish Republic during the cold war (1980–1990) in Chapter 3. Turkey's post–cold war foreign policy objectives and strategies toward the United States are examined in Chapter 4 while those with Western Europe are explored in Chapter 5. Chapter 6 looks at the former Soviet republics and the Middle East as new arenas for Turkish foreign policy.

NOTES

1. John J. Mearsheimer, "Back to the Future," *International Security* 15.1 (Summer 1990): 5–56; Joseph S. Nye, Jr., *Bound to Lead* (New York: Basic Books, 1990), 238; Samuel P. Huntington, "The Clash of Civilizations?" *Foreign Affairs* 72 (Summer 1993): 22–49; John Gerard Ruggie, "Territoriality and Beyond: Problematizing Modernity in International Relations," *International Organization* 47 (Winter 1993): 139–174; Kenneth Waltz, "The Emerging Structure of International Politics," *International Security* 18 (Fall 1993): 44–79.

2. Dankwart A. Rustow, *Turkey: America's Forgotten Ally* (New York: Council on Foreign Relations Press 1987), 88.

3. Udo Steinbach, "The European Community, the United States, the Middle East, and Turkey," *Politics in the Third Turkish Republic*, ed. Metin Heper (Boulder, Colo.: Westview Press, 1994), 104.

4. Erik Zurcher, *Turkey: A Modern History* (London: I. B. Tauris, 1993), 290.

5. A. Suat Bilge, *"Birinci Kibris Uyuşmazliği ve Turkiye-Sovyetler Birliği Munasebetleri," Olaylarla Turkiye Dis Politikasi* (Ankara: Siyasal Kitapevi, 1993), 426.

6. Sabri Sayari, "Turkey: The Changing European Security Environment and the Gulf Crisis," *Middle East Journal* 46.1 (Winter 1992): 9–21.

7. Rustow, *Turkey: America's Forgotten Ally*, 85.

8. Ferenc A. Vali, *Bridge Across the Bosphorus: The Foreign Policy of Turkey* (Baltimore: Johns Hopkins University Press, 1971), 68.

9. Steinbach, "The European Community, the United States, the Middle East, and Turkey," 103.

10. "Information Bank," *Home Page of the Turkish Ministry of Foreign Affairs*, June 1996 <http://www.mfa.gov.tr>.

11. Duygu Bazoğlu Sezer, "Turkey's Grand Strategy Facing a Dilemma," *International Spectator* 27 (January-March 1992): 22.

12. Robert J. Art, "A Defensible Defense: America's Grand Strategy after the Cold War," *International Security* 15.4 (1991): 6.

13. Morton Abramowitz, "Dateline Ankara: Turkey After Özal," *Foreign Policy* 91 (Summer 1993): 164.

14. Graham E. Fuller, "Turkey's New Eastern Orientation," in *Turkey's New Geopolitics*, eds. Graham E. Fuller and Ian O. Lesser with Paul B. Henze and J. F. Brown (Boulder, Colo.: Westview Press, 1993), 89.

15. "Information Bank," *Home Page of the Republic of Turkey, Prime Ministry, The Undersecretariat of Foreign Trade*, June 1996 <http://www.foreigntrade.gov.tr>.

16. Fuller, "Turkey's New Eastern Orientation," 89.

17. Süha Bölükbasi, "Ankara's Baku-Centered Transcaucasia Policy: Has It Failed?" *Middle East Journal* 51.1 (Winter 1997): 82.

18. "The Elusive Golden Apple: The War That Cannot Speak Its Name," *The Economist* (8 June 1996): 15.

19. Robert Powell, "Guns, Butter and Anarchy," *American Political Science Review* 87.1 (March 1993): 115–127.

20. Waltz, "The Emerging Structure of International Politics," 54.

21. Baran Tuncer, "External Financing of the Turkish Economy," *Turkey's Foreign Policy in Transition: 1950–1974*, ed. Kemal Karpat (Leiden: E. J. Brill, 1975), 25.

22. Zurcher, *Turkey: A Modern History*, 290.

23. Vali, *Bridge Across the Bosphorus*, 318.

24. Vali, *Bridge Across the Bosphorus*, 320.

25. Rüsdü Saracoğlu, "Liberalization of the Economy," in *Politics in the Third Turkish Republic,* ed. Metin Heper (Boulder, Colo.: Westview Press, 1994), 63.

26. Saracoğlu, "Liberalization of the Economy," 66.

27. Andrew Mango, *Turkey: Challenge of a New Role* (Westport, Conn.: Praeger, 1994), 58–61.

28. Atila Eralp, Muharrem Tunay, and Birol A. Yesilada, eds., *The Political and Socioeconomic Transformation of Turkey* (Westport, Conn.: Praeger, 1993), 3.

29. Robert O. Keohane and Joseph S. Nye, *Power and Interdependence*, 2nd ed. (Glenview, Ill.: Scott, Foresman and Company, 1989), 11.

30. Waltz, "The Emerging Structure of International Politics," 63.

31. James M. Goldgeier and Michael McFaul, "A Tale of Two Worlds: Core and Periphery in the Post–Cold War Era," *International Organization* 46.2 (Spring 1992): 467–491.

32. Keohane and Nye, *Power and Interdependence*, 11.

33. Keohane and Nye, *Power and Interdependence*, 23–29.

34. Waltz, "The Emerging Structure of International Politics," 59.

35. Ali E. Hillal Dessouki and Bahgat Korany, "A Literature Survey and Framework for Analysis," in *The Foreign Policies of Arab States*, 2nd ed. (Boulder, Colo.: Westview Press, 1991), 17.

36. Sayari, "Turkey: The Changing European Security Environment and the Gulf Crisis," 10.

37. Ian O. Lesser, "Bridge or Barrier? Turkey and the West After the Cold War," in *Turkey's New Geopolitics*, eds. Graham E. Fuller and Ian O. Lesser with Paul B. Henze and J. F. Brown (Boulder, Colo.: Westview Press, 1993), 104.

38. Lesser, "Bridge or Barrier?" 107.

39. Lesser, "Bridge or Barrier?" 99.

40. "Tomorrow's Empires," *The Economist* (21 September 1991): 15–16.

41. *Facts on File* 48 (December 1988): 901.

Chapter 1

The Foundations of Turkish Foreign Policy

This chapter examines several important aspects of Turkey's domestic environment, the factors that either enhance or constrain its foreign policy options: geography, population, social structure, economic capability, military capability, and political structure.

GEOGRAPHY

It has repeatedly been said that "Turkey's historical role and relative political importance rest, in large measure, on her incomparable geographical location" because various aspects of Turkey's geography have played an important role in shaping its foreign policy.[1] Some features of Turkey's geography that are most relevant to its foreign policy are: its strategically important seas and straits; its status as a country that rests in both Asia and Europe; its geopolitical position as a state bordered by the Soviet Union during the cold war and successor republics in the post–cold war; and its location and history in the Middle East. Turkey is surrounded on three sides with seas—to the north, the Black Sea; to the northwest, the Sea of Marmara; to the west, the Aegean Sea; and to the south, the Mediterranean. It provides a natural passage between Europe and Asia as the country rests on both continents. The vast majority of the country's land mass is on the Anatolian peninsula, while a much smaller portion of the country's territory is in Europe. The passageways between the two continents are controlled by the straits of Bosporus and the Dardanelles. These straits have always played a prominent role in Turkey's foreign affairs. During various periods in Turkish history, for example, possessing the straits saved the country from annihilation. Neither Napoleon and Alexander I, nor Hitler and Stalin, for example, could agree on how to divide this strategically crucial area between themselves, and neither of them could relinquish it to the other, and thus allowed the Turks to continue their control of the straits.[2] Furthermore, throughout history, the straits increased Turkey's importance in the world arena because of its power to deny passage through the waterways, and its commitment that it would not hesitate to so if this were required for the country's safety in times of war. Turkey's exclusive control of the straits of Bosporus and the Dardanelles even contributed to its entry as a central figure into cold war politics.

POPULATION AND SOCIAL STRUCTURE

Ethnic Minorities

According to the most recent census (1990), Turkey's population is 56.5 million with an annual rate of population growth averaging 2.17 percent from 1985 to 1990.[3] Fifty-nine percent of the population lives in urban centers and 41 percent in rural areas. The high rate of migration from rural to urban areas is reflected by an urban growth rate of 4.31 percent and a rural depreciation rate of 0.556 percent. Turkey's population today is almost entirely Muslim—about four-fifths are Sunni and the remainder, Shiite (or in Turkish, *Alevi*). Turkey, therefore, is an extremely homogeneous country in terms of religion. One important reason for the religious homogeneity of Turkey's population structure is that as the Ottoman Empire shrank, it lost its territories in Africa, Europe, and Arabia. Minorities that remained were either deported, such as the Armenians at the end of World War I, or exchanged in population exchanges, such as the Greeks after the Turkish War of Independence.

There are, however, ethnic differences among Turkey's religiously homogeneous population. The most significant minority is the country's Kurdish population. Estimates of Turkey's Kurds vary between 7.1 percent of the population (the official figure) and 24 percent (according to Kurdish sources), although a better estimate is around 17 or 18 percent (thus between 10 and 11 million people).[4] Ankara's relations with this rather large minority has played a crucial role in Turkish domestic as well as foreign policy since the foundation of the Republic. Although the Kurds, like the Turks, are mostly Sunni Muslims, they have their own language. The Kurdish language belongs to the Indo-European family of languages whose various dialects are closer to Iranian than to Turkish. While language is one characteristic that sets the Kurds apart, socioeconomic status is another. About half the Kurdish population lives in southeastern Turkey, the most underdeveloped region of the country. Per capita gross domestic product (GDP) in the region is less than half the national average and unemployment is twice the national average at around 25 percent. The inadequacy of the social services are reflected in social development indicators. While the national literacy rate is 77 percent, in Mardin (a prototypical province in the southeast) it is only 48 percent. Only 9 percent of children in the southeast graduate from high school and only 18 percent ever start high school. As such, the Kurds in Turkey are significantly worse off than the Turks.[5] One reason is that the ethnonationalist ideology developed by Mustafa Kemal Atatürk in the early days of the Republic—Kemalism—claimed that the different citizens of modern Turkey would define themselves as Turkish, despite what their ethnic backgrounds may be. Accordingly, the Kurds were defined as "Mountain Turks."[6] They did not receive any special benefits, and in fact, laws were instituted in order to deny, and even erase, the separate identity of the Kurds. For example, traditional Kurdish dress was banned, the use of the Kurdish language was restricted, and various villages with Kurdish names were forced to adopt Turkish ones.

As a result of these policies, Kurds have been staging armed rebellions against the Turkish state since the revolt of Sheik Sait in 1925. Other notable revolts occurred in 1930 and between 1936 and 1938. All of these were contained rather quickly by the Turkish military but "the fact that three major armed rebellions against the state were led by Kurds and based in the Kurdish region of the state firmly established the Kurds in Turkish minds as the originators of the primary challenge to their independent existence."[7] Turkey did not face any further significant dissent from the Kurds until the 1970s when the Kurdish issue once again arose as a source of violent antistate activity. The Kurdish Workers Party (PKK) was founded in 1978 and launched an armed struggle against the government forces in 1984.[8] The PKK—declared to be a terrorist organization not only by the Turkish government but also by the United States and several European countries—contends that the Kurds are entitled to a separate, independent state because of the discrimination they face in Turkey. It has been fighting a brutal guerrilla war with the Turkish military forces in order to achieve its goal of an independent Kurdistan. This fighting claimed more than fifteen thousand lives between the years 1982 and 1995, has caused thousands of peasants to flee their villages, and has contributed to the vast migration from rural areas to Turkey's major cities as people afraid for their lives move to urban areas in search of a better life.

The Turkish government has been pursuing several avenues to deal with the Kurdish insurgency. First, the government in Ankara has given the military a central role in formulating policy on the subject of the PKK insurgency and a free hand in pursuing PKK terrorists. In addition, ten provinces in the southeast of the country have been under a state of emergency since 1987, with extended powers given to the governor for the area and increased restrictions imposed on the media. Second, the government maintains that (despite laws that restrict the use of the Kurdish language and other similar measures that infringe on the freedoms of the Kurds) all Turks are treated as equal members of the state, with equal opportunities and equal duties. Ankara argues, therefore, that there are no barriers to the advancement of Kurds in Turkey. In fact, it is true that many Kurds have achieved high positions within the Turkish establishment—as cabinet ministers, members of parliament, businessmen, etc. Some scholars argue, however, that until about 1989, only Kurds who suppressed their Kurdish identity were able to get ahead, and those who embraced their ethnicity were treated with suspicion and even faced persecution.[9] A third avenue in dealing with the Kurdish crisis is through economic means. The government has realized that the economic backwardness of the southeast region contributes to Kurdish unrest. It launched, therefore, the Southeast Anatolian Project (GAP), which seeks to rejuvenate the economy of the region. This project is based on utilizing the Atatürk dam for irrigation and power generation and seeks to raise the standards of living in the southeast as well as to connect this region more closely to the rest of the country. Critics contend, however, that the beneficiaries of the project will be Turks who are already better off, rather than the impoverished Kurds and Turks.

What makes the Kurdish problem more complex is the fact that not only is it a domestic policy issue, but a foreign policy issue as well. Only about half of the Kurds live in Turkey; the rest are dispersed in Iraq, Syria, and Iran. Ankara, therefore, has to take into account its neighbors' relations with their own Kurdish minorities when making decisions. Sometimes, the Kurdish issue creates shared interests among the four countries. For example, Turkey's and Iraq's interests have often converged over the years and led to cooperation on issues such as border penetration (crossing each other's borders in order to pursue terrorists and attack their bases). Following the uprising of the Kurds during the Iranian revolution, the head of the Turkish armed forces, General Kenan Evren even went to Baghdad to sign an agreement on the suppression of Kurdish separatism in the border regions of the three countries. At other times, however, the Kurdish issue weakens relations between Turkey and its Middle Eastern neighbors as one state can manipulate its own Kurds to harm the interests of the other states. Although the PKK operates exclusively against the Turkish state and does not even have allies among the Kurds in other countries, it has set up bases in Syria, Iran, and Iraq. The alleged support of these countries for the PKK guerrillas continues to be a serious source of conflict between Turkey and its neighbors. Furthermore, the Kurdish issue also influences Turkey's relations with its Western allies. Ankara's strategies in dealing with the armed insurgency are often criticized by the European and American media and politicians as violating basic human rights. Germany, for example, briefly imposed an arms embargo on Turkey protesting that the weapons Turkey bought from Germany were being used in the war against the PKK.

Economic Inequalities

Turkey's population has been growing at a very fast pace—adding over a million people to its population every year. The World Bank estimates that Turkey's population will grow to 68 million by the year 2000 and to 92 million twenty-five years later.[10] Another assessment says that 60 percent of the population is less than twenty years old.[11] The reason for such high growth rates is that, although the birth rate has remained above 2 percent, there has been a steady decline in death and infant mortality rates since the 1950s. Another trend has also had a significant affect on Turkey's social structure—the mass migration from rural areas to the cities. During the 1950s, over a million people moved to the cities and contributed to their growth at an annual rate of 10 percent. The migration to the cities that occurred during this time differed from what had taken place before. Previously, people would move to the urban centers for a part of the year in order to work in the mines while keeping their families based in the villages. During the 1950s, however, peasants started to move to the cities permanently, bringing their families with them and requiring a whole array of social services from the government. Few of the migrants found permanent jobs in the industrial sector, which, although growing, remained small. Instead, they became day laborers and street vendors. The lack of adequate government services in housing, health care, and education meant they had to fend for themselves. They built their own houses, the *gecekondus* (meaning built at night), at the outskirts of the cities and survived without basic infrastructure such as roads, electricity, and sewers. Their ability to build such illegal housing was facilitated "by the provision of Middle Eastern customary law that any dwelling that is built on unused land and has four walls and a roof by morning may not be torn down."[12]

Even Turkey's high levels of economic growth could not keep up with its population growth. Therefore, large sectors of the population remained in poverty, needing an extensive array of social services such as education, health care, and housing, which the government has not been able to provide. Although there was substantial economic progress in the 1980s, it only benefited a small sector of the population. In fact, the liberalization reforms had the overall effect of worsening the distribution of income in Turkey. The net result of the 1980 reforms was a shift in income distribution from popular sectors, such as agriculture, wages, and salaries, to profits, rents, and interest income.[13] As real wages for the working classes dropped, in other words, the earnings of the wealthy rose. The vast inequality in Turkey's distribution of income can be seen by the fact that 5 percent of income goes to the lowest 20 percent of the population, while 50 percent goes to the richest 20 percent.[14] This inequality is compounded by considerable differences between regions and between rural and urban communities. The incomes of households in eastern Anatolia, for example, are half those in the major cities of Ankara, Istanbul, and Izmir.[15]

Such gross inequality between urban and rural areas has contributed to the continued migration to the urban centers as villagers leave their homes with hopes of finding better paying jobs and better social services, causing Turkey's major cities to grow at an annual rate of 6 percent during the 1980s. Even the fast-paced industrialization of the decade could not create enough jobs to absorb this rapidly expanding workforce, and most of the migrants could not afford the rents of even low-income housing and had to move into the *gecekondus* that lined the margins of such cities as Ankara, Istanbul, Izmir, and Adana. The size of these neighborhoods grew such that in 1993, over half of the built-up surface of Ankara consisted of *gecekondus*, and more than half of the inhabitants of the city lived in them. It is important to note at this point that the *gecekondus* in Turkey are quite different from the slum neighborhoods of many cities. Although they did not have basic infrastructure such as roads, electricity, water, and sewage systems when they were first erected in the 1950s, they had not only acquired these by the 1980s but many of the houses in these areas even had televisions and washing machines. The communities in the *gecekondus* were able to maintain their customs and traditions with strong ties to the villages they came from. Adding to the sense of community in these areas was the fact that the population of a certain neighborhood usually consisted of people from one area of the country. Nevertheless, the inhabitants of these squatter communities felt somewhat estranged from mainstream Turkish society because the majority of the migrants who came to the cities with inflated hopes and dreams could not find jobs in the industrial or service sectors. Furthermore, the fact that the expansion of services and amenities had not kept up with such high rates of urbanization meant that the quality of life in Turkey's large cities had declined.[16]

ECONOMIC CAPABILITY

Turkey's geography and climate make it a country with tremendous economic potential. It has a diverse terrain that includes fertile plains, pine tree forests, mountainous regions, as well as endless seashores. The variation in topography is accompanied by rather different types of climate: the average annual temperature varies between 18 to 20 degrees centigrade on the Mediterranean coast, and fluctuates between 4 to 18 degrees in the interior areas.[17] The vegetation is also quite diverse: the western Mediterranean, Aegean, and Marmara coasts have olive and citrus trees, while the Black Sea coast is famous for its forests of deciduous and coniferous trees as well as apples, pears, cherries, hazelnuts, mandarin oranges, and tea. Furthermore, there are parts of Turkey, namely, the eastern Mediterranean shores, where the vegetation is tropical, with banana, palm, and citrus trees. Because of such diversity in climate and topography, Turkey is able to produce a wide variety of agricultural products and does not need to import goods in order to feed itself. Despite significant natural resources and economic potential, however, Turkey has not been able to achieve economic self-sufficiency. One reason for this is the path of economic development followed by the leaders of the country since the inception of the Republic in 1923.

The founders of the country, determined to convert Turkey into a politically, socially, culturally, and economically Western nation, believed that Turkey would become a strong nation only if it westernized. Economic development, therefore, was a part of the overall objective: "In the 1920's, social and humanitarian considerations were hardly prominent; the purpose of economic and technological progress was to strengthen the Turkish state as a political and military entity."[18] The economic goal of Turkey in the first decades of the Republic was achieving self-sufficiency—the new leaders of Turkey did not want to repeat the mistakes of Ottoman economic and financial dependence that characterized the last years of the empire. In the first decades of the Republic, suspicious of foreign interference, Ankara relied exclusively on its own resources, which were not enough to achieve any significant degree of economic development. Not only was the country in the process of recovering from the devastation of World War I and the War of Independence, but the emigration of Greeks, Armenians, and Jews, who had dominated the business fields (while the Turks were farmers and soldiers), created a situation in which there was a lack of entrepreneurial and technically skilled manpower. Furthermore, protectionist policies that were adopted as a temporary measure to isolate Turkey from the harmful impact of the Great Depression and trade cycles remained the economic policy after the end of the Depression.[19] As such, the state was to be the major driving force behind the economy: state economic enterprises (SEEs) dominated domestic production, and import substitution was adopted as an economic measure to ensure Turkey's independence. The economic arena, therefore, was highly regulated, with "licensing requirements, quotas, tariffs, and other levies [and] surrender requirements on external receipts, foreign exchange allocation schemes, and voluminous and complex foreign exchange regulations."[20] Tobacco, oil, shipbuilding, and many other industries became state monopolies and were highly protected from outside competition. Despite such heavy regulation, however, the economy was still facing difficulties, which were compounded by the strains of World War II.

By the end of the war, the policy of statism increasingly came under attack both from Turkish business circles, the opposition, and the Americans. Consequently, the governing Republican People's Party (CHP) realized that in order to qualify for American foreign assistance, it would have to abandon its autarkic, interventionist economic policies and adopt a more free market-oriented approach. Consequently, in 1947 it took a number of liberalizing measures, such as the devaluing of the Turkish lira by 120 percent, to integrate Turkey into the world economy. This move toward liberalization was reinforced when Turkey became a founding member of the Organization for Economic Cooperation (OEEC, later OECD) in 1948 and was included in the Marshall Plan. By 1950 Turkey received close to $183 million in economic assistance and about $200 million in military assistance under the auspices of the European recovery program.[21] After this time, reliance on foreign assistance became a crucial aspect of Turkish economic policy.

The rise to power of the Democratic Party (DP) in May 1950 furthered the free-market reforms in Turkey. At the core of the Democrats' economic reforms lay their emphasis on the agricultural sector as well as their desire to encourage private enterprise (if necessary, at the expense of the state sector). They provided cheap credits to farmers and maintained artificially high prices for agricultural goods. The substantial amounts of foreign aid received were invested in machinery and infrastructure. The DP policies adopted in the early 1950s led to rapid growth for the Turkish economy and, combined with favorable weather conditions, to impressive harvests. The second half of the decade, however, brought severe economic difficulties. Production slowed down and inflation grew. Foreign investment never surpassed 1 percent of total private investment during the decade and domestic private investments did not grow at a pace desired by the DP government. The aversion of Prime Minister Adnan Menderes to economic planning meant that the government did not have a coordinated, long-term economic policy. As a result, for example, the government built sugar refineries in places where the farmers had not yet started to plant sugar beets and highways where there were essentially no vehicles.[22] In addition, investment decisions were often driven by political considerations, resulting "in factories being put up in economically unpromising locations and in the wrong sectors, leading, for instance, to a disastrous overproduction of sugar, which had to be dumped on the world market at a loss."[23] In other words, "there was a complete lack of planning, coordination and priorities in investments," and thus the Democrats were not able to achieve the kind of economic development that would have ensured their political longevity.[24]

The 1960s, therefore, saw a return to central planning in the Turkish economy. Article 129 of the 1961 constitution even established a State Planning Office, which was to formulate five-year plans for economic development. The next decade in Turkish economic history was thus characterized by the prevalence of such import-substituting industrialization (ISI) policies as direct investment incentives, subsidies, tax rebates, import restrictions, and high tariffs. State economic enterprises provided about 40 percent of total production.

One of the greatest difficulties faced by the economy during this time was that new industries depended heavily on the import of foreign parts and on the availability of foreign reserves to pay for them. In addition, there were persistent trade and balance of payment deficits that led to foreign exchange shortages. Despite these problems, the Turkish economy was relatively healthy and entered the 1970s with moderately high economic growth rates. Real GNP increased at an annual rate of about 7 percent during the 1968–1973 period, the current account of the balance of payments improved steadily, and extremely heavy remittances from Turkish guest workers helped finance the trade deficit. By the end of 1973, Turkey's gross international reserves equaled more than twelve months of imports (at $2 billion); total external debt (excluding IMF purchases) was under $3 billion; and the debt-service ratio stood at a low 5 percent.[25] At 13 percent, even the rate of inflation proved low by Turkey's traditional standards.

The 1973–1974 oil shocks, which led to the quadrupling of crude oil prices, however, reversed these positive trends. After the oil shocks, not only did Ankara have to pay exorbitant prices for its oil imports, on which it had grown increasingly dependent, but the stagflation in industrialized countries depressed the demand for Turkish exports and increased the price of nonoil Turkish imports. Furthermore, the labor market in Europe slackened, reducing the remittances from emigrants from $1.4 billion in 1975 to $980 million in 1977 and 1978. By this time, Turkey was facing a severe economic crisis. The current account of the balance of payments reached a deficit of $3 billion and external debt, $11 billion (1977).[26] Meanwhile, successive weak coalitions that ruled between 1974 and 1977 failed to take restrictive measures to correct the situation. In fact, various governments contributed to increasing the public sector deficit and fueling increased inflation.

Although a series of negotiations with the IMF resulted in the implementation of a stabilization program in April 1978, this package was not adequate in dealing with the severity of the problem. Despite a small improvement in the current account, public-sector finances continued to worsen (especially due to the inefficiency of the SEEs). After reaching a standby agreement with the IMF, the government started negotiations on debt rescheduling with commercial banks as well as with the member countries of the OECD consortium for Turkey.[27] After several rounds, an agreement was reached that stated that Turkey's debts would become payable in a five- to eight-year time frame and that the consortium would provide Turkey with a new loan of $407 million. It was based, however, on the condition that Turkey use these credits mostly to pay for its imports of goods originating from the OECD consortium countries.

These agreements had not led to significant improvements in Turkey's economic situation. In fact, inflation had reached 80 percent, and unemployment, 20 percent of the working population by 1979.[28] The GNP growth rate fell to 1.7 percent, which was less than the population growth rate, and which led the GNP to decrease in real terms. The public-sector deficit increased from under 2 percent of GNP in 1974 to over 8 percent in 1979.[29] The cost of living index rose by 72 percent in Ankara and 82 percent in Istanbul.[30] Exports stagnated at extremely low levels, and an effort to improve the balance of trade by cutting imports led to shortages of fuels, vegetable oils, sugar, coffee, light bulbs, medicines, medical equipment, newsprint, and cigarettes. Schools as well as factories had to close down because of a lack of heating oil and electricity. These economic problems, which constituted the worst economic crisis in the history of the Turkish Republic, were "exacerbated, if not caused in good part, by the chaos that permeated political life."[31]

On the one hand, the mounting deficits of the inefficient state economic enterprises had been a major cause of the economic crisis. On the other hand, the years of borrowing to meet the demands of import-substituting industrialization made Turkey lose its credibility in the eyes of the lending institutions and countries. In order to deal with this mounting economic crisis, therefore, on January 24, 1980, Prime Minister Demirel adopted a medium-term structural adjustment program under the auspices of the IMF and with the support of the World Bank and the OECD. The guiding principles of this program included liberalization of the economy, the adoption of free-market reforms, outward-orientation, deregulation, and the promotion of the private sector. The strength of the program contributed to convincing the OECD governments and lending institutions to postpone the due dates on principal and interest payments, and secured additional loans. Turkey received close to $1.6 billion in structural adjustment loans between 1980 and 1984, and, in return for the loans, agreed to implement "a large number of policies which affected almost every sphere of economic life [such as] the liberalization of imports, promotion of exports, reformation of the public sector and the capital market, and the transformation of the agricultural and energy sectors."[32] Although this adjustment program was aimed at stabilizing the economy and restructuring it to achieve growth and development, it did not yield immediate results because, in the face of the political crisis that plagued Turkey at the time, the government failed to implement the policy changes.

It was not until the military establishment seized power in a coup carried out on September 12, 1980, that the January 24 reforms were really carried out in Turkey. The armed forces removed obstacles (such as unions, strikes, and dissent by the opposition) that had been impeding the successful implementation of the stabilization program. The military regime also quickly established sociopolitical order, a requirement for the economic reforms. Turgut Özal, who had been the architect of the January 24 reforms as undersecretary for economic affairs in charge of planning in Demirel's government, was appointed to be the undersecretary of the State Planning Organization (in which position he served until he was forced out of office as a result of financial scandals).

A number of economic reforms were adopted in accordance with the economic liberalization package. The Turkish lira was devalued by 33 percent vis-à-vis the U.S. dollar, followed by continuous minidevaluations and flexible exchange rates. Interest rates were liberalized and ceilings on interest rates lifted.[33] In order to make competition for the SEEs and force them to become more efficient to ensure their survival, the government lifted controls and subsidies on most items (except bread, coal, fertilizer, and sugar) and liberalized the determination of private-sector commodity prices. Price controls on agricultural products were gradually removed. The long-standing policy of import substitution was replaced with a strategy of outward-oriented export promotion. The most important aspects of the reform package included reducing the role of the state in the economy, focusing on the development of the country's infrastructure—roads, communications, and sources of energy—and opening up the Turkish economy to the world market. As a result of the rather comprehensive reforms carried out after the coup, the economy stabilized rather quickly. By 1981 the economic growth rate reached 4.1 percent (from negative growth in 1980), and inflation decreased from 107 percent in 1979 to 26 percent in 1981.[34]

The reforms to liberalize the Turkish economy were intensified even further after the return to competitive party politics in 1983. Turgut Özal became prime minister and vowed to incorporate Turkey into the world economy as a competitive player. Özal asserted that the protectionism of previous decades had forced Turkish industry to be inefficient, expensive, and uncompetitive and argued that everyone would benefit from a liberalized economy, "especially the consumer who would have cheaper and high-quality goods."[35] His government thus focused on opening up the economy to international competition and adopted policies to increase significantly the amount of goods being imported to Turkey. It further liberalized trade and payment regulations and encouraged foreign investments. Tourism was heavily promoted as an important source of revenue for the country. The Özal government also instituted reforms in the financial sector and in January 1985, with the introduction of a 10 percent value-added tax (VAT), adopted a comprehensive overhaul of the country's tax system in order to broaden the tax base. As such, "Turkey embarked on a new policy designed not only as a comprehensive program of economic stabilization, but also as a basic reorientation of economic programs away from detailed government regulation and control toward greater reliance on market forces, foreign competition, and foreign investments."[36] Meanwhile, foreign assistance played an important role in the Turkish economic reforms. In addition to IMF credits and the postponement of loan payments, the Turkish economy received $13 billion from abroad between 1980 and 1987, which contributed to its growth rate of around 5 percent during that time.[37]

The economic liberalization program of the 1980s led to exceptional progress in the Turkish economy. The bottlenecks in foreign exchange and foreign credit, which kept trade stagnant, were removed, leading to substantial increases in exports as well as imports. Exports, which stood at $2.9 billion in 1979, increased to $13 billion by 1991.[38] The nature of exports also changed; agricultural products, which had constituted 60 percent of Turkish exports in 1979, comprised only 20 percent in 1988, allowing industrial goods to compose the majority of exports.[39] Imports also increased from $5 billion in 1979 to $14.4 billion in 1989. International competition forced Turkish businesses to be more efficient and productive. Meanwhile, GNP grew at an annual rate of 4.7 percent for the decade. The relatively low inflation rate combined with high interest rates and political stability led Turkish workers in Europe to deposit their money in Turkish banks, thus increasing the savings and investments rates in Turkey. Turkey's donors hailed the economic liberalization reforms as a major success, and their new confidence in the country's economic potential improved its creditworthiness in the international financial community. As a result, loans from the OECD, IMF, World Bank, some OPEC (Organization of Petroleum Exporting Countries) countries, and international banking institutions flowed into Turkey, improving the balance of payments. The 1980 reforms, in other words, were very successful at restructuring the Turkish economy, which was transformed from a stagnant and unstable economy based on import substitution to a growing one based on export promotion.

Nevertheless, the economic liberalization reforms also had some detrimental effects on the Turkish economy as well as on Turkish society. For example, despite a brief drop in 1981 and 1982, the inflation rate remained high for most of the decade. Although the IMF and World Bank had recommended decreasing the role of the state in the economy, the state's economic influences actually grew as state support increasingly focused on exporters. Most seriously, the stabilization program led to the worsening of the distribution of income and increased unemployment in Turkey. Constant "price increases, suppression of wages, low floor prices for agricultural products, and the increasing tax burden on the masses all led to a significant decrease in the standard of living of the people, but at the same time resulted in a transfer of resources to capital."[40] The differences between the rich and the poor increased substantially as certain sectors of the society (those engaged in import, export, and construction) grew extremely wealthy while the incomes of other sectors (such as blue-collar workers and those in the informal sector) either stagnated or dropped. The outcome of the economic policies of the 1980s was:

a regression in income distribution from popular sectors (agriculture, wages, and salaries) to profits, rents, and interest income. Factor shares as percent of national incomes for agriculture (farmers' income) declined from 26.7 in 1980 to 13.2 in 1988. During the same period, the share of wages and salaries fell from 23.9 percent to 15.8 percent. On the other hand, the share of rents, profits, and interest income increased from 49.5 percent in 1980 to 71 percent in 1988.[41]

Between 1980 and 1988, the transfer of resources from agriculture and wages to capital was worth about $51.1 billion.[42] As a result of these developments, the purchasing power of the majority of Turks had been substantially reduced by the end of the decade. Many people in middle and lower classes joined the ranks of the poor; and World Bank reports placed Turkey among the seven countries with the worst levels of income disparity.[43]

Meanwhile, the government did not have any long-term plans to alleviate the inequitable distribution of income.[44] Although it implemented policies to adjust wages for inflation, to maintain high interest rates, to encourage workers to become shareholders in the companies they worked for, these measures were not a part of a comprehensive strategy. In fact, the government's structural adjustment policies worsened the existing inequalities in income distribution in the country. An important reason for this emanated from the role given to agriculture in the development plans. The state subsidies to the agricultural sector, long a characteristic of Turkish economic policy, were not compatible with the structural adjustment program. Therefore, the IMF and World Bank insisted that they, along with state controls, be removed. In addition, the government took steps to let prices adjust to world prices and incorporate small producers into the market economy. Consequently, the share of agriculture in the national income decreased from 23.9 percent in 1980 to 14 percent in 1988.[45] Farmers were thus among the groups that were harmed the most from the economic reforms of the 1980s.

The liberalization policies also sharpened the inequality in the distribution of land and the distribution of wealth by region. The already sharp contrast between industrialized western Anatolia and the agricultural east increased in the face of reduced government subsidies, protection of local businesses, and so forth. The incomes of the households in eastern Anatolia were less than half of those in Ankara, Istanbul, and Izmir.[46] This inequality fueled the migration of peasants and villagers to Turkey's major cities discussed above.

Meanwhile, widespread poverty remained not only among the migrants but also among those who had stayed in the countryside. In 1988, for example, 11 percent of the Turkish population lived in conditions of absolute poverty, unable to afford such necessities as an adequate diet, clothing, and shelter. The worst poverty was prevalent among the small peasants, agricultural and unskilled workers, as well as those self-employed in the informal sector. The next income level consisted of skilled and white-collar workers, artisans, and government officials while industrialists, traders, and professionals in private businesses earned the highest incomes in society. The poverty in the *gecekondus* seemed particularly acute because it existed side by side with the extreme wealth prevalent among the upper classes of society. The numbers of the very wealthy grew significantly greater as well as more visible in the 1980s, with, for example, the opulence of celebrity weddings being written about (complete with pictures) in the front pages of such mainstream newspapers as *Hürriyet* and *Milliyet*. Successive governments during the decade were particularly inept at either alleviating some of the poverty or equilibrating the distribution of income. In fact, state expenditure on health and education actually declined during the 1980s.[47]

The unequal distribution of income was also exacerbated by high levels of unemployment in Turkey during this time. The uneducated and unskilled inhabitants of the squatter neighborhoods ranked among the groups that suffered the most from the high unemployment rate, which (in both the agricultural and nonagricultural sectors) increased from 14 percent in 1979 to an average of 16.8 percent during 1982–1986. In order to support their (often large) families, migrants had to become porters, street vendors, day laborers, or janitors—not the types of occupations they had envisioned when leaving their villages—while many others joined the growing ranks of the unemployed. Meanwhile, the state could not provide for such basic needs as cheap bread, health services, and education. Although many politicians made grand campaign promises to the people in the *gecekondus* during election time, they largely ignored the needs of these communities after being elected. As a result, many of the migrants grew extremely dissatisfied with the ruling governments. Turkish politicians, traditionally from the upper classes, seemed far more concerned with their own political survival than with improving the living conditions of the disfranchised sectors of the society. Unemployment and underemployment in the squatter communities, which led to the migrants' inability to realize their expectations, contributed to making these communities extremely jaded with the ruling governments. In addition, migrant communities (in Turkey's urban centers as well as in Europe) "tended on the whole to become more, rather than less, traditional when confronted with the unfamiliar surroundings of an industrial society."[48] As a result, they became the base of support of the Welfare Party (*Refah Partisi*, RP), which espoused traditional values and presented itself as the only effective alternative to the types of governments that had ruled in the past with no concern for the well-being of the poor sectors of the society. The success of the Welfare Party in attaining a narrow plurality in the December 1995 elections thus emanated from the ability of its leaders effectively to exploit the discontent prevalent in the *gecekondu* neighborhoods and in the rural areas.

The 1980s constituted a period of transformation for Turkey. Not only did the economy experience a drastic break from the past with the implementation of economic liberalization reforms, but Turkish society also saw some major changes. The free-market reforms led to the growth of the economy, privatization of some state enterprises, and an emphasis on the export sector. National wealth grew as businessmen and rentiers made huge profits. The massive foreign borrowing that financed the economic reforms, however, threatened Turkey's economic independence. The economy was also burdened with a colossal foreign debt that required an increasing amount of resources to service: 60 percent of export earnings in 1987 went to service the debt. The economic policies of the decade also sharpened income inequality in Turkey. While some sectors of society catapulted to the levels of the very rich, others saw significant declines in their standard of living. Unemployment hovered around 15 percent during the decade; inflation remained high; and workers did not even have the right to strike to protest these conditions. Despite the dismal situation of the urban workers, millions of peasants migrated to the cities in search of better jobs and living conditions, only to find housing in squatter communities and, if lucky, jobs in the informal sector. Consequently, many people became increasingly dissatisfied with the political elite, who instead of talking about social welfare and justice "spoke only of how to make money and how best to consume it."[49] Many of the developments of the 1990s were based on this transformation of the Turkish economy and society.

The governments during the post–cold war period kept Turkey on a path of economic liberalization while working toward the goal of being fully integrated into the world economy. In addition, despite the frequent references to Turkey's development potential—as an emerging market with 62 million people and an invaluable location at the crossroads of Europe and Asia, the Balkans, the Caucasus, and the Middle East—the economy remained on the verge of taking off rather than actually taking off. Furthermore, the failure of the governing coalitions to work on the fundamental problems facing the economy (such as extremely high inflation, lofty public sector borrowing, and high unemployment as well as a huge budget deficit and trade gap) led to the worst economic crash in Turkey's history in 1994. Bülent Gültekin, the governor of the Central Bank until early 1995, asserted that "the budgetary deficit could not be reduced because [Prime Minister] Çiller did not embark on such needed measures as the privatization of state enterprises, the reform of the social security system (. . .), the elimination of direct and indirect subsidies to the private sector, and the reform of the notoriously inadequate fiscal system."[50] In January 1994, two rating agencies downgraded Turkey's international credit rating, and despite an intervention by the Central Bank, the Turkish lira dropped by 60 percent against the major currencies during the first quarter of 1994.[51] The economy had overheated, and the situation was worsened by the spending of the Çiller government in preparation for the local elections scheduled for March 1995. Huge sums of money were poured into the economy by giving significant raises to public sector employees and other measures. Consequently, inflation rose to more than 100 percent. A rescue operation finally came when, soon after the local elections, the government initiated a major economic stabilization program that aimed "to strengthen Turkey's growth prospects and competitiveness by introducing structural reforms in several key areas."[52] The austerity package raised interest rates, reduced government spending, elevated prices on state-controlled products, and imposed new taxes. In addition, the government agreed to reduce its short-term borrowing from the Central Bank from 15 percent of its budget to 3 percent by 1998 in accordance with the stabilization program.

Although this IMF-backed package succeeded in bringing about stability to the market and in raising foreign exchange reserves, the Turkish economy suffered significant losses in 1994. The economy shrank by 6.5 percent and real wages dropped by more than 30 percent. There was a significant decline in imports and in domestic demand. Many workers were laid off from their jobs. Meanwhile, the construction of homes and factories around cities continued at a rather brisk pace. Exports remained high, and in fact, rose in response to the devalued lira. A high level of remittances from Turkish workers abroad and healthy profits from the tourism sector contributed to getting the economy on a path of recovery by the end of 1994.[53]

The economic crisis of 1994 defined the pattern of economic ups and downs experienced by the Turkish economy in the 1990s: periods of healthy economic activity were often followed by crisis situations that threatened to crash the economy. The most important reason for the troubles in the economy was the instability in the domestic political arena. As *The Economist* reported in June 1996, "Turkey's elections never produce an absolute majority for any party, and the coalitions needed to form governments have encouraged short-term thinking. Essential reforms have been neglected, and successive governments have borrowed to fund their vote-catching programmes."[54] As a result, the Turkish economy in the post–cold war era remained saddled with a number of important problems. The Turkish lira remained weak compared with the dollar. The inflation rate (considered relatively low at 87 percent in March 1996) remained much higher than the 40 percent targeted by the International Monetary Fund. Although industrial exports rose, the deficits in foreign trade, the balance of payments, and the state budget deteriorated. In addition, Turkey became one of the eight most indebted nations in the world per capita when its foreign debt reached a record high of $73.6 billion in 1996.[55] The enormous cost of the war with the PKK—$8.2 billion in 1994, 20 percent of the state budget—in the southeastern region of the country augmented these economic difficulties.

Furthermore, the unemployment rate remained slightly above 10 percent between 1990 and 1995. Official estimates showed that during this time, four out of ten young people (in a country where 70 percent of the population was under the age of thirty) were searching for jobs.[56] Meanwhile, although there was not an enormous level of absolute poverty, income inequality remained high, with substantial differences between regions and rural and urban communities. The economic policies followed in the 1990s furthered the income disparities as well as social polarization in the country by enriching a small minority while failing to remedy the rising unemployment and large drops in the purchasing power of wage earners.

MILITARY CAPABILITY

The military has played an important role in Turkish politics as an institution with an unchanging worldview, that stands above society and acts independently in order to pull the country out of crisis situations. A powerful force in Turkish politics, the army has seized power to restore order and stability, as well as to defend the integrity of the constitution when the generals believed it was necessary to do so: in May 1960, March 1971, and September 1980. In each of these instances, the military leaders declared that their taking of power was a temporary measure and that they intended to return power to civilian government once they fulfilled their objectives. Although the role of the armed forces in politics diminished after 1983 with the return to democracy and civilian government, the central place that the military has occupied in Turkish society dates back to Turkey's Ottoman history.

The Ottoman Empire was a great military power that conquered vast amounts of territory in Africa, Asia, and even went as far into Europe as Vienna. The army that had threatened much of the world, however, became involved in palace politics and began to threaten the sultan during the days of Ottoman decline. When the Ottomans were attempting to revitalize the empire through reform, the soldiers, along with religious groups, impeded the reform process. One of the first goals of the sultans of the late eighteenth and early nineteenth centuries, therefore, was to modernize and transform the army. They set up military academies modeled after the schools in the West and "out of these institutions emerged a new generation of reformist officers dedicated to the salvation of the state and the empire."[57] The Turkish army was also the most important force in the founding of the modern Turkish Republic. General Mustafa Kemal (later known as Atatürk, the father of the Turks) organized the nationalist forces who not only resisted the invading powers in the aftermath of World War I but also restored Turkish authority over the Anatolian peninsula.

The military establishment went through a number of stages in the history of the Turkish Republic before attaining the position it had in the late 1990s. During the first decades of the Republic, the army was completely isolated from political life. Military officers had to retire if they wanted to enter politics, and soldiers were not even allowed to vote. Marshall Fevzi Çakmak, the chief of the general staff from 1925 to 1944, did not approve of his soldiers reading newspapers or engaging in "un-military" activities such as playing the violin.[58] Although the military was quite respected during this time, it became the instrument of the single-party state. Turkey's entry into NATO, however, changed the role of the army in Turkey as the Korean War highlighted the importance of the military, and the armed forces became more drawn into politics and society. Meanwhile, a division arose between the generals, who were considered to be politically significant by the ruling elite and the junior officers. While the generals were politically connected and economically well-off, the junior officers were dissatisfied with the direction the country was taking as well as with their role in society. The reform of the military structures that they demanded had not occurred, the prestige of the services was declining, and their already modest living standards were falling. The military intervention of May 27, 1960, therefore, was carried out in an environment of tension between the junior officers, who had started to voice their discontent in a language similar to the opposition party's rhetoric, and the generals, who were allied with the ruling elite. The goal of the coup d'état was not only to bring about a change of government, but also to institute structural changes in society; changes that were introduced in a new and more liberal constitution that, for example, gave trade unions the right to strike and the socialists the right to form a party and criticize society. The lesson that the generals learned from this intervention was that they had to establish rigid hierarchical control as well as political consensus in the armed forces in order to prevent similar uprisings from below in the future. The politicians, on the other hand, learned that the military had to be integrated into the decision-making process so that it would have a strong interest in maintaining the status quo.

Consequently, the 1960s saw another transformation of the military establishment. A number of dissenting officers were purged; an Armed Forces Union was formed by the High Command; and the National Security Council was created. The Armed Forces Union was to control and regulate the activities of all groups in the services, while the National Security Council—composed of the president; prime minister; ministers of defense, foreign, and interior affairs; the chief of general staff; commanders of the army, navy, air force; and the general commander of the gendarmerie—was to assist the government "in the making of decisions related to national security and coordination."[59] These new institutions had the overall effect of giving a significant degree of independence to the military, which could no longer be manipulated by the major parties. Furthermore, the soldiers perpetuated the belief that the armed forces were to be the guardians of the new regime they had created. The military systematically restructured the political system and included in the new constitution elements that were new to Turkish society, such as the guarantee of all civil rights and liberties and an overhaul of the electoral system. They became greatly involved in all aspects of Turkish society, their prestige increased, and their most important aim became the maintenance of stability and social peace. They made it clear that they were willing to overthrow any government that threatened the ideals on which the second Turkish Republic was built. The two subsequent interventions were thus carried out as the generals believed that the government had lost its legitimacy and threatened the stability of the regime.

The succession of presidents with military backgrounds in the 1960–1980 period reinforced the important role of the military in Turkish politics. The 1980 intervention, however, took the privileged role of the military one step further as the armed forces assumed full executive and legislative powers following the coup. They closed all political parties, purged and centralized universities, censored the press, and banned former politicians from politics. The authoritarian 1982 constitution gave the military continued power over civilian governments. Article 1, for example, said that upon returning to civilian rule, the leader of the military regime would become president (with extensive powers of appointment and supervision) of the Republic for seven years.[60] General Kenan Evren, who had presided over the coup, thus became president of Turkey after the country returned to democratically elected government in 1983.

The military's power in Turkish politics, however, started to decline after 1983. In the elections held during that year, the party that the generals favored lost while the one that they had actively discouraged people from voting for—the Motherland Party (*Anavatan Partisi*, ANAP)—won by a landslide. The official role of the military in Turkish politics was reduced further when, on October 31, 1989, the Grand National Assembly elected Prime Minister Turgut Özal as the first civilian president since 1960. The military, however, continued to play a rather significant role, especially over issues that related to Turkey's national security, mostly from behind the scenes. During the Persian Gulf Crisis, for example, the generals prevented President Özal from making an even more open commitment to U.S. policy than he had already done.

In the 1990s, an era of civilian politics in Turkey, there were two different avenues through which the military exercised influence over governmental policy making. One was through its representation in the National Security Council: according to the 1982 constitution, the Council of Ministers had to give priority to policy decisions made by the National Security Council. Second, through emphasizing the possibility that if the armed forces were dissatisfied with the direction in which the country was headed, they would not hesitate to stage another intervention. As Feroz Ahmad said, "The possibility of another coup is always present so long as the Turkish army perceives itself as the guardian of the republic and its Kemalist legacy."[61] The Turkish military, therefore, acted as a constraint on the choices that were available to politicians in the making of domestic as well as foreign policy, and prevented them from undertaking policies that strayed too far from the status quo.

POLITICAL STRUCTURE

The structure of the Turkish political system is one in which competitive party politics exist alongside the important role given to the military establishment. On the one hand, the intensity of the military's involvement in the everyday politics of the country has prevented a real multiparty system from flourishing. On the other hand, this same involvement has repeatedly prevented the country from sinking into deeper levels of chaos. While the active participation of the military is one characteristic of Turkish politics, another is the prevalence of political violence in the society. Throughout the history of the Turkish Republic, there have been battles between government forces and Kurdish nationalist guerrillas as well as clashes between leftist and rightist extremists. In the political environment of the mid-1990s, in addition to the PKK violence, there were clashes between Islamist Sunni groups and the more secular Alevis. Assassinations (or assassination attempts) of controversial journalists and writers still occurred, and the possibility of violence loomed large at mass demonstrations and political rallies.

A third characteristic of the Turkish political structure is the high degree of polarization among parties. Relations between the major party leaders are usually so hostile at a personal level that compromise becomes impossible to achieve. C. H. Dodd states that "it has often been claimed that there is an oppositional mentality in Turkish political culture which makes compromise difficult to achieve. The basic qualities which are stressed among children and youth, like courage and loyalty, do not perhaps develop a spirit of compromise, especially if the rightness of revenge is stressed."[62] He adds, however, that the influence of such cultural traits are often exaggerated, and that Turkish politicians would be able to get along with one another if they had enough time to get to know one another. One reason for the high degree of polarization among leaders of political parties is the very personal nature of Turkish politics. Politicians, who often share similar views regarding Turkey's foreign and economic policies, tend to attack each other's personal characteristics during campaigns and find it difficult to work together after the campaigning is over. In addition, the emergence of the Welfare Party as a major player in the post–cold war era has led to an increasingly polarized electorate as well. While one component of society is staunchly secular and believes that the future of Turkey lies in the West, another part believes that religion should play a greater role in Turkish society and that Turkey should enhance its relations with Islamic countries.

The significant role that the military plays in the political process, the high degree of political violence, and a polarized political system have contributed to the disorder and instability prevalent in Turkish democracy. In addition, Turkish democracy is characterized by the constant formation and fragmentation of a large number of major and minor parties. "Multiparty democracy in Turkey means a multiplicity of parties that are continually fragmenting and reforming."[63] Dissenting groups within parties break off to form new political parties and contribute to the tendency of governments to operate in the context of coalitions. These coalitions are often fragile because coalition partners usually share little besides the desire to hold office. Politicians are not reluctant to change their ideological orientations or party affiliations in order to be elected into office. While Turkish politics is dominated by right-of-center and left-of-center parties (with the rightist parties consistently slightly more popular than the leftist), extremist parties on both sides of the political spectrum have always existed on the fringes. Despite such a high degree of instability (what can sometimes best be described as chaos) in Turkish domestic politics, however, there has also been a remarkable degree of stability in the conduct of foreign policy.

NOTES

1. Ferenc A. Vali, *Bridge Across the Bosphorus: The Foreign Policy of Turkey* (Baltimore: Johns Hopkins University Press, 1971), 42.

2. Vali, *Bridge Across the Bosphorus*, 44.

3. Metin Heper, *Historical Dictionary of Turkey* (Metuchen, N.J.: Scarecrow Press, 1994), 60.

4. Philip Robins, "The Overlord State: Turkish Policy and the Kurdish Issue," *International Affairs* 69.4 (1993): 661.

5. Robins, "The Overlord State," 663.

6. Robins, "The Overlord State," 661.

7. Robins, "The Overlord State," 660.

8. George E. Gruen, "Turkey's Emerging Regional Role," *American Foreign Policy Interests* 17.2 (April 1995): 15.

9. Michael M. Gunter, *The Kurds in Turkey: A Political Dilemma* (Boulder, Colo.: Westview Press, 1990), 46.

10. Paul B. Henze, "Turkey: Toward the Twenty-First Century," *Turkey's New Geopolitics*, eds. Graham E. Fuller and Ian O. Lesser with Paul B. Henze and J. F. Brown (Boulder, Colo.: Westview Press, 1993), 13.

11. Celestine Bohlen, "In a Search for 'Turkishness,' Turks Reveal Their Diversity," *New York Times* (18 May 1996): A1.

12. Dankwart A. Rustow, *Turkey: America's Forgotten Ally* (New York: Council on Foreign Relations Press, 1987), 33.

13. Atila Eralp, Muharrem Tunay, and Birol A. Yeşilada, eds., *The Political and Socioeconomic Transformation of Turkey* (Westport, Conn.: Praeger, 1993), 233.

14. "Turkey," *Trends in Developing Economies 1995* (New York: Oxford University Press, 1995), 519.

15. William Hale, *The Political and Economic Development of Modern Turkey* (New York: St. Martin's Press, 1981), 135.

16. Heper, *Historical Dictionary of Turkey*, 60.

17. Heper, *Historical Dictionary of Turkey*, 59.

18. Vali, *Bridge Across the Bosphorus*, 318.

19. Rüsdü Saraçoğlu, "Liberalization of the Economy," *Politics in the Third Turkish Republic*, ed. Metin Heper (Boulder, Colo.: Westview Press, 1994), 63.

20. Saraçoğlu, "Liberalization of the Economy," 63.

21. Hale, *The Political and Economic Development of Modern Turkey*, 74–75.

22. Mehmet Yaşar Geyikdaği, *Political Parties in Turkey: The Role of Islam* (New York: Praeger, 1984), 77.

23. Erik J. Zurcher, *Turkey: A Modern History* (London: I. B. Tauris, 1993), 236.

24. Z. Y. Hershlag, *Turkey: The Challenge of Growth* (Leiden: E. J. Brill, 1968), 142.

25. Saraçoğlu, "Liberalization of the Economy," 64.

26. Saraçoğlu, "Liberalization of the Economy," 65.

27. Saraçoğlu, "Liberalization of the Economy," 65.

28. Hale, *The Political and Economic Development of Modern Turkey*, 128.

29. Saraçoğlu, "Liberalization of the Economy," 66.

30. Geyikdaği, *Political Parties in Turkey*, 133.

31. Geyikdaği, *Political Parties in Turkey*, 135.

32. Zulkuf Aydin, "The World Bank and the Transformation of Turkish Agriculture," *The Political and Socioeconomic Transformation of Turkey*, 116–117.

33. Atila Eralp, Muharrem Tunay, and Birol Yeşilada, Introduction, *The Political and Socioeconomic Transformation of Turkey*, 2.

34. Ahmet Kiliçbay, *Türk Ekonomisinin Son 10 Yili* (Istanbul: Milliyet Yayinlari, 1991), 14.

35. Feroz Ahmad, *The Making of Modern Turkey* (London: Routledge, 1993), 204.

36. Birol A. Yeşilada and M. Füsunoğlu, "Assessing the January 24, 1980 Economic Stabilization Program in Turkey," *The Politics of Reform in the Middle East*, ed. H. J. Barkey (New York: St. Martin's Press, 1992), 187.

37. Ahmad, *The Making of Modern Turkey*, 207.

38. Kiliçbay, *Turk Ekonomisinin Son 10 Yili*, 225.

39. Zurcher, *Turkey: A Modern History*, 310.

40. Aydin, "The World Bank and the Transformation of Turkish Agriculture," 117.

41. Yeşilada and Füsunoğlu, "Assessing the January 24, 1980 Economic Stabilization Program in Turkey," 200.

42. Aydin, "The World Bank and the Transformation of Turkish Agriculture," 117.

43. Ahmad, *The Making of Modern Turkey*, 204.

44. Kiliçbay, *Turk Ekonomisinin Son 10 Yili*, 228.

45. Aydin, "The World Bank and the Transformation of Turkish Agriculture," 117.

46. Hale, *The Political and Economic Development of Modern Turkey*, 138.

47. Halis Akder, "Turkey: Country Profile," *Human Development Report 1990* (Ankara: United Nations Development Programme, 1990), 13.

48. Zurcher, *Turkey: A Modern History*, 285.

49. Ahmad, *The Making of Modern Turkey*, 209.

50. Eric Rouleau, "Turkey: Beyond Ataturk," *Foreign Policy* (Summer 1996): 80.

51. "Turkey," *Trends in Developing Economies 1995* (New York: Oxford University Press, 1995), 519.

52. "Turkey," 520.

53. "Survey Turkey: A Disaster That Hasn't Quite Happened," *The Economist* (8 June 1996): 11.

54. "Survey Turkey: A Disaster That Hasn't Quite Happened," 8.

55. Rouleau, "Turkey: Beyond Ataturk," 80.

56. Rouleau, "Turkey: Beyond Ataturk," 80.

57. Ahmad, *The Making of Modern Turkey*, 2.

58. Ahmad, *The Making of Modern Turkey*, 9.

59. Ahmad, *The Making of Modern Turkey*, 12.

60. Ahmet Evin, "Demilitarization and Civilianization of the Regime," *Politics in the Third Turkish Republic*, 25.

61. Ahmad, *The Making of Modern Turkey*, 213.

62. C. H. Dodd, *The Crisis of Turkish Democracy* (Huntingdon, United Kingdom: Eothen Press, 1983), 30.

63. Henze, "Turkey: Toward the Twenty-First Century," 17.

Chapter 2 _____

From Neutrality to NATO

Examining a state's foreign policy orientation means exploring what governments seek to do—the purposes and objectives that states have—and the strategies they employ to achieve them.[1] Furthermore, "a nation's general strategy or orientation is seldom revealed in any one decision, but results from a series of cumulative decisions made in an effort to adjust objectives, values, and interests to conditions and characteristics of the domestic and external environments."[2] Consequently, this chapter will examine Turkey's foreign policy orientation from the inception of the new Turkish state to its alliance with the North Atlantic Treaty Organization (NATO).

1923–1945: THE PERIOD OF NEUTRALITY

Foreign Policy Objectives and Strategies

Turkey's most important foreign policy objective throughout its history has been security—protecting its independence and sovereignty from encroachments by foreign powers. Although this goal is a natural one for any country, it became particularly important for Turkey because the mere existence of the Turkish state was threatened in the aftermath of World War I.[3] The deteriorating Ottoman Empire had not been ready militarily, economically, or politically to enter World War I, but convinced that isolation from world affairs would mean the end of the empire, the Ottomans formed an alliance with the Germans, an alliance that would eventually lose the war. By the time that the Ottomans surrendered to the entente powers on October 31, 1918, with the armistice of Mudros, they faced the threat of losing control over Anatolia—"their only base for a homeland left eight centuries after their arrival from Central Asia."[4] This armistice was devastating for the Ottomans; it had provisions that called for the military occupation of the straits of Bosporus and the Dardanelles, the control by the entente of all railways and telegraph lines, the demobilization and disarmament of the

Ottoman troops (allowing only a few small contingents to keep law and order), the surrender of the Arab provinces under Ottoman control, and the freeing of all entente prisoners of war in Ottoman hands while Turkish prisoners would remain indefinitely under entente detention.[5] A further clause in the armistice, one that threatened the sovereignty of the country even more, claimed that the entente had the right to occupy any part of the Ottoman Empire if it considered its security to be in jeopardy.

Soon after the armistice of Mudros went into effect, representatives of the entente arrived in Istanbul to supervise the execution of the armistice terms. Their job was facilitated by Sultan Mehmed VI Vahidettin, who pursued policies of appeasement in order to get a favorable peace treaty.[6] His main goals included the preservation of the dynasty and the maintenance of the seat of the caliphate (the office of the spiritual leader of Islam) in Istanbul, and he was willing to cooperate with the entente as long as the peace treaty being drafted guaranteed the continuance of these institutions. Meanwhile, the entente formulated an elaborate partition plan to divide western Anatolia into separate Greek, Italian, and French zones. In addition, the straits would not only be permanently demilitarized but would operate under the administration of an allied commission.[7] These harshly unfavorable conditions, formulated as the Treaty of Sèvres, were accepted by the sultan's government. Although nationalist groups operating from the interior of Anatolia firmly rejected the peace treaty and its provisions, power still rested in the hands of the sultan. Therefore, the Treaty of Sèvres was signed on August 10, 1920.

By this time, the Ottoman Empire had been stripped down to consist of a small area in northern Asia Minor with Istanbul as its capital. Eastern Thrace and the area around Izmir were given to Greece. An independent Armenian republic was created in eastern Anatolia. France established mandates in Syria and Lebanon, while Britain did so in Palestine, southern Syria, and Iraq. Italy established a sphere of influence in the southwestern part of Asia Minor, and an area called Kurdistan was created and given the right to appeal for autonomy within a year. Meanwhile, the straits of Bosporus and the Dardanelles were internationalized. Realizing the harshness of the terms of the treaty, the entente had anticipated resistance from either the Ottoman government or opposition movement forces, and as a precautionary measure, had occupied Istanbul.

Although the Ottoman rulers readily accepted the brutal terms of this treaty, an opposition movement not only to the entente occupation but also to the government in power had started to form. Local leaders had set up regional organizations called Societies for the Defense of Rights in various parts of Anatolia to resist the entente's scheme to divide Turkey. These independent societies were organized into a cohesive nationalist resistance on May 19, 1919, when Mustafa Kemal went to the city of Samsun to formally launch an opposition movement.[8] At this time, Mustafa Kemal and other nationalist leaders made clear that the very existence of the Turkish homeland was threatened, and they emphasized the need to take action to save their country. The different branches of the Societies for the Defense of Rights all over the country had already begun working to mobilize a weakened and war-weary population against the entente's occupation. While they were having various degrees of success, the Greek occupation of Izmir, also in May 1919, provided a significant boost to their efforts. Not only had Greece allied with the entente toward the very end of the war but it also had not won any of its battles against the Ottoman troops. Therefore, the Greek army's occupation of Izmir was seen as a great injustice by the Turks.[9] Furthermore, in addition to occupying the areas agreed upon in the Treaty of Sèvres (Izmir and Ayvalik), the Greeks went on to take over a much larger area. After May 1919, therefore, the nationalist movement started to gain momentum as the masses increasingly became convinced that they would have to fight for the possession of the disputed provinces. Meanwhile, a series of congresses convened by the nationalist opposition adopted "The National Pact"—a political document that defined and declared the territorial boundaries of the new political entity that Mustafa Kemal and his followers were determined to establish.

Although the Ottoman army had been significantly drained by the defeats of World War I, as well as by numerous epidemics and desertions, almost all of its leading officers supported the resistance. Despite instances of guerrilla fighting with the occupying powers, however, a war of resistance was not launched until the political structures and institutions of the nationalist movement were founded. The efforts of the Societies for the Defense of Rights to establish these structures and institutions culminated in the first meeting of the Turkish Grand National Assembly in Ankara on April 23, 1920. This gathering was attended by 92 parliamentarians and 232 representatives elected by the local branches of the Defense of Rights movement. By this time, the headquarters of the nationalist movement in Ankara resembled a complete government and the nationalists declared that all legislation passed by the Istanbul government after March 16 was void. They also made clear that they would not accept the terms of the Treaty of Sèvres, and that they were ready and willing to fight to preserve the Ottoman dynasty and the caliphate. (Mustafa Kemal only talked about abolishing the caliphate and establishing a republic after December 1922). During the War of Independence of the next two years, the nationalist armies defeated their adversaries on many fronts: the Greeks in the west, the Armenians and Georgians in the northeast, and the French and the British in the southeast. Consequently, Mustafa Kemal emerged from the war as the undisputed leader of Turkey. He made clear to the entente powers that a new peace treaty that reflected the victories of the Turkish nationalists during 1921 and 1922 would have to be negotiated. Ismet İnönü, one of Mustafa Kemal's closest allies and a prominent general from the War of Independence, represented Turkey in Lausanne where a new peace treaty—the Treaty of Lausanne—was drawn up.

The nationalists had attained their most important goal by the time this treaty was signed on July 24, 1923; Turkey had emerged as a completely sovereign state. Furthermore, this new treaty (which replaced the Treaty of Sèvres) granted the nationalists most of the territorial demands outlined in the National Pact. The main exceptions were two former Ottoman Arab territories—the oil-rich provinces of Mosul-Kirkuk in northern Iraq (which was a British mandate), and the *sancak* of Alexandretta in northern Syria (known as Hatay in Turkey, which was a French mandate). In addition, except for Imroz and Tenedos, the Aegean Islands that Turkey had claimed remained with Greece and Italy. The straits zone was internationalized under a commission chaired by a Turk and demilitarized (except for a contingent of twelve thousand troops in Istanbul). Despite these relatively minor setbacks, however, the Treaty of Lausanne was considered to be a tremendous victory for Turkey. The entente's efforts to establish supervision over Turkey's judicial system had failed, and everyone living in Turkey, including foreigners, was subject to Turkish laws and Turkish courts. All of the reparation claims outlined in the Treaty of Sèvres were renounced. Furthermore, the treaty contained a clause in which "Turkey bound itself to protect its citizens, regardless of creed, nationality or language," giving Turkey autonomous power over the minorities living within its borders.[10] This clause referred to the religious minorities in Turkey, such as the Greeks and the Armenians, as the Turkish negotiators in Lausanne had refused to recognize ethnically based minorities. As such, the Kurds were not defined as a minority and were prevented from being able to claim any special status or provisions.[11] By the time the last of the entente troops left Turkey on October 1, 1923, Turkey had become a completely independent and sovereign nation.

The foreign policy objectives of this new state—the Republic of Turkey— were very much colored by the experiences and the hardships that it underwent to claim its independence and territorial integrity. The fact that the Turkish homeland was nearly lost during World War I led the rulers of the new republic to be very clear in identifying and defining their most important foreign policy goal—the "physical protection of the country against potential or actual threats endangering or violating its territorial integrity, especially those originating in the immediate surroundings."[12] The objective of maintaining the state's security and territorial integrity remained stable throughout the history of the Turkish Republic, but Ankara often shifted the policies it pursued to reach this goal.

Turkish foreign policy from 1923 to the end of World War II in 1945 has been described as "cautious, realistic and generally aimed at the preservation of the status-quo and the hard won victory of 1923."[13] Having learned a lesson from the Ottomans' permanent involvement in various wars and conflicts that ultimately led to the downfall of the empire, the leaders of the new Turkey aspired to be totally independent.[14] They also believed that such independence could only be achieved if Turkey maintained a policy of neutrality in international disputes. During this time, therefore, Ankara became involved only in a few minor disputes with Western European powers, most of which resulted from the fact that the Treaty of Lausanne had left a number of problems unresolved.

One such conflict, for example, was with the United Kingdom over the province of Mosul—an oil-rich area occupied by the British that was mostly inhabited by Kurds, but that also had significant Arab and Turkish minorities. The National Pact had demanded that Mosul be included in the borders of the Turkish Republic. The British, however, had insisted that this province be a part of Iraq. The dispute was submitted to the League of Nations when, amid persistent border scuffles, the two sides could not reach a settlement. The League (of which Turkey was not yet a member) reached the decision in September 1925 that the province should be included in Iraq. In return for officially concurring in June 1926, Turkey was to receive 10 percent of Mosul's oil profits for the next twenty-five years. Ankara, however, soon abandoned this claim in exchange for a compensation of £700,000 from the United Kingdom. A similar conflict occurred with France over the *sancak* of Hatay. This was an area within the borders of Syria with a significant Turkish community that closely followed the developments in Turkey. The People's Party of Hatay had even carried out such Kemalist policies as the hat and alphabet reforms, which introduced Western attire and the Latin script to Turkish society. France's announcement in September 1939 that it would grant independence to Syria and that it intended to include Hatay in the Syrian state, therefore, was unacceptable to the Turks. This issue was also brought before the League of Nations, and at this time, the League ruled in favor of Turkey, concluding that the Turkish community was the majority. Hatay proclaimed independence in 1938 and in July 1939, it announced that it was forming a union with Turkey—leading this dispute to be solved to Turkey's satisfaction. The parameters of Turkey's current territory were established after Hatay became a part of the country.

Other sources of disagreement with Western powers included, for example, France and Britain's refusal to move their embassies to Ankara, the new capital of the Turkish Republic, and their concerns about the jurisdiction of the Turkish Ministry of Education over the diplomatic missions' schools. Despite these relatively minor disputes, however, Ankara focused on adhering to Atatürk's basic foreign policy slogan, "peace at home and peace in the world." The 1920s and 1930s saw an improvement in Turkey's relations with countries such as Italy, Greece, Yugoslavia, Romania, Iran, Iraq, and Afghanistan with which it signed friendship treaties or formed pacts and alliances. Meanwhile, Turkey's relations with the Soviet Union were excellent, and the Treaty of Friendship signed by the two countries on March 16, 1921, was one of the pillars of Turkish foreign policy during this time. World War II, however, disrupted this relatively harmonious foreign policy arena.

Turkey's foreign policy strategy during World War II was one of "active neutrality." Ankara devoted considerable energy to staying out of the war, as it felt that the country was not ready militarily, economically, or politically to be involved in another major war so soon after World War I and the War of Independence. Its strategy was termed "active neutrality" because, in addition to remaining impartial in the war, Turkey would actively seek to mediate between the two sides. Although its offers of mediation did not lead anywhere, the core of Turkey's wartime strategy consisted of maintaining cordial but distant relations with the warring parties. For example, although Ankara had signed a treaty of mutual support with France and the United Kingdom in October 1939, it insisted on the attachment of a separate protocol that stipulated that Turkey would not have the obligation to become involved in conflicts that could entangle it in a war with the Soviet Union. By invoking this protocol, and by signing a treaty of friendship with Germany in 1941 (at the time of Germany's invasion of the Soviet Union), Turkey succeeded in remaining neutral and on the sidelines of the war until the very end. It did not break diplomatic relations with Germany until August 2, 1944. Although the Soviets had previously agreed with the British and the Americans that Turkey should be convinced to enter the war, by late 1944 Moscow preferred that Ankara stay out of the conflict. The Soviet press condemned Turkey's severance of diplomatic relations with Germany as a half-measure and announced that Turkish entry into the war on the side of the Allies was no longer desired by the Soviet Union. Meanwhile, the United States, the United Kingdom, and the Soviet Union decided at the Yalta

Conference in February 1945 that only the states that had fought the Axis powers, or declared war on Germany by March 1, 1945, would be invited to the forthcoming United Nations Conference. Not wanting to be left out of this upcoming conference, Turkey declared war on Germany and Japan on February 23, 1945. This declaration of war was only a symbolic action, however, because, for all practical purposes, the war was over by this time. The Soviet armies were within 50 kilometers of Berlin and the Anglo-American forces were closing in on Cologne. Turkey's wartime policies were not only criticized as being "immoral and reneging on the treaty [with France and Britain] of 1939" by the Allied powers but also damaged its international reputation.[15] Turkish citizens as well as politicians, however, saw Turkey's ability to stay out of the war as a great political success. While the Ottoman Empire had allowed itself to be used as a pawn by the Germans during World War I, the young Turkish Republic had managed to assert its independence and sovereignty while protecting its territorial integrity.

The Decision-Making Process

The foreign policy and domestic decisions of 1923–1945 were made by a highly authoritarian political structure. During this time, Turkey was a single-party state in which the Republican People's Party (CHP) had a monopoly on power. This political system was established soon after the War of Independence when Mustafa Kemal centralized power in his own hands, as well as in the hands of his party, the CHP. Although the role of the caliph had already been reduced to a purely religious function in 1922, for example, the fact that many people continued to see the caliph as a head of state, and that his jurisdiction extended to the entire Muslim world, led Mustafa Kemal to want to abolish the institution as a whole. For similar reasons, he also wanted to do away with the Ottoman dynasty and to establish a republic. Despite some opposition, Mustafa Kemal's proposal for a republic that would have an elected president, a prime minister appointed by the president, and a cabinet was accepted by the majority of the Grand National Assembly delegates. The Republic of Turkey was thus proclaimed on October 29, 1923. The caliphate was abolished on March 1, 1924, and the members of the Ottoman dynasty were told to leave the country. Many of the decisions that led to these significant changes were made in a rather authoritarian manner. During the debate and decision period for these momentous changes, a number of important personalities from the War of Independence who may have been opposed to these alterations were not in Ankara. Various factions within the CHP harshly criticized the government for its heavy-handed tactics and denounced the declaration of the republic as premature. As a result of the disagreement that arose over this issue, as well as over some other sources of contention, thirty-two deputies defected from the CHP to form an opposition party on November 17, 1924. Although this new party—the Progressive Republican Party—also had a secular and nationalist ideology, it objected to the CHP's radical, centralist, and authoritarian inclinations. The creation of an opposition party scared the CHP; because certain sectors of society were dissatisfied with the ruling party, they were willing to support any opposition group, threatening the CHP's grip on power.

A Kurdish rebellion led by Sheikh Sait of Piran in February 1925 in the southeast region of Turkey, however, provided the context in which the CHP clamped down on opposition movements in the country. Sheikh Sait's goal was to establish a traditional Islamic order in Turkey, and he was supported not only by Kurds but also by groups dissatisfied with the secular direction the country was taking. He and his followers succeeded in occupying a third of Kurdish Anatolia before their uprising was suppressed. To fight this rebellion, the Grand National Assembly passed the Law on the Maintenance of Order in March 1925. This law, which remained in effect until 1929, provided the administrative basis for the government's authoritarian tendencies. It gave the government the right to ban any organization or publication that it considered to be a cause of disturbance to law and order. Although the law was passed to fight the Kurdish insurrection, it was also used to suppress other groups. Eight major newspapers and journals, for example, were closed down, and all of the most influential journalists from Istanbul were brought before the Independence Tribunal and not allowed to resume their work even after being released. Furthermore, the government used the Law on the Maintenance of Order to close down the Progressive Republican Party, charging that its members had not only assisted the Kurdish rebellion, but also used religion to further their political agenda, which was prohibited under the strictly secular constitution of 1924.

Although the 1924 constitution placed all power in the Grand National Assembly as the only legitimate representative of the sovereign will of the nation, it was not a democratic institution as it did not allow any meaningful, open debates to take place among the delegates. Because the CHP did not want to see more defections or further dissent within its ranks, the party leadership tightened party discipline and limited open discussion to closed party meetings. Not even these internal meetings, however, were unrestricted: they served more as a forum in which the cabinet would announce and explain its decisions. Some issues such as economic policy were discussed and debated more freely, whereas other issues, such as foreign affairs, were not open for deliberation. Because foreign policy decision-making was left entirely to the cabinet, the party meetings only served as a place where foreign policy decisions would be legitimized and rubber-stamped. Delegates were bound by the majority decision reached in these closed meetings and obligated to support it in the assembly. As a result, the voting in the Grand National Assembly was not much more than a formality.

Although Turkey was a highly authoritarian single-party state during the 1923–1945 period, there was a brief experiment with multiparty democracy in 1930, showing that Atatürk was not ill-disposed toward liberal democracy.[16] By this time, there was widespread discontent within the country about the authoritarianism of the CHP, the corruption in the party, the lack of civil liberties, and the economic difficulties that the government could not alleviate. In order to channel this social discontent, expand participation, and encourage some healthy criticism, therefore, Atatürk urged his friend Fethi Bey to found another political party.[17] Fethi Bey formed the Free Republican Party after getting assurances that the government would allow it to function freely, and that Atatürk himself would remain impartial. Although the citizenry showed great enthusiasm for the Free Republican Party's promotion of more liberal economic policies and a more open political system, it succeeded in winning only 30 of the 512 councils in the local elections held in October 1930. Dissatisfied with these results, Fethi Bey accused the CHP of election fraud, and, in return, was assailed by the CHP for committing high treason. Furthermore, Atatürk informed Fethi Bey that he could not remain impartial in such a tense atmosphere. This experiment with multiparty democracy thus came to an abrupt end when Fethi Bey closed down the Free Republican Party on November 16, 1930.

After having failed at the attempt to create a multiparty state in Turkey, the Republican People's Party officially declared Turkey a single-party state in the 1931 party congress. Consequently, the party grew more authoritarian, and the state and the party became very closely identified with each other. Meanwhile, the parliamentary elections that were held every four years served only a ceremonial function because the "slates of candidates for parliamentary seats were drawn up by the chairman of the party, the executive chairman and the secretary-general and then ratified by the party congress and there was no way in which citizens, even if they were active party members could stand for parliament on their own initiative."[18] Its experience with the Free Republican Party also led the CHP to clamp down on a number of independent social and cultural organizations, fearing that they would be the breeding ground for opposition movements. A law passed in 1931 gave the government the right to shut down newspapers or journals that published articles that contradicted the "general policies of the country." The closeness between the state apparatus and the party organization was institutionalized at the 1936 party congress. As a result, for example, the governor of a certain province would automatically become the head of the CHP branch in that province.

The decisions that were made during the 1923–1945 period, especially foreign policy decisions, thus emanated from the upper echelons of the CHP. Foreign policy was not an area that was open to debate, and not even the opposition parties (during their brief existence) questioned the validity of the decisions taken by the CHP leadership in this area. During this time, Ankara worked single-mindedly to achieve the maintenance of national security, or as Atatürk said "peace at home, peace in the world."

1945–1960: ALLIANCE WITH THE WEST

Foreign Policy Objectives and Strategies

The drastic alterations that occurred in the structure of the international system in the aftermath of World War II led to major changes in the policies Ankara pursued in maintaining Turkey's national security. The United States had emerged from World War II as the strongest major power, and the Soviet Union soon became its ardent enemy. It was becoming clear to many nations in the world that they could not maintain cordial relations with both the United States and the Soviet Union now that the world had been divided into two opposing camps. Turkey did not have a great deal of choice as to which side it should ally with because Joseph Stalin's desire to establish control over the Turkish straits, as well as his claims to the Turkish provinces of Kars and Ardahan (which had been part of Georgia from 1878 to 1921, but had been returned to Turkey in 1921) soon after the end of the war convinced Turkish politicians that their neighbor to the northeast was not only hostile but expansionist as well. As a result of these threats, Ankara concluded that Washington should become its most important ally, and its protector. Writing about the Soviet demands in later years, Nikita Khrushchev said that Lavrenti Beria, who was the head of Stalin's large police network, had urged Stalin to make these claims, arguing that a Turkey considerably weakened by World War II would not be able to resist the Soviets' advances.[19] Khrushchev thus concluded that Beria and Stalin had "succeeded in frightening the Turks right into the open arms of the Americans."[20]

Ankara's foreign policy strategy during the post-war period, therefore, focused on being included in as many vehicles of the Western alliance as possible in order to ward off the Soviets' demands. Although this involvement in Western institutions was a process that changed and deepened over the years, "at no time in history was the westernization of Turkey so intensive and one-sided as in the period after WWII, and this thanks to the pressure coming from the Soviet Union."[21] Turkey's desire to westernize encompassed the economic, political, and military arenas. In fact, Ankara was operating under the assumption that inclusion in Western institutions (such as the Marshall Plan, Council of Europe, and the North Atlantic Treaty Organization) would not only enhance Turkey's security considerations, but also help procure material resources necessary for the country's economic growth and development.[22] Consequently, Turkey developed a linkage between its economic and its foreign policy. Meanwhile, Turkish foreign policy during the 1945–1960 period was governed by pragmatism, except when the issue became the rights of Turks living outside Turkey, such as in Cyprus. Situations in which the well-being of the so-called outside Turks were jeopardized brought a certain degree of uncertainty to Turkish foreign policy, an uncertainty that threatened the single-minded pursuit of security through alliance-building strategies.

Turkey's first success in the endeavor of becoming a part of the institutions of the Western alliance was its inclusion in the Truman Doctrine. On March 12, 1947, U.S. President Harry S. Truman delivered a speech to Congress in which he stressed that Greece and Turkey were being threatened "by direct or indirect aggression [which would] undermine the foundations of international peace and hence the security of the United States." Consequently, "it must be the policy of the United States to support free peoples who are resisting attempted subjugation by armed minorities or by outside pressure."[23] According to Truman's plan, which became known as the Truman Doctrine, the United States would provide financial and military assistance to help defend "free nations" being threatened by foreign pressure. Accordingly, Turkey started to receive foreign aid from the United States and was included in the Marshall Plan, which was to provide massive financial support to European countries to help them rebuild their war-ravaged economies. Turkey also aspired to membership in NATO, which was created in 1949. Its application in 1950, however, was met with resistance, especially from countries like Britain, Denmark, and Norway, who argued that Turkey (along with Greece, whose membership application was also being considered) was neither an Atlantic nor a democratic country. Prime Minister Adnan Menderes, however, saw the North Korean invasion of South Korea in June 1950 as Turkey's best chance to overcome this hurdle and prove its loyalty to the West. One of the first countries that offered to contribute troops, Turkey eventually sent 25,000 soldiers to Korea and suffered significant casualties. Inspired by Turkey's brave actions during the Korean War, the United States heavily promoted Turkey's membership in NATO and succeeded in convincing countries who had objections to drop them. Turkey, therefore, became a member of NATO on February 18, 1952. Their country's entry into NATO was celebrated by Turks as a great foreign policy success as membership in the organization was seen as "a guarantee against Soviet aggression and as guaranteeing the flow of western aid and loans which would make the modernization of Turkey possible [as well as] a sign that Turkey had finally been fully accepted by the western nations on "equal terms."[24]

Subsequently, Turkey's membership in NATO and its role in the cold war contributed significantly to determining other aspects of the country's foreign policy. Its relations with the Arab world were difficult, for example, because of Turkey's position in the Israeli-Palestinian conflict. Although it had expected the new Israeli state to be pro-communist and sided with the Arab countries at first, Turkey recognized Israel's independence and established diplomatic relations once the United States forged close relations with the young state. Furthermore, at the insistence of the Americans, Ankara entered into a number of regional alliances. The Baghdad Pact, for example, was formed in February 1955 with Britain, Pakistan, Iraq, and Iran as members and the United States as an observer. Although it had verbally supported Egypt in the Suez crisis of 1956, Turkey as well as the Baghdad Pact were heavily criticized as puppets of Western imperialism. The fact that Americans used their bases in Turkey to intervene in the Lebanese civil war in 1958 added to such criticisms of Turkey by the Arabs. The Baghdad Pact was transformed into the Central Treaty Organization (CENTO) in 1960 when the new regime in Iraq withdrew from the organization and the United States joined as a member. Neither the Baghdad Pact nor CENTO, however, had been effective in contributing to regional security or cooperation because member countries were too distrustful of each other to trade military secrets or to adopt any substantive cooperative measures.

Similarly, Turkey's relations with its Balkan neighbors were conditioned by its position in the Western alliance, and once again, Turkey entered into a regional alliance under the guidance of the Americans. The Balkan Pact, concluded in February 1953 among Turkey, Greece, and Yugoslavia, however, proved to be as ineffective as the Baghdad Pact and CENTO. Turkey's biggest conflict in the Balkans was with the Soviet-backed regime in Bulgaria. A crisis, for example, had occurred when the regime expelled 250,000 of their Turkish-speaking Muslim citizens as a reaction to Turkey's sending troops to Korea. Totally unprepared for such an influx of people, Turkey closed its borders. The crisis was solved when Bulgaria allowed the people to return in 1953, but then adopted another policy condemned by Ankara that would not allow any Muslim Bulgarians to leave the country.

Perhaps also due to the importance Ankara placed in becoming a central figure in the Western alliance, it succeeded in maintaining cordial relations with its old enemy, Greece, until the first Cyprus crisis. Although the Greek Cypriot (80 percent) and Turkish Cypriot (20 percent) inhabitants of Cyprus had lived together under British rule since 1878, the movements by the Greek nationalists, who wanted to liberate Cyprus from the British and unify the island with Greece, escalated into riots and terrorist attacks on the British in 1954.[25] Moreover, the possibility of such a union with Greece was totally unacceptable to the Turks. Years of tense negotiations among the interested parties led to the signing of an agreement, which made Cyprus an independent republic on August 16, 1960. The independence, territorial integrity, and constitutional order of the island were to be guaranteed by Greece, Britain, and Turkey. The agreement signed at the time stated that the three countries would work together in order to jointly uphold the guarantees, but if they were unable to do so, each one could act unilaterally. (This provision of the agreement, Article 3, would be used years later to justify the Turkish military intervention in Cyprus.)

While the structure of the international system had changed drastically during the time between the beginning and the end of World War II, there had been significant changes in the Turkish domestic arena between the years 1945 and 1960. Turkey had been an authoritarian single-party state from 1923 until 1945 but adopted major reforms in the aftermath of World War II that placed it on the path to becoming a multiparty democracy. The Republican People's Party, which had a monopoly on power in the first decades of the Republic, was replaced by the Democratic Party in 1950, which rose to power through free and fair elections. But the corruption and mismanagement of the Democrats led to military intervention on May 27, 1960.

The Decision-Making Process

It was not until the end of World War II that Turkey had its first real experience with democracy. Consequently, the 1945–1960 period was characterized by Ankara's transition from a single-party to a multiparty system. This democratization process resulted from the external pressures for democratization, as well the domestic demands for change. The defeat of the Axis powers in World War II was seen as a victory for democratic values, and the Western bloc "appeared to be increasingly concerned with promoting democracy as the mainstay of the 'free world.' "[26] Ankara, therefore, "had a feeling of isolation, of being regarded as undemocratic or 'fascist' in a world which, under the Charter of the United Nations, paid lip service to democracy and human rights" and was thus eager to "join the Democratic Club."[27] In addition, despite the satisfaction among the populace with President Inönü's ability to keep Turkey out of World War II, there was widespread disapproval of the government. The peasants—about 80 percent of the total populace—had not seen significant improvements in their standards of living, and the business community was disappointed with the government because of an extremely unpopular taxation system that imposed punitive taxes on excess profits (the property tax).[28] Meanwhile, the entrepreneurs who had prospered economically during World War II wanted their new economic power to lead to a certain degree of political power, and "hence, to break down the power monopoly of the bureaucratic elite."[29]

Because of these pressures for democratization, Inönü had signaled that Turkey might be ready to democratize its political institutions prior to the end of the war. Perhaps because of the feeling that a transition to democracy was approaching, therefore, the parliamentary discussion regarding the Land Distribution Law (aimed at providing land to farmers by distributing unused state lands) in May 1945 became the first time that the government was openly and severely criticized. An opposition faction in parliament condemned not only various articles of this law but also the way in which the government had controlled the debate—laying down the seeds for dissent in the governing party. Soon afterward, on June 7, 1945, Adnan Menderes, who had led the opposition, and three other prominent deputies submitted a memorandum to the governing CHP in which they called for the establishment of a democracy in Turkey.

The multiparty period in the history of the Turkish republic officially started in July 1945 when a leading businessman founded an opposition party—the National Development Party—that was neither effective nor popular because it did not have any experienced politicians or representation in the Grand National Assembly. Despite its existence, therefore, Inönü proclaimed on November 1, 1945, that the lack of an opposition party was the major weakness of the Turkish political system. He said that the general elections planned for 1947 would be free and fair and contested by opposition parties. This declaration thus allowed those who had been ousted from the CHP to found the Democratic Party (DP) in January 1946 under the leadership of Menderes. The elections of July 1946 (moved forward from July 1947 to give the DP less time to organize and campaign) were far from being free and fair; there was no guarantee of secrecy during the casting of ballots, no impartial supervision of the elections, and a significant degree of vote-rigging. As a result, the DP only managed to win 62 out of the 465 seats in parliament. In the next general elections in May 1950, which were free and fair, however, the Democrats won over 53 percent of the vote and took office as Turkey's first democratically elected government.[30]

Once in power, the Democrats concentrated on reforming Turkey's economic policies but did not make significant alterations in other arenas. The economic platform of the DP promoted economic liberalization and focused on the development of the agricultural sector as the base of the Turkish economy. These new economic policies brought some important changes to Turkish society, and, consequently, to Turkish politics. The investment of large amounts of capital in the agricultural sector in the first years of DP rule led to a significant increase in the earnings of farmers. However, these policies also raised rural communities' expectations of what their standard of living should be. Because the government could not adequately meet these expectations and satisfy the demand for material improvements, enormous numbers of people from rural areas began to migrate to the urban centers. By the end of the decade of the 1950s, over a million people had abandoned their villages and farms, causing the cities to grow at an annual rate of 10 percent.[31] The newly emerging industrial sector could not absorb the influx of people searching for employment and the state could not provide basic services. Although the urban migration did not have tremendous repercussions at this time, it came to play a significant role in Turkish politics in later decades.

Although the Democrats had risen to power with great popular support, a number of serious problems in Turkey led to the demise of their power by the end of the 1950s. One important problem emanated from their economic policies. Although the country experienced significant rates of growth in the first years of DP rule, the efforts to expand and liberalize the economy at too fast a pace, coupled with some substantial mistakes in economic planning, led to a major economic crisis. As the economic situation deteriorated, the government relied increasingly on using Turkey's strategic importance in the cold war to secure significant amounts of American loans. These loans, in turn, were used to purchase large amounts of modern machinery and materials, increasing the trade deficit. An inefficient system of taxation, high levels of inflation, and a large black market compounded the country's economic problems.

This economic crisis combined with difficulties in the political arena. Even though the Democrats had campaigned on the platform that they were going to implement policies of economic liberalization along with policies of political liberalization, they grew more and more authoritarian when faced with unceasing criticisms from the CHP, the leftists, and other members of the opposition. For example, they expelled dissenters from the party and retired civil servants, judges, and university professors who they believed were still loyal to the CHP.[32] The DP also established tight government controls over the press, suspended a number of newspapers from publication, and prosecuted journalists for insulting the government.[33]

While economic crises and the lack of political liberalization may not have been enough to bring down the regime, these problems, coupled with the threat of religious fundamentalism, ultimately led to its downfall. By the time the 1957 elections took place, the DP was quickly losing support in the urban areas. Even the repressive measures it took could not prevent the intellectuals, the bureaucrats, and the military, which had always been suspicious of the DP, from voicing their criticisms of the ruling party's shortcomings. In order to increase its support, therefore, the DP began courting the religious vote in Turkey. Although it upheld the secularist ideology that religion was not to play a part in Turkish politics, the DP took certain measures that increased the role of Islam in society. It allowed the call to prayer to be in Arabic (which had been forbidden by Atatürk), permitted the broadcast of Koran recitations on the radio, introduced religion to school curricula, expanded religious education, increased the numbers of mosques being built, and reopened an Institute of Islamic Studies. By "directly or indirectly encouraging private initiatives favoring religion," the DP contributed to the increase in the number of pilgrims going to Mecca, the rise in the numbers of people who visited the tombs and shrines of holy figures, and an increased observance of fasting during Ramadan.[34] The 1950s, in other words, saw a revival of religion in the daily lives of the Turkish people. The concessions that the Democrats made to religion, however, were heavily criticized by the CHP, the intellectuals, and the military as using religion for political purposes. Clashes between secularists (or Kemalists) and Islamists grew more violent, and the society, more divided over this issue.

The growing authoritarianism of the Democrats, the increasingly dismal economic situation, and the greater role that the DP gave to religion created a situation in which many influential sectors of society were greatly dissatisfied with the Democrats' rule. Perhaps the most important of these groups constituted a large segment of the armed forces. While the Democrats had wooed army generals during their tenure, they had largely neglected the junior officers. The purchasing power of the fixed-income military officials had diminished due to the high levels of inflation, and their already meager standard of living had deteriorated under DP rule. Furthermore, many army officers were upset that the Menderes government had not implemented the "thorough-going reform of the entire military structure" that they had been hoping for.[35] In addition, the prestige of the armed services declined during the Democrats' rule. As a result of the grievances with their own situation as well as with the circumstances in the country, on May 27, 1960, the military ousted the government of Menderes. The objective of the coup d'état was not only to change the government but also to carry out significant changes in the political structures of the Turkish Republic. The changes implemented after the military intervention affected foreign policy decision-making in Turkey for years to come.

The 1945–1960 period was significant for foreign policy decision-making in Turkey because whereas foreign policy decisions were made by a small groups of state elites until 1945, the decision-making arena was expanded in the 1950s with the entry of the Democratic Party into Turkish politics. The rise to power of the DP, however, did not democratize the decision-making process because the Democrats were just as autocratic as their Republican predecessors in restricting dissent. The only real change that this period ushered in was the expansion of the foreign policy decision-making arena. During the single-party era, questions regarding Turkey's foreign affairs were discussed and decided by an extremely limited group of party leaders who were mostly bureaucrats and retired military officers. The DP, on the other hand, was composed of a rather diverse group of people including "private industrialists, commercial groups, landed interests, and the peasantry."[36] The different composition of the governing party reflected the different priorities of the party—the focus on the liberalization and development of the Turkish economy—as well as the convergence of economic and foreign policy (i.e., using Turkey's strategic position in the cold war to garner foreign assistance).

Foreign Policy Behavior

As an ally of the West, Turkey made many foreign policy decisions and took many actions that were closely aligned with American interests. One of the first such decisions was the pro-Israeli position it assumed in the Arab-Israeli conflict. As a member of the Palestine Conciliation Commission along with France and the United States, Turkey became one of the first countries to recognize Israel diplomatically in 1949. Its decision to do so, which enraged Turkey's Arab neighbors, signaled to the world that its sympathies as well as the direction of its foreign policy lay with the countries of the West.

Its involvement in the Korean War a few years later solidified Ankara's position as an integral part of the Western bloc.

For the next few decades, Turkey's foreign policy behavior was dominated by Turkish decision-makers' desire to demonstrate their allegiance to the West, especially to the United States. In 1954, for example, it signed the first bilateral military aid agreement with the United States that provided the basis for a greater degree of security cooperation between the two countries. Two years later, the Americans stationed high-altitude U-2s at the Incirlik Air Base near Adana, installed equipment to gain information from the Soviet Union along the Black Sea region, and, after another year, positioned strike aircraft with tactical nuclear weapons. Furthermore, American forces stationed in the Middle East used Turkish bases as a staging area during the U.S. intervention in the war in Lebanon in 1958.

The Turkish-American relationship intensified a few years later when Turkey became the only country in NATO that, in spite of strong objections from the Soviet Union, accepted the stationing of American nuclear missiles on its territory. An agreement between Ankara and Washington that detailed the deployment of a squadron of Jupiter missiles was reached in October 1959. It took several more years to install the missiles (owned by Turkey but under the operational control of the Supreme Allied Command Europe [SACEUR]), which finally became operational in the spring of 1962. Although the technology of the Jupiter missiles became obsolete even before they were deployed (because the negotiations preceding their deployment had taken so long and new weapons technologies had been developed during that time), their deployment on Turkish territory made Turkey a central figure in one of the defining events during the cold war—the Cuban Missile Crisis. A part of the compromise that resulted from the secret discussions between the Soviets and Americans during the crisis, to which Turkey was not a party, was the agreement that in exchange for the removal of Soviet missiles from Cuba, the United States would remove the missiles deployed in Turkey.

By 1960 Turkey had established itself as a close ally of the United States and an integral actor in containing Soviet expansionism. The various governments in power had worked consistently and single-mindedly toward this foreign policy objective, and despite failures in many other aspects of politics, they had been successful in achieving this goal.

NOTES

1. K. J. Holsti, *International Politics: A Framework for Analysis*, 6th ed. (Englewood Cliffs, N.J.: Prentice-Hall, 1992), 83.

2. K. J. Holsti, *International Politics: A Framework for Analysis*, 3d ed. (Englewood Cliffs, N.J.: Prentice-Hall, 1977), 109.

3. Kemal H. Karpat, Introduction, *Turkey's Foreign Policy in Transition: 1950–1974* (Leiden: E. J. Brill, 1975), 4.

4. Duygu Bazoğlu Sezer, "Turkey's Grand Strategy Facing a Dilemma," *International Spectator* 27 (January-March 1992): 18.

5. Erik J. Zurcher, *Turkey: A Modern History* (London: I. B. Tauris, 1993), 138.

6. Zurcher, *Turkey: A Modern History*, 142.

7. William Hale, *The Political and Economic Development of Modern Turkey* (New York: St. Martin's Press, 1981), 33.

8. George S. Harris, *Turkey: Coping with Crisis* (Boulder, Colo.: Westview Press, 1985), 55.

9. Zurcher, *Turkey: A Modern History*, 154.

10. Zurcher, *Turkey: A Modern History*, 170.

11. Philip Robins, "The Overload State: Turkish Policy and the Kurdish Issue," *International Affairs* 69.4 (1993): 660.

12. Sezer, "Turkey's Grand Strategy Facing a Dilemma," 19.

13. Zurcher, Turkey: *A Modern History*, 209.

14. Udo Steinbach, "The European Community, the United States, the Middle East, and Turkey," *Politics in the Third Turkish Republic*, ed. Metin Heper (Boulder, Colo.: Westview Press, 1994), 104.

15. Zurcher, *Turkey: A Modern History*, 14.

16. C. H. Dodd, *The Crisis of Turkish Democracy* (Huntingdon, United Kingdom: Eothen Press, 1983), 7.

17. Dodd, *The Crisis of Turkish Democracy*, 7.

18. Zurcher, *Turkey: A Modern History*, 185.

19. Bruce R. Kuniholm, "Turkey and the West Since World War II," *Turkey Between East and West: New Challenges for a Rising Regional Power*, eds. Vojtech Mastny and R. Craig Nation (Boulder, Colo.: Westview Press, 1996), 45.

20. Strobe Talbott, *Khruschev Remembers: The Last Testament* (Boston: Little, Brown, 1974), 295–296.

21. Karpat, *Turkey's Foreign Policy in Transition*, 4.

22. Atila Eralp, "Turkey and the European Community," in *The Political and Socioeconomic Transformation of Turkey*, eds. Eralp, Muharrem Tunay, and Birol A. Yesilada (Westport, Conn.: Praeger, 1993), 194.

23. Donald R. McCoy, *The Presidency of Harry S. Truman* (Lawrence: University Press of Kansas, 1984), 121.

24. Zurcher, *Turkey: A Modern History*, 246.

25. Suat Bilge, "The Cyprus Conflict and Turkey," *Turkey's Foreign Policy in Transition*, 135–148.

26. Ali L. Karaosmanoğlu, "The Limits of International Influence for Democratization," in *Politics in the Third Turkish Republic*, 120.

27. Ferenc A. Vali, *Bridge Across the Bosphorus: The Foreign Policy of Turkey* (Baltimore: Johns Hopkins University Press, 1971), 64.

28. Hale, *The Political and Economic Development of Modern Turkey*, 70.

29. Ziya Önis, "The State and Economic Development in Contemporary Turkey," in *Turkey Between East and West*, 158.

30. Dodd, *The Crisis of Turkish Democracy*, 7.

31. Zurcher, *Turkey: A Modern History*, 237.

32. Dodd, *The Crisis of Turkish Democracy*, 9.

33. Mehmet Yasar Geyikdaği, *Political Parties in Turkey: The Role of Islam* (New York: Praeger, 1984), 80.

34. Geyikdaği, *Political Parties in Turkey*, 77.

35. Feroz Ahmad, *The Making of Modern Turkey* (London: Routledge, 1993), 10.

36. Önis, "The State and Economic Development in Contemporary Turkey," 158.

Chapter 3 _____

Fluctuations in Cold War Foreign Policy

Although maintaining national security and territorial integrity remained Turkey's foremost foreign policy objective during the rest of the cold war period, there were several shifts in the strategies Ankara pursued to achieve this goal. Successive governments concentrated on increasing Turkey's strategic value for the United States and Western Europe so that these allies would not only maintain their commitment to Turkey's defense but would also continue to provide Turkey with financial and military assistance. Despite Ankara's desire to uphold strong relations with its Western allies, however, several sources of friction led to alterations in its foreign policy objectives and strategies.

1960–1980: COOLING OFF WITH THE UNITED STATES

Foreign Policy Objectives and Strategies

Turkey entered the 1960s with its close relationship with the United States as the foundation of its foreign policy. In addition to their association in NATO, the two countries were also bound together by fifty-six separate agreements, which allowed the Americans the right to build and operate military installations and bases in Turkey. These bases (which even housed Jupiter nuclear missiles after 1957), however, became problematic when many Turks resented the financial burden on their government imposed by the responsibility for the expropriation costs of land for the bases, the protection of the bases, the storage and care of weapons, and the maintenance of environmental security. Furthermore, they were irritated at the rights and privileges granted to American personnel, such as juridical privileges, a private postal service, and tax-free shopping. These irritations might not have risen to the forefront of the political arena in earlier decades, but the liberal constitution of 1961 (which had been written in the aftermath of the 1960 coup d'état) had granted greater liberties to the people, such as the freedom of speech. Left-wing intellectuals, like people connected to the journal *Yön* (*Direction*) or those with ties to the Workers Party, therefore, were now able to speak openly against government policies. Criticizing the government for making Turkey too dependent on the United States and NATO, they organized anti-American and antigovernment protests.[1] Meanwhile, the government maintained its allegiance to the United States and NATO and tried not to pay too much attention to public opinion that was becoming more and more anti-American. Several incidents that occurred during the 1960–1980 period, however, questioned NATO's commitment to protecting Turkish interests and led Ankara to seek ways of diversifying its foreign policy.

The first such event was the Cuban Missile Crisis in 1962–1963, when U.S. President John F. Kennedy yielded to Soviet demands that the U.S. missiles based in Turkey be withdrawn in exchange for the Soviet Union not installing missiles in Cuba. Although the Jupiter missile system in Turkey was rather obsolete and its value rather questionable, this occurrence gave Turks "the feeling that [Turkey] was no more than a pawn in the American game."[2] Furthermore, as Bruce Kuniholm said,

in the aftermath of the Cuban Missile Crisis a seed of doubt about NATO's commitments was planted among the Turks. They began to appreciate the fact that possession of particular weapons systems, while providing certain assurances and addressing some of their security needs, could also make them a target and render them vulnerable to decisions that were made in Washington. From now on they would be far more sensitive to the possibility that the alliance could pull them into a crisis that was of no direct concern to them.[3]

The Cuban Missile Crisis also made Turkish leaders realize that despite American commitments to Turkish security, Washington was willing to forgo its assurances to Turkey when American interests were at stake. The way in which the crisis was resolved made Turkish politicians and the public acknowledge the fact that the Americans would guarantee Turkey's security only if it was to their advantage. Furthermore, the fact that Ankara had not been invited to participate in the negotiations to resolve the crisis contributed to the perception that Turkey was no more than a pawn in cold war politics. While Turkish officials may have been naive for not coming to these realizations earlier, the Cuban Missile Crisis was a sort of rude awakening for them, and Ankara was eager to follow a more balanced foreign policy in the aftermath of the crisis.

Although the Cuban Missile Crisis had brought the world to the brink of war, its aftermath saw a de-escalation in cold war hostilities and the onset of détente. During this time, "which began with the Nuclear Test-Ban Treaty in 1963 and lasted through the . . . 1970s the nuclear threat seemed much less imminent, and relations [between the United States and USSR] took on a character of a stable competitive rivalry."[4] This relaxation of tensions between the superpowers meant that Turkey's dependence on the United States for protection from the Soviets was significantly reduced. Consequently, Ankara made efforts to diversify its foreign policy and improve relations with the Soviets in the first years of détente. Immediate improvements in Turkish-Soviet relations manifested themselves in the exchange of a number of official visits during which both sides declared their intentions for bettering their relationship. Nonetheless, Ankara's warmer relations with Moscow did not affect its close ties to Washington right away as both Turkish policymakers and the Turkish public still valued their country's alliance with the United States. For example, there was a general outpouring of sympathy in Turkey when President Kennedy was assassinated in November 1963; public places of entertainment were closed, and a major street was named after the late U.S. president.[5]

The aftermath of the Cuban Missile Crisis also saw an intensification of Turkey's relations with the European Community (EC, later known as the European Union, EU). Turkey had joined the EC as an associate member in 1964 and increased considerably trade with its member countries. In fact, Turkish trade with the EC surpassed that with the United States and the EC replaced the United States as Turkey's most important trading partner. Furthermore, economic growth in Europe created a demand for Turkish labor and thousands of workers moved to Europe, with the greatest numbers going to Germany. This reduced unemployment in Turkey, and the remittances from the Turkish workers in Europe soon became an important source of foreign exchange, easing foreign exchange shortages and balance of payments deficits. The number of Turkish "guest workers" in Germany, for example, went from 22,054 in 1963 to 528,475 in 1973.[6]

Another event that caused both the Turkish public and the politicians to question America's commitment to its security and interests was the 1963–1964 Cyprus crisis. The conflict started when Cypriot president Archbishop Makarios's government moved to change the island's constitution, a change that would limit the autonomy of the Turkish minority. A number of Turkish villages were besieged and clashes ensued between the Turkish and Greek Cypriots. The Turkish government decided to physically intervene in the island in order to protect the rights of the Turkish minority; and, operating under the assumption that the United States was its most important NATO ally, Ankara informed Washington of its intentions. President Lyndon Johnson's reply, however, came in a letter that stated that "NATO allies have not had a chance to consider whether they have an obligation to protect Turkey against the Soviet Union if Turkey takes a step which results in Soviet intervention without the full consent and understanding of its NATO allies."[7] Furthermore, the letter also said that the United States would not allow Turkey to use any American-donated military equipment in the invasion. Even U.S. Undersecretary of State George Ball declared that the so-called Johnson letter was "the most brutal diplomatic note [he had] ever seen."[8] The strong American reaction to the possibility of Turkish intervention in Cyprus, articulated in such harsh terms, prevented Turkey from invading Cyprus at this time. Johnson's letter, however, was leaked to the press and created widespread anti-American feelings among Turks. Meanwhile, both the public and the politicians had realized that neither NATO nor the United States was concerned about protecting Turkey's vital interests and that the foreign policy strategies they had been pursuing were no longer adequate. Reactions to the letter came in the form of widespread demonstrations during which university students shouted such slogans as "No to NATO" and "[Down with] American imperialism," and called on the government to sever ties with the West as prominent opposition politicians, journalists, and writers fervently called for the withdrawal of American troops from Turkish soil.[9]

Consequently, the next few years were characterized by a significant cooling off of Turkish-American relations. During this time, Ankara intensified its efforts to establish more cordial relations with its traditionally hostile neighbor, the Soviet Union. The Soviets were also eager to improve relations with Turkey. During an official visit to Turkey in January 1965 (the first visit to Turkey by a Soviet parliamentary delegation in more than twenty-five years), Soviet president Nikolay Podgorny reiterated the statements of Stalin's successors over ten years previously that the "inappropriate and incorrect statements" made in the Soviet Union had harmed Turkish-Soviet relations and that such events would not be repeated in the future. Podgorny's declaration, perceived as an indirect admission of responsibility for the tensions that had existed between the two countries, markedly improved relations.[10] More official exchanges followed Podgorny's visit during which declarations of friendship were made and agreements of economic cooperation and assistance were signed.

After establishing more friendly relations with the Soviets, Turkish officials made some foreign policy decisions that repudiated the wishes of the United States. During the 1967 Arab-Israeli War, for example, Ankara did not permit the United States to use the bases in Turkey for refueling and supply activities. Similarly, the Americans were not permitted to use the bases for direct combat or logistical support in 1973. This new reluctance to allow the use of their facilities for non-NATO contingencies was a marked departure from earlier times, such as when the United States had used the Turkish bases to support its intervention in the war in Lebanon in 1958. Although Ankara employed a more pragmatic approach to foreign policy during the 1960s, it was not completely opposed to the United States; in both the 1967 and 1973 wars, the Americans were allowed to utilize the bases as communications stations. Furthermore, the Americans conducted the evacuation operations of American citizens from their bases in Turkey during the Jordanian civil war in 1970 and the Iranian revolution in 1979.[11]

Meanwhile, other disagreements between the United States and Turkey transpired over rather insignificant issues. One such episode resulted from Washington's efforts to curb the extensive amount of opium production in Turkey. As drugs were becoming a serious problem in the United States in the late 1960s, a large percentage of the opium and heroin used there was being produced in Turkey. Washington, therefore, pressured Ankara to ban the growing of poppies—a crop that yielded a good income for the peasants. The decision of Prime Minister Nihat Erim's government in 1971 (during the time that democracy was briefly suspended by a military intervention) to sign an agreement banning the growing of poppies after 1972, therefore, was greatly unpopular among the Turks. Turkey did not have a drug problem, and no other crop could yield the peasants the income that poppies could. Although the agreement was reversed in 1974, it had once again contributed to the feeling that Turkish interests were being subordinated to American ones.[12]

Another Cyprus crisis in 1974 was a much more significant event that prompted questions about Washington's commitment to Turkey's vital interests. The junta in Athens masterminded a coup d'état by the Cypriot National Guard to overthrow President Makarios and his government on July 15, 1974, and to replace him with Nikos Sampson. The ultimate objective of the coup was to declare the "Hellenic Republic of Cyprus" and end the independence of the island by forming a union with Greece (*enosis*)—a prospect that was unacceptable to Turkish Cypriots and to Turkey. Turkish Prime Minister Bülent Ecevit demanded that the powers that had guaranteed the independence, territorial integrity, and security of Cyprus (Turkey, Great Britain, and Greece) intervene. Ecevit was resolved to prove that Turkey could act independently, and when no such intervention was forthcoming five days later, he ordered the Turkish army to land troops in Cyprus and occupy a section of the northern part of the island. Within hours of the Turkish landing, the Cypriot National Guard attacked and occupied many

Turkish Cypriot villages, while the Turkish troops occupied Kyrenia and prepared to push inland. Although unprepared to do so, Greece declared that it was in a state of general mobilization with the intent of attacking Turkey and forcing it to withdraw its troops. When the United Nations Security Council called for a cease-fire on July 21, 1974, Greece and the Greek Cypriots complied immediately, and Turkey did so two days later.[13] The cease-fire, however, did not end the hostilities, and the Turkish troops began another offensive on August 14, bringing about 40 percent of the island under Turkish control. Although Ecevit's actions were hailed within Turkey, the Turkish intervention in Cyprus was a public-relations disaster for Turkey. Washington suspended military aid to Turkey after December 10, 1974. This embargo, which was intensely supported by the vocal and important Greek-American community, remained in place until 1978 and led Ankara to suspend U.S. operations at military installations in Turkey. Also to Turkey's detriment, the United Nations passed a number of resolutions calling for the withdrawal of the Turkish troops from Cyprus as well as for the reunification of the island.

As Turkey's relations with the United States deteriorated, those with the Soviet Union proceeded to improve. "By 1978, the Soviet Union was aiding forty-four different development projects in Turkey and by the end of the decade Turkey received more Soviet economic assistance than any other country in the third world except Cuba."[14] Ankara also increased its efforts not only to mend its ties with the Soviet Union, and intensify them with Europe, but also worked to heal its relations with the Arab world. Despite several attempts at Turkish-Arab cooperation in the form of joint ventures and a number of symbolic gestures, such as Turkey's admittance as a full member of the Organization of the Islamic Conference (OIC), however, there was no significant improvement in Turkey's relations with Arab countries. The main reason for continued troubles was Ankara's pro-Israeli stance in the Arab-Israeli conflict, which led many Arabs to regard Turkey as a traitor. Although these views were difficult to overcome, in a symbolic gesture Turkey became a full member of the OIC in 1978.

The Decision-Making Process

The anti-American sentiments of the 1960s and 1970s would probably not have been able to flourish in previous times. The coup d'état carried out by the armed forces on May 27, 1960, however, brought new civil liberties to the Turkish people who were able to more openly express their views and opinions after the 1961 constitution was instituted. The coup was executed by military officers who had been highly critical of the growing authoritarianism of the Democratic Party, their courting of the religious vote, and the economic crisis in the country. On May 27 they transferred the powers of the Grand National Assembly to themselves, organized into the National Unity Committee (NUC), and arrested all DP ministers and deputies, Prime Minister Menderes, and President Celâl Bayar.[15] They also formed a provisional government with General Cemâl Gürsel as head of state, prime minister, and minister of defense. Although this government also had fifteen civilian ministers, it was clear that supreme legislative and executive decision-making power was in the hands of the NUC.[16] The NUC banned all types of political activity, but also declared that military rule was a temporary solution to a crisis situation, and that it would return power to a democratically elected government when the country was ready.

The NUC supervised the drafting of a new constitution that had mechanisms that would prevent any single party from establishing a monopoly on power in the future. The power of the Grand National Assembly was balanced by the creation of a second chamber, the Senate, and all legislation would have to pass through both chambers. To give minor parties a role in the legislative process, a system of proportional representation was adopted. Furthermore, an independent constitutional court was created, and the judiciary, academia, and the media were given full autonomy. The constitution also granted all Turkish citizens full civil rights and liberties—allowing for a much wider spectrum of political activity than the 1924 constitution. When in 1961 the military leaders lifted the ban on political activity and allowed parties to register for the elections scheduled for that year, new parties that were further from the center on both sides of the political spectrum emerged.

Although the expectation was that the NUC would attack Islam and reinstate the intensely secular policies that existed before 1950, it did not usher in a return to the anti-religious policies of the single-party era.[17] The NUC realized that religion was an important part of the lives of the Turkish people and that it would be counterproductive to attempt to remove Islam from society. Rather, they wanted to establish some controls to prevent reactionary groups from using religion for their own political gain. Instead of repressing the religious tendencies of the society, the government assumed an enhanced role in religion, paying more attention to the building of mosques as well as to religious education in schools.[18] The goal was to bring to Turkey a more modern version of Islam, a version that was nationalist and progressive, and one that would not contradict the westernization of the society. Promoting this new image of Islam on a tour of Anatolia, President Gürsel stated that "Islam orders us to work and advance towards perfection. Those who blame religion for our backwardness are wrong. No, the cause of our backwardness is not our religion but those who have misrepresented our religion to us."[19] It is important to note, however, that the second Republic did not abandon the principle of secularism. In fact, an article in the new constitution prohibited the use of religion for political purposes. After the new constitution was approved by a national referendum on July 9, 1961, Turkey returned to democratically elected government with the elections of October 15, 1961. The only restriction in the elections was that the competing parties were not allowed to make the coup, or the ongoing trials of the former DP politicians, a campaign issue.

The democracy of the second Republic was significantly different from the democracy of the 1950s because the 1961 constitution brought about two contradictory developments. One was the unprecedented level of freedom granted to the Turkish people, and the other was the greater role given to the military establishment. Whereas the increased civil liberties furthered democratization in Turkey, the enhanced role of the military—institutionalized in the National Security Council (NSC)—brought an authoritarian element. The NSC (officially established in March 1962), which consisted of the chief of the general staff and the commanders of land, sea, and air forces, was originally created to assist the cabinet "in taking decisions and ensuring necessary coordination" in the area of national security.[20] The cabinet had to give priority consideration to the decisions of the NSC, which was to act as a legal mechanism in which the senior military commanders could voice their views and concerns to the country's civilian leaders. Soon after its establishment, however, the NSC expanded its power to not only become a significant player in foreign policy decision-making but also to become the guardian of democracy and secularism in Turkey and the protector of the new constitution.

One party that rose to prominence in the 1960s was the Justice Party (*Adalet Partisi*, AP). After serving as a junior partner in the coalition government of 1962, the AP became the governing party after the October 1965 general elections. Seen as the continuation of the Democratic Party, it was a politically conservative party that wanted to strengthen Turkey's capitalist institutions, liberalize the economy, and allow the freedom of expressing religious beliefs. The AP and its leader Süleyman Demirel dominated the Turkish political scene and remained in power until 1970. The supporters of the party included a diverse group of industrialists, small traders, artisans, peasants, large landowners, religious reactionaries, and Western-oriented liberals.

The AP succeeded in achieving an economic growth rate averaging around

8 percent during the 1965–1969 period.[21] The major beneficiaries of this growth, however, were not the masses of the population but rather large industrial capitalists. As the income levels of these groups were rising, those of the smaller merchants and blue-collar workers were declining due to a high inflation rate. Hence, the gap between the rich and the poor was growing rapidly. As Prime Minister Demirel was struggling with the increasingly unequal distribution of income, he was also grappling to unite behind a coherent ideology the different groups that supported his party. He adopted religion as the unifying theme for his party, and in order to increase his party's support base, Demirel emphasized the AP's Islamic character. He emphasized how much the AP embraced traditional, religious values and engaged in strong anticommunist propaganda. Because of the AP's antileftist stance, left-wing organizations and individuals were often harassed and pressured. Despite coercion by the government to purge universities of leftist professors and persecute those who published communist propaganda and translated socialist writings, however, the mechanisms of checks and balances adopted by the 1961 constitution helped protect the rights of individuals. The police, for example, could not go onto university campuses unless they had been invited by the rector. The new constitution also guaranteed the independence and freedom of the press, which was often very critical of the government.

Meanwhile, a significant social phenomenon in the 1960s was that during this time, the Turkish public became more socially and physically mobile. A growing student population, as well as an increasing number of urban workers became politically active. Groups who had remained outside the political arena entered it for the first time during the second Republic. Although people from the business community started to become politically involved in the 1950s, the political arena became more diverse than ever as farmers and people involved with religious affairs also became politically active in the 1960s.[22] Under the 1961 constitution, these different groups that had diverse views and interests were allowed to engage in intellectual debates about a whole array of political and social issues. Many of these discussions took place in political debating societies (often called Idea Clubs) that were formed in all the major universities. Independent newspapers and journals flourished and, for the first time in the history of the Turkish Republic, had the freedom to criticize government policies. As a result of the increased freedoms, a vibrant left-wing movement emerged, and Marxist groups engaged in lively debates as to whether Turkey was ready for a socialist revolution. Some of these groups, like the Turkish Workers and Peasants Liberation Army, however, were not content to limit themselves to rhetorical discussions and also carried out terrorist activities to destabilize the government.[23] There were bombings, robberies, kidnappings, and violent clashes with the police and the military. This militant activity of the far left became much more deadly when it was matched, and surpassed, by the activity of the far right. The violence carried out by the youth organization of the ultra-conservative Nationalist Action Party (*Milliyetci Hareket Partisi*, MHP), the "Gray Wolves" (*Bozkurtlar*), was particularly deadly. This group became notorious because of the vicious campaign it started in December 1968 to intimidate leftist students, teachers, publicists, bookstore owners, and politicians.

Another far right party that emerged during this time was the National Order Party (*Milli Nizam Partisi*, MNP) formed by Necmettin Erbakan in January 1970. Although Erbakan had been a prominent member of the AP, he left when his attempts to take leadership of the party failed. He was then elected as an independent representative from Konya before founding the MNP. The MNP used euphemisms for Islam such as morals and virtue in its party program, and criticized the AP "for being subservient to big business and, especially, foreign capital [and] denounced [it] for being an instrument of the freemasons and Zionists which had turned its back on Islam."[24] As the political arena grew more and more fragmented and polarized with the emergence of such extremist parties and groups, Turkey was swept up in an atmosphere of violence.

The situation of political violence and disarray did not cease after the Justice Party's victory in the 1969 elections. The party itself was in disarray and by 1971, forty-one conservative members of parliament had left the Justice Party; some had resigned voluntarily, while others had been forced to leave. Demirel's government had been considerably demoralized by these defections and was having an increasingly difficult time governing the country. The clashes between left-wing and right-wing extremists had spread and involved large-scale unrest among students as well as workers. The increasing instability in Turkey at this time led the armed forces to issue a memorandum to the government (which was, for all effective purposes, an ultimatum) on March 12, 1971. It stated that unless a government capable of ending the prevailing anarchy was formed, the military would perform its constitutional obligation by seizing power. The military leaders justified this intervention in politics by saying that the government had been so weak and inefficient as to be a "source of anarchy and instability which threatened the very foundations of the state which the armed forces were guardians."[25] Consequently, as Prime Minister Demirel resigned, the generals installed a provisional government. On April 27, 1971, in the face of more terrorist violence, the National Security Council announced that martial law would be implemented in eleven provinces, including Ankara, Istanbul, and Izmir. The armed forces thus began to crack down on terrorists, especially left-wing extremists, who were seen as the main forces behind the instability that had engulfed the country. The persecution of the left was not merely a witch-hunt, however, because a number of radical left-wing groups had instigated deadly attacks, such as on May 22, 1971, when members of the Turkish People's Liberation Army kidnapped and murdered the consul general of Israel in Istanbul. The coercion of leftist elements in society grew more intense after this incident, as around five thousand people—some of whom were leading writers, journalists, trade unionists, and academics—were arrested. The Workers Party was shut down, and in order to show that the antiterrorist campaign conducted by the military was not only directed at the left, so was Erbakan's National Order Party.

Although there was some instability in the provisional government of Prime Minister Erim—eleven cabinet members defected in December 1971—it did succeed in adopting a number of amendments to the constitution. The 1961 constitution, which had given significant liberties to the people, was blamed for the crisis situation in Turkey. The new government thus wanted to amend the constitution in such a way that extremist groups would not be able to flourish unrestrained by the government once again. One measure, for example, gave the government the power to suspend civil liberties under certain circumstances. Another one ended the autonomy of radio, television, and the university system. Limitations on the powers of the constitutional court and the freedom of the press were introduced. Furthermore, the National Security Council was given a greater role in the governing of Turkey; its powers were extended to enable it to give unsolicited, binding advice to the cabinet.

As in the 1960 intervention, after making these changes to the political system, the military wanted Turkey to return to competitive party politics and held parliamentary elections on October 14, 1973. The inability of any party to win a majority in this election, and in every other election during the 1970s, led to rule by a variety of coalition governments. The first coalition of the decade was formed in January 1974 and was an uneasy alliance between the Republican People's Party and Erbakan's National Salvation Party (*Milli Selamet Partisi*, MSP, a reincarnation of his National Order Party). The MSP was an Islamist party that had campaigned with religious slogans and promoted socioeconomic and welfare reform. The entry of the MSP into government as a junior coalition partner was significant because this was the first time that an overtly pro-Islamic party gained such a prominent position in the history of the Turkish Republic. Although the combination of the left-wing CHP and the right-wing MSP was rather peculiar, the two parties proclaimed a shared distrust of Western influence on Turkey, a wariness toward big business, and a desire to abolish the restrictions on the freedom of thought and belief. The coalition, however, crumbled soon afterward due to a number of disagreements (over such issues as the Cyprus crisis of 1974 and the role of religion in society). The breakdown of the CHP-MSP coalition did not surprise anyone because, although the two parties shared some common goals, they had been at the opposite ends of the political spectrum. Many of the coalition governments that followed were equally mismatched, and thus, equally weak and short-lived. As a result, the political system was very unstable. Although the two biggest parties, the CHP and the AP, would have been able to create the strongest coalition government, they refused to put their differences aside in order to cooperate for the well-being of the country. They depended on the smaller parties to form coalitions and thus allowed for minor radical groups to wield too much power. The political system became increasingly polarized because of the ideological differences between the parties and the personal rivalries between the party leaders. The crisis in the political situation was reflected in the failure of the assembly to elect a successor to President Korutürk whose term ended in 1980 despite one hundred rounds of voting.[26] Just as the AP had been unable to deal with the political, economic, and social crises in Turkey in the late 1960s, the instability and weakness of successive coalition governments in the late 1970s meant that they were not able to deal effectively with the wide array of problems facing the country at the time.

Political violence, which had been suspended by the military action of 1971, became a major problem once again, and by the end of the 1970s, leftist extremists battled rightist radicals. Much of the violence occurred on university campuses, but a significant amount was also carried out in the streets. Schoolchildren were drilled on what to do if they were caught in a cross-fire. As bombs exploded on a daily basis in the major cities, people were afraid to venture outside, especially at nighttime. Even self-imposed curfews did not provide an adequate feeling of safety as members of the extremist groups went door-to-door to collect donations or to distribute propaganda materials. Recruiting members was an easy task for the radical groups because many of the youth had few alternatives. The university system could accept only 20 percent of the thousands of applicants each year, and the growing economic crisis led to extremely high unemployment rates. The lack of job and educational opportunities left the young with literally nothing to do and vulnerable to the propaganda of extremist groups. The political violence among these organizations resulted in many casualties: the number of victims increased from 230 in 1977 to between 1,200 and 1,500 two years later.[27] It was also at this time that the secessionist, neo-Marxist Kurdish Worker's Party (PKK) was formed to carry out terrorist attacks with the goal of establishing a Kurdish state.

In an apparent power vacuum, "law and order came to a point of total collapse as the number of assassinations approached thirty a day."[28] Terrorists not only killed one another but also assassinated members of parliament, journalists, and university professors. While the violence continued to rise, the economic situation in Turkey deteriorated. By 1980 the annual inflation rate reached 140 percent; GNP actually decreased in real terms; oil imports alone exceeded the total exports; and the balance of trade showed major deficits.[29] The government was not in a position to deal with the anarchic political situation or the very distressing economic conditions. These problems were compounded by the threat of Islamic fundamentalism. The Islamic revolution in Iran in January 1979 had encouraged the MSP and other Islamist groups in Turkey to become increasingly vocal in their demands to bring a more religious type of society to the country. On September 6, 1980, for example, they organized a mass demonstration in Konya, called for the return to *sharia*—the Islamic holy law—and refused to sing the Turkish national anthem.[30] The combination of these problems led the military to take control of the government for the third time in two decades, on September 12, 1980.

The 1960–1980 period in Turkey thus saw three important developments: (1) the role of the military in foreign policy decision-making was institutionalized with the creation of the National Security Council; (2) the liberties and freedoms introduced by the 1961 constitution allowed debate of foreign policy issues for the first time in the history of the Turkish Republic; and (3) religion became a more visible part of the lives of the Turkish people and an increasingly important part of the political process in the country. In fact, during this period, the military leaders became the unofficial makers of foreign policy as the members of the National Security Council became the guardians of the regime they had created. As such, successive governments operated under the assumption that the NSC would not hesitate to intervene in the political system (as it did in 1971) if it felt that Turkey's security was being threatened, either externally or internally. The NSC had a particular interest in ensuring that Ankara followed a rational, stable foreign policy because Turkey's national security and territorial integrity had been threatened by external forces throughout its history.

Whereas the increased role of the military brought an authoritarian element to Turkish foreign policy decision-making, another development introduced a more pluralistic element; the 1961 constitution expanded the foreign policy arena in that it allowed many groups to debate foreign policy issues by increasing people's rights and liberties. The liberalism of this constitution gave scope to the leftist groups who were able openly to criticize government policies for the first time. They condemned Turkey's pro-American and pro-NATO foreign policy stance and argued that Turkey should be allied with the third world rather than with the West. Whereas these declarations would not have been tolerated in earlier decades, they became a part of the foreign policy debates in the 1960s. It is important to note, however, that while there was increased discussion and debate, Ankara mostly dismissed the left-wing and right-wing calls for a change in Turkey's foreign policy, and despite some minor alterations, the government continued to pursue status quo policies—alignment with the United States and membership in NATO.

The third development of the 1960–1980 period was the increased role of Islam in Turkish politics. The courting of the religious vote had led to the downfall of the DP in 1960; thus, the military leaders of the coup wanted to control religious forces in society. Despite their efforts to establish command over religion by taking charge of religious development in the country—building mosques, conducting religious education in schools, and so forth—the military was unable to control the strong forces of religion in politics. The formation of Erbakan's pro-Islamic National Order Party in 1971 and its entry into the governing coalition as junior partner in 1974, then renamed as the National Salvation Party, brought the role of religion in politics to a whole new level. Although not able to influence foreign policy in such a way as to change its direction, the MSP nonetheless played an important role in that it challenged some of the basic tenets of Turkish foreign policy. For example, Erbakan vehemently opposed Turkey's entry into the European Economic Community in 1970, saying that Turkey's 35 million people would be assimilated economically and culturally by a "Christian world with 400 million inhabitants," and that the Common Market was the result of a "new crusader mentality."[31]

Because of these three major developments in the 1960s and 1970s, Ankara's foreign policy strategies were more complex than they had been during the first fifteen years of the cold war period. During this time, Turkey ventured beyond merely following the United States in the conduct of its foreign policy, attempted to diversify its foreign policy partners, and even improved relations with the Soviets.

Foreign Policy Behavior

The period between 1960 and 1980 was one of significant change for Turkish foreign policy behavior. In less than two decades Turkey had gone from being an exclusively pro-American country to one that not only worked on diversifying its foreign policy but also defied the wishes of the Americans when its own interests were at stake. There were several factors that contributed to this change in Turkish foreign policy behavior. One factor was the shift in the structure of the international system. The international system was defined by an intense level of hostility between the superpowers prior to the successful resolution of the Cuban Missile Crisis. During this time, Turkey had to be closely aligned with the United States in order to garner protection from Soviet encroachments. Relaxation of cold war tensions meant that Ankara and Washington were less dependent on each other. Consequently, Turkish policymakers were able to engage in foreign policy behavior that was more independent from American interests. As a result, they started reestablishing relations with the Soviets, forging economic ties with the Europeans, and attempting to mend relations with their Arab neighbors. They were not ready to engage in foreign policy behavior that contradicted American demands right away, however, and adhered to Washington's wishes in the Cyprus crisis of 1963. Although it contributed to a shift toward more independence in Turkish foreign policy behavior, the structure of power in the international system was thus not its only determinant. If it had been, the onset of détente would have meant that Turkish officials would have acted more autonomously in 1963.

While détente set the stage for increased independence in the making of Turkish foreign policy actions and decisions, another factor that contributed to Turkey's shifting behavior was the U.S. response to the first Cyprus crisis. The so-called Johnson letter prompted Turkish policymakers not only to reevaluate Washington's commitments to Turkish security but also led to the realization that the Americans would not assist Turkey in matters crucial to Turkish national interests that did not directly affect the United States. The actions of the U.S. government, therefore, also contributed to the worsening of Turkish-American relations in the late 1960s and early 1970s. If the Americans had been more conciliatory in the first Cyprus crisis instead of being so confrontational, the situation may not have escalated to the point in which Turkey openly defied the United States by invading Cyprus in 1974. By this time, the United States was facing a variety of problems at home—the energy crisis of 1974, the subsequent recession and hyperinflation, and "the feeling of national weakness following American disengagement from Vietnam in 1975."[32] These developments within the United States may have contributed to its imposition of an arms embargo on Turkey following the Cyprus crisis of 1974.

A third factor contributing to the shift in Turkish foreign policy was the domestic situation in Turkey in the 1960s. As discussed above, the military intervention of 1960 and the subsequent constitution created an environment in which people were allowed to openly criticize government actions for the first time in the history of the Turkish Republic. The Cuban Missile Crisis and the Cyprus crisis of 1963 thus coincided with a time in which the Turkish people were granted an unprecedented level of rights and liberties and were exercising their freedom of expression, speech, and assembly for the first time ever. Anti-American feelings among various groups in Turkey were thus articulated in street demonstrations and newspaper articles. Although foreign policy decision-making was still in the hands of a small group of elites, the more democratic leaders at least were willing to listen to public opinion. Furthermore, the new government wanted to distance itself from the disastrous rule of the Menderes government of the 1950s and did not feel obliged to stick to the intensely pro-Western foreign policy behavior it had pursued.

1980–1990: THE THIRD TURKISH REPUBLIC DURING THE COLD WAR

Foreign Policy Objectives and Strategies

By 1980, hostilities between the United States and the Soviet Union had reemerged at the forefront of international politics. Concerns about American security reached a peak after the seizure of American hostages following the Iranian revolution and the Soviet invasion of Afghanistan in late 1979.[33] Growing support for increased military spending in the United States combined with a deteriorating sense of security in Turkey to draw Turkish foreign policy into alignment with U.S. interests once again. On March 29, 1980, for example, Washington and Ankara finally reached enough compromises to conclude the U.S.-Turkish Defense and Economic Cooperation Agreement (DECA) that they had been haggling over for five years. Two years later, they signed a Memorandum of Understanding for the modernization of close to a dozen airfields in eastern Turkey. In addition, Washington steadily increased the total amount of foreign assistance extended to Turkey. In fact, by 1981 American aid to Turkey quadrupled from the pre-1974 amount, only three years after the end of the four-year arms embargo. At this time, Washington also decided to take its support of Turkey's military systems one step further by helping to finance the country's efforts to modernize its troubled air defenses and its defense industry program. One reason for this intensification of the Turkish-American alliance was policy changes in the United States. The American defense budget increased significantly, and was coupled with hostile rhetoric toward the Soviet Union, during the first Reagan administration. President Ronald Reagan advocated taking a strong stand against possible Soviet encroachments by bolstering American military power. The defense program of his administration was thus based on sharp increases in defense spending (which was escalated by about 7 percent a year from 1981 to 1985) and the development of new defense strategies to neutralize the Soviet strategic buildup (i.e., the Strategic Defense Initiative [SDI]).[34] The American rearmament program also reaffirmed American interests in Turkey due to this country's strategic importance for American security. As Assistant Secretary of Defense Richard N. Perle stated at the time,

in the time that it would take the United States to deliver a division to the upper Gulf in the event of an emergency there, the Soviets could easily deliver 10 divisions. . . . If Turkey is strong then a Soviet military commander considering a move into a critical region like the Gulf would have to think twice. He would have to think twice because eastern Turkey is within striking distance of those critical Soviet forces based in the Transcaucasus.[35]

There were also developments within Turkey that contributed to improving relations with the United States. The 1980 military takeover had ended the "experimental phase in the conduct of Turkish foreign policy" that had defined the previous decade.[36] The "conservative philosophy and worldview of the military regime [which had seized power in a coup d'état in September 1980] promoted strong pro-American and pro-NATO policies."[37] The Americans, on the other hand, were happy with the fact that the coup had brought stability to a country that was in a state of near chaos in the late 1970s. A stable Turkey, in a region of instability, was in the best interest of the Americans. They were thus eager to lend their support first to the military regime and then to its successors.

Despite this renewed sense of cooperation between the United States and Turkey during the 1980s, there were still some issues that led to, or which had the potential to lead to, conflict. The Americans, for example, were dissatisfied with the fact that Turkey was not willing to give unlimited access to bases in Turkey for American troops stationed in the Persian Gulf and the Middle East.[38] They also did not like the fact that the Turkish Cypriots had declared an independent Turkish Republic of Northern Cyprus in the fall of 1983, and that Ankara had recognized this entity as an independent country.[39] Meanwhile, the Turks were never fully content with the amount of American military and economic assistance they received. They also resented the powerful Greek-American and Armenian-American lobbies in Washington that campaigned against Turkey in Congress.

The mid- to late-1980s, however, saw some significant changes in the structure of the international system. Mikhail Gorbachev assumed power in March 1985 with such goals as reforming domestic political processes, developing better relations with the West, and improving the Soviet economy. Gorbachev espoused a different attitude toward the West than his predecessors in that he was "confident that the United States would not deliberately attack the Soviet Union."[40] With the belief that the Soviet Union would be able to fix its declining economy only after establishing peaceful relations with the West, Gorbachev pursued a relationship of accommodation rather than confrontation with the United States and its allies. The Geneva summit between Reagan and Gorbachev in November 1985 set the stage for further talks on arms reduction proposals, loosening of trade restrictions, and exchange of spies and political prisoners.[41] Although the next few years were characterized by alternating periods of cooperation and hesitation between the United States and the Soviet Union, a watershed event in Soviet-American relations came with the signing of the Intermediate Range Nuclear Forces (INF) Treaty in 1987. The treaty called for the total elimination of Soviet and American medium- and short-range weapons within three years, and its signing meant that the nuclear arms race between the superpowers was finally being reversed.[42] Soon afterward, Soviet troops withdrew from Afghanistan, and the Treaty on Conventional Forces in Europe was signed. As a result of this "new thinking" in the Soviet Union, Turkish-Soviet relations proceeded to improve. There were several official visits exchanged by the countries' chiefs of staff in 1985 and 1986. In 1988, Turkish officers were invited to watch Soviet military maneuvers, and the two countries stepped up their efforts to cooperate more in the economic arena.

Obstacles to a close relationship between the two countries remained, however, as they continued to disagree over a number of crucial issues. Moscow, for example, supported the Greek claims that Turkish troops had to be withdrawn from Cyprus before an agreement about the future of the island could be reached. Other sources of conflict between Turkey and the Soviet Union included fishing rights in the Black Sea (which the two countries shared), and the Soviet toleration of the repression of the Turkish minority in Bulgaria.[43]

Another parameter of the 1980s was Turkey's strained relations with its European allies. The European Community alienated many politicians as well as the public in Turkey by focusing on the country's adverse human

rights record. The reason for Europe's harsh criticisms was its close geographical proximity to Turkey, which meant that the many Turkish refugees who
received political asylum in various European countries became a burden on
these countries. The Council of Europe suspended Turkey from the organization in May 1981 due to its poor human rights record. Despite its unfavorable standing in Europe during the 1980s, however, Turkey stepped up
its efforts to be admitted into the European Community at this time. Resolved to become accepted finally as an equal partner by European countries,
Turkey applied for membership in April 1987. As Udo Steinbach states,
"after having been forced to side closely with the United States in the climate
of the cold war, and subsequently, in the 1970s, experimenting with new
openings in its foreign relations, the Turkish government appeared to seek
stability in accordance with the political, economic, and cultural policies it
adopted under the Third Republic."[44] The economic restructuring and
growth Turkey had undergone since 1980 led politicians to be confident that
not only did they have a good chance of being admitted but also that they
had the right to be accepted. They believed that EC membership would be
the foundation of the crucial role that Turkey would play in Europe, as well
as the realization of the long-standing goal of westernization. The Europeans,
however, rejected Turkey's application for membership, citing human rights
abuses in the country, a relatively backward and unstable economy, and
disputes with Greece as reasons for this rejection. There was a general feeling
among the public and the population in Turkey, however, that Turkey—its
culture, its religion, and its people—were simply being snubbed by Europe.[45]
The failure of this foreign policy strategy also made many Turks question
the validity of the foreign policy tactic of westernization. It also led certain
political factions to exploit these feelings in order to expand their support
base by engaging in anti-European rhetoric.

Meanwhile, relations with the countries of the Middle East and the Balkans remained strained, if not openly hostile, in the 1980s. Because it valued
its own security and territorial integrity above all else, Turkey tried to stay
out of the turbulent politics of the Middle East. For example, it maintained
a strict neutrality in the Iran-Iraq war, which dominated the political arena
of the region during this time. It had relatively cordial relations with both
countries, with Iran becoming Turkey's most important export market in
1983–1984, and Iraq pumping oil through the Turkish pipeline. After the
end of the war in 1988, however, it developed closer ties with Iran than with
Iraq. Relations with Iraq, as well as with Syria, deteriorated due to disagreements over the flow of water from the Euphrates and Tigris Rivers. These
downstream countries were concerned about the flow diminishing as a result

of the building of the huge Atatürk Dam on the Euphrates and thus they tried to put pressure on Turkey to guarantee the flow of water by supporting Kurdish guerrillas. Relations with Greece also remained difficult. A number of attempts by the United Nations to start negotiations between the Turkish and Greek sides over the Cyprus issue were all unsuccessful, and the two countries continued to clash over such issues as oil rights on the continental shelf and rights to airspace. Turkey also experienced another crisis with Bulgaria, when in 1989 the Bulgarian government accelerated its policies of forced assimilation of the Turkish-Muslim minority, coercing 344,000 Bulgarian Turks to escape across the border into Turkey.[46] The situation was very tense and created a wave of nationalist feeling in Turkey. The crisis was dissipated when most of the refugees, who could not find jobs or housing in Turkey, gradually returned to Bulgaria.

The Decision-Making Process

The decade of the 1980s was rife with significant changes in the political arena. The unstable and weak governments in office during the late 1970s had not been able to deal effectively with the numerous challenges facing the country. As mentioned previously, there were severe economic, social, and political problems. Consequently, on September 12, 1980, the leaders of the armed forces announced that they had taken over political power because the organs of the state had stopped functioning. Presiding over the coup, the Chief of Staff General Kenan Evren said that the warnings that the military had issued to the various governments in the past two years about the increasingly critical state of affairs in Turkey had failed to remedy the crisis situation. He added that the military was stepping in to reunify a citizenry, one that shared the same religious and national values but that had been divided into opposing camps by politicians seeking to further their own political agendas. Evren declared, in other words, that the armed forces would fill the power vacuum that had been created by the incompetence of the elected politicians, restore order, and change some of Turkey's political institutions in order to ensure that such a crisis would not arise in the near future. The military leaders immediately suspended the constitution, dissolved parliament, closed down political parties, detained party leaders, and lifted the political immunity of the members of the Grand National Assembly. They also proclaimed a state of emergency.

As a result, power was removed from the hands of politicians (not just members of parliament and political parties, but also mayors and municipal politicians) and consolidated in the hands of the National Security Council.

General Evren presided over the NSC and was officially declared head of state on September 14. In a press conference two days later, he announced that democracy would be restored once significant reforms had been implemented to make the political system more efficient and more effective. He said that the National Security Council "was determined to remove all obstacles which had hindered the healthy working of the democratic order in a way that would preclude forever the need for similar interventions in the future" and that all policy arenas, except foreign policy and economic liberalization, would undergo major changes.[47] The generals believed that these changes would be possible only if they undid the work of their predecessors who had carried out the May 27, 1960, coup. In a symbolic gesture, they even went so far as to abolish May 27 as a national holiday.

On September 21, the NSC announced that retired admiral Bülent Ulusu would become prime minister and head a twenty-seven-member cabinet appointed by them. There would be a Consultative Assembly but its powers would be limited because final decision-making power rested in the hands of the NSC. The NSC also appointed regional and local commanders whose powers under martial law extended to education, the press, chambers of commerce, and trade unions. Furthermore, President Evren said that the military envisioned no place in politics for former politicians who were considered to be the cause of Turkey's troubles. By a decree passed by the NSC in 1982, the public discussion of political matters was banned and the old politicians were prohibited from discussing publicly the past, the present, and the future.

As the NSC established a monopoly on power, their forces all over the country began a campaign of arrests. Before the end of October, 11,500 people were arrested, 30,000 by the end of the year, and a total of 122,600 by September 1981.[48] As a result of these arrests, political violence decreased by over 90 percent. Trade unionists, politicians, university professors, teachers, lawyers, and journalists—anyone who had expressed views even slightly sympathetic to either the leftists or the Islamists—were rounded up for questioning. The use of torture was widespread, and many suspects and prisoners died under suspicious circumstances while in police custody. Furthermore, legal proceedings were initiated against many politicians: the leaders of the National Action Party (accused of right-wing terrorism), and the National Salvation Party (accused of violating secularism) were among the thousands tried.

The military also worked on establishing state control over many of the institutions that had been given autonomy under the 1961 constitution. The Higher Education Authority (*Yüksek Ögretim Kurulu*), for example, was founded in order to establish centralized authority over the universities and was directly responsible for the appointment of all rectors and deans. The NSC also wanted to form mechanisms to control religion in society but was more tolerant of Islam than had been expected. Although it prohibited obvious violations of secularism, it also took measures to teach religion to both Turkish children and adults. The Ministry of National Education and the Faculty of Theology formulated a compulsory course on religion and ethics that was to be taught every year from fourth grade to the senior grade of high school. Meanwhile, the Ministry of Justice started to teach classes on religion and ethics to more than eighty thousand jailed prisoners all over the country. This religious education was coupled with literacy classes, with the belief that literacy "[opens] the door for knowledge and skills which help the integration of the individual in society and reduce feelings of inferiority and alienation, [and, it decreases] the likelihood of . . . susceptibility to religious exploitation."[49]

The military recognized, however, that it could not hold power indefinitely in the face of increasing demands for elections. This realization became especially acute after West German Foreign Minister Hans Dietrich Genscher visited Ankara in November 1981 and warned that the authoritarian nature of the military regime could lead to Turkey's expulsion from the Council of Europe as well as to the suspension of economic aid. The constitution that would return Turkey to electoral politics was thus submitted to a referendum on November 7, 1982, and adopted by 91 percent of the eligible voters.[50]

Those who drafted the 1982 constitution believed that the 1961 constitution had allowed so much freedom that these freedoms were exploited and abused by politicians and various groups. Therefore, they attempted to reverse some of its provisions. The new constitution increased the power of the president, who "could dissolve parliament and call a general election if parliament was paralyzed; rule by decree if he believed there was a 'national emergency'; and select members of the constitutional court from nominations provided by the courts and councils."[51] The 1982 constitution also replaced the former bicameral legislature with a unicameral Turkish Grand National Assembly. Furthermore, like countless other constitutions, it stipulated that sovereignty was in the hands of the people and that all citizens were equal before the law, no matter what their religion, language, race, gender, or political beliefs were. A further article (Article 14), however, indicated that these rights and freedoms could not be used to divide the country, endanger the existence of the Turkish state, have the state ruled by an individual or a class, establish the rule of one social class over others, or discriminate based on language, religion, or race.[52] In addition, the people's

freedoms and rights could be annulled, suspended, or limited in the event
of a war, martial law, or other extraordinary circumstances, or if they con-
flicted with the national interest, public order, national security, danger to
the republican order, and public health. The freedom of the press was limited
by a clause in the constitution that prohibited the publication of "inaccurate
and untimely reports," and the freedom of trade unions was restricted by
provisions allowing the right strike only under "carefully defined circumstances."[53] Furthermore, a temporary article in the new constitution indicated that General Evren would automatically become president for a
seven-year term if and when the constitution was adopted, and the other
four members of the NSC would become the presidential council during his
term.

While the generals wanted Turkey to return to democracy, they did not
want this democracy to bring to power once again the politicians who had
dominated the political arena in the 1970s. Consequently, on April 4, 1983,
the Consultative Assembly announced the Law on Political Parties, which
imposed certain restrictions on the formation of political parties. It stipulated,
for example, that the right of citizens to establish a political party could not
contradict the principles of the constitution, such as secularism and the in-
divisibility of the country, or use religion for political ends.[54] Most important,
the Law on Political Parties disqualified politicians who had been active before the September 1980 coup from engaging in politics for the next ten
years. The goal was that, instead of relying on the old parties (or new parties
that were still led by these politicians), Turkish democracy would be re-
invigorated with the creation of new parties and the entry of new politicians
into the political arena. The Law on Political Parties was followed by the
Law on the Election of Deputies, which stipulated that political parties that
did not get at least 10 percent of the vote in the general or partial elections
could not have any deputies in the assembly. This law was passed in order
to prevent the experience of the previous decade during which minor parties
had become increasingly and somewhat disproportionately important in the
political process, forcing the major parties to depend on their support to gain
majorities in parliament and to provide concessions to them.

The National Security Council declared that only three of the fifteen new
parties formed after these laws were passed had satisfied the conditions to
compete in the November 1983 elections: the Party of Nationalist Democracy, the Populist Party, and the Motherland Party. The military establishment had clearly supported the Party of Nationalist Democracy, and to a
lesser degree the Populist Party. The Motherland Party, however, under the
leadership of Turgut Özal, won a landslide victory with over 45 percent of

the vote in the elections.[55] One reason for Özal's success was that he was the only truly democratic candidate (the only one not supported by the military) who projected a "liberal, anti-statist, anti-bureaucratic image and the promise of a quick return to civilian rule."[56] Despite President Evren and Prime Minister Ulusu's overt campaign to get the Party of Nationalist Democracy elected, it came in third in the elections, signifying the fact that the military had not rigged the elections. The elections, however, were not completely free and fair because some important parties, namely the Social Democratic Party (*Sosyal Demokrat Partisi*, SODEP, led by Professor Erdal Inönü, the son of Ismet Inönü), and the True Path Party (*Dogru Yol Partisi*, DYP, under the guidance of Demirel) had been kept out of the elections. Regardless, Turgut Özal became prime minister and dominated the political arena for the next decade.

Özal and his party were supported by a rather diverse group of interests, many of which had joined ANAP because they had no other viable alternatives. Özal was able skillfully to hold together a rather disparate coalition (which included business interests who favored economic liberalization, Islamists, and nationalist right-wing groups) because not only was he a major proponent of economic liberalization and had a background in private industry but also was known to be religious and closely linked with the Islamists. Özal also claimed that his party would work to benefit all the Turks who had largely been ignored by the elitist parties of the past—the lower and middle classes he termed the "central pillar" of society (*orta direk*). Promising that Turkey would soon prosper, and that this prosperity would benefit the lower-middle classes, he won the support of this large group.

The Motherland Party benefited from the fact that there were no real alternatives to its rule. The opposition parties represented in parliament had been demoralized, while the parties not represented in parliament were divided and disorganized. Meanwhile, the politicians who might have been able to gather support and mobilize the electorate were still banned from engaging in political activities. Some of them had risen as the unofficial leaders of a number of political parties: Demirel was behind the True Path Party; Ecevit, the Democratic left; Erbakan, the Welfare Party; and Turkes, the Nationalist Labor Party. In fact, as it became clear that the former politicians were the real power behind these parties, their popularity rose once again, and Özal's prevalence started to decline. His main challenge came from Demirel (although still officially prohibited from engaging in politics) and the center-right True Path Party. As the more liberal and democratic members of the center-right groups started congregating around the DYP, Özal became increasingly Islamist in order to expand his support base. Even his move to the right did not placate the public, and Özal came under a lot of pressure to restore the political rights of the old politicians. Declaring, therefore, that he wanted further democratization in Turkey, Özal called for a referendum to decide on the restoration of political rights to his rivals. Although the Motherland Party actively campaigned against it, a provision of a 1982 basic law banning former politicians from public office was rescinded on September 6, 1987, by a 50.2 percent margin.[57] Consequently, Demirel became the leader of the True Path Party, and Erbakan, the leader of the Welfare Party. Although neither of these parties were able to surpass the Motherland Party in the elections of November 1987, their prominent leaders were now able legally to act as opposition leaders, constantly taunting and criticizing the governing party.

The political arena during the late 1980s was dominated by the question of who would succeed President Evren when his term expired in November 1989. Because Özal's popularity was declining as a result of his government's inability to curb inflation and improve the economy, he realized that the general elections scheduled for 1992 would probably bring an end to his political career. Becoming president, however, would keep him in office for the next seven years. When Özal announced that he would run for president, the opposition was so outraged that they boycotted the session of the assembly in which the new president was elected. The Motherland Party's majority in the assembly thus ensured that Özal became the eighth president of the Turkish Republic. He was only the second civilian to hold this post.

One issue that had become increasingly important for Turkey during the 1980s was the growing Kurdish insurgency. Although this could have remained a domestic policy issue, it became a foreign policy issue when the Kurdish Workers Party (PKK) set up its training camps in neighboring countries, and when the tactics used by the government to fight the insurgency were criticized by the Western world. Western European countries as well as the United States condemned Turkey for denying basic human rights to its Kurdish population and for waging a full-fledged war against the PKK. They were justified in some of these criticisms. The expression of Kurdish identity was vehemently suppressed in the years immediately following the 1980 coup: the use of the Kurdish language in private conversations was officially banned, and Kurdish people would often be indicted for "weakening national sentiments." A famous singer, Ibrahim Tatlises, for example, was charged with engaging in separatist propaganda when he expressed regret at not being able to sing a folk song in his mother tongue, Kurdish.[58] Such repressive measures fueled the dissatisfaction of many Kurds—often the poorest groups in society—with the government in Ankara. Capitalizing on this dissatisfaction, the PKK directed its efforts at mobilizing the poor and the ill-educated who felt that they were marginalized from mainstream Turkish society. The founder and leader of the PKK, Abdullah Ocalan, set up his bases in Syria in 1980 where members of his organization were trained by Syrian and Palestinian officers. Although the PKK engaged in guerrilla activity in Turkey in the early 1980s, it intensified its violent campaign to gain independence after the celebrations of Kurdish new year (*Nevroz*) in March 1984, which had been banned by the government. From this time on, southeastern Turkey was engaged in a civil war. The fighters of the PKK (which numbered between five and ten thousand) directed their attacks against government property, government officials, Turks living in Kurdish regions, Kurds accused of collaborating with the government, foreigners, and Turkish diplomats. The Turkish military had devoted tens of thousands of soldiers as well as counter-revolutionary Kurdish groups (called village guards) to fight the PKK. During the six years between 1984 and 1990, 2,500 people had died in the fighting with the PKK, "a great majority of whom were Kurdish civilians."[59]

Meanwhile, the economic liberalization policies pursued since January 24, 1980, had led to some significant problems in Turkey during the 1980s. Although the country saw significant economic growth as a result of these policies, it also endured an extremely high inflation rate and worsened standards of living for the middle and lower classes. Despite Özal's proclamations that the middle classes would see improvements in their living conditions, this sector of the society became much more worse off. The fact that the Motherland Party was perceived as being corrupt, nepotistic, and plagued by scandals added to the masses' dissatisfaction with the government. Perhaps as a result of this discontent, the people increasingly turned to Islam as the solution to their problems. Consequently, this decade saw an expansion in the visibility of Islam in Turkish life. Even the military started to recognize Islam as an essential element in holding together the increasingly fragmented and polarized society.[60]

There were several reasons why the military leaders allowed the growing influence of Islam in Turkey. One reason was that the Muslim countries of the Middle East became important trading partners and diplomatic allies for Turkey at a time when its relations with Western Europe were deteriorating, pressuring "the Turkish leaders to look favorably to the Islamic countries of the region."[61] Another reason was that military officials realized that religion could work not only to legitimize their policies but also to placate the forces that pulled the country toward leftist terrorism and anarchy. As a result of this permissive attitude toward religion, new mosques were built; the number of *imam-hatip* (preacher) schools, as well as the number of students attending them, rose dramatically; and the number of religious publications and book-stores increased. Schoolbooks and radio and television programs became much more focused on religion. There were several incidents over the years, during the holy month of Ramadan, when people who were smoking or drinking instead of fasting were attacked. Perhaps the biggest break with the past was seen when members of the cabinet increasingly took part in religious ceremonies. This development was harshly criticized by the press and by certain elites as an effort to undermine the secular nature of the state. One scandal that led to broad concern among these groups about the secular nature of the Turkish state ensued after a December 1986 investigation revealed that thirty-three cadets in a military academy (the Kuleli Military *Lycée* in Istanbul) had engaged in fundamentalist activities.[62] Clearly, however, there were also groups who embraced the growth of religion in Turkish society and who wanted to bring Turkey closer to Islam. In fact, a number of state institutions were penetrated by Islamic groups and became "vehicles for the promotion of fundamentalist ideas and interests."[63] The personnel departments of some ministries recruited graduates of the imam-hatip schools, who then engaged in intense campaigns to promote Islam. As such, many sectors of society, especially students and people living in the shanty-towns who were particularly susceptible, were influenced by the growing religious sentiments in the country. Although the state apparatus that existed at the beginning of the Turkish Republic was strictly secular, by the end of the 1980s parts of the state had been penetrated by the Islamists.

The changes in the Turkish political system that occurred during the 1980s, from yet another military intervention to the return to democracy, did not have major repercussions for foreign policy decision-making in the country. This was because the military kept a close watch on developments in foreign policy even after handing power to civilian government in 1983. The fact that the president was a general from the armed forces made the active role of the military in the foreign policy decision-making process almost natural. In addition, the 1982 constitution had given the National Security Council the role of final arbiter on issues considered to be vital for the long-term interests of the country.[64] These included law and order, elementary education, and of course, foreign policy. When the NSC felt that the actions of the elected leaders threatened Turkey's vital interests, it did not hesitate to intervene verbally. In May 1988, for example, President Evren warned that the military would not be able to remain silent if the government failed to address the incidents of leftist violence that had occurred on several occasions.[65] The military establishment justified its involvement in politics by pointing to the threats that emanated from Turkey's fragile geopolitical situation as well as from separatist activities and Islamic fundamentalism. It did, however, limit its engagement to issues that related to Turkey's national security and territorial integrity, leaving all other issues to be dealt with by various governments.

The extensive domestic institutional and political changes that occurred during the transition from authoritarianism to a unique type of democracy in Turkey, therefore, did not have any significant effects on foreign policy. There was a high degree of stability, especially during the cold war, because the foreign policy decision-making arena was in the hands of the state elites— the bureaucratic, military, and academic elites—who favored status quo policies. It was only during the mid- to late-1980s that certain developments in the country "[released] unprecedented social and political forces, including the rise of a new business class and a concerted attack on the entrenched étatist bureaucracy" which allowed increased discussion, debate, and change in the foreign policy arena.[66] Turkey's foreign policy orientation, in other words, remained stable because of the institutional monism that existed in the foreign policy decision-making arena.

NOTES

1. Mehmet Gönlübol, "NATO and Turkey," in *Turkey's Foreign Policy in Transition: 1950–1974*, ed. Kemal Karpat (Leiden: E. J. Brill, 1975), 20.

2. Erik J. Zurcher, *Turkey: A Modern History* (London: I. B. Tauris, 1993), 288.

3. Bruce R. Kuniholm, "Turkey and the West Since World War II," in *Turkey Between East and West: New Challenges for a Rising Regional Power*, eds. Vojtech Mastny and R. Craig Nation (Boulder, Colo.: Westview Press, 1996), 54.

4. William Schneider, "'Rambo' and Reality: Having It Both Ways," in *Eagle Resurgent? The Reagan Era in American Foreign Policy*, eds. Kenneth A. Oye, Robert J. Lieber, and Donald Rothchild (Boston: Little, Brown and Company Limited, 1987), 50.

5. Kuniholm, "Turkey and the West Since World War II," 55.

6. Kuniholm, "Turkey and the West Since World War II," 57.

7. Udo Steinbach, "The European Community, the United States, the Middle East, and Turkey," in *Politics in the Third Turkish Republic*, ed. Metin Heper (Boulder, Colo.: Westview Press, 1994), 104.

8. George W. Ball, *The Past Has Another Pattern: Memoirs* (New York: W. W. Norton and Co., 1982), 350.

9. Gönlübol, "NATO and Turkey," 20.

10. Kuniholm, "Turkey and the West Since World War II," 57.

11. Kuniholm, "Turkey and the West Since World War II," 57.

12. Zurcher, *Turkey: A Modern History*, 289.

13. Kemal H. Karpat, "War on Cyprus: The Tragedy of *Enosis*," in *Turkey's Foreign Policy in Transition*, 199.

14. Kuniholm, "Turkey and the West Since World War II," 57.

15. Mehmet Yaşar Geyikdaği, *Political Parties in Turkey: The Role of Islam* (New York: Praeger, 1984), 88.

16. William Hale, *The Political and Economic Development of Modern Turkey* (New York: St. Martin's Press, 1981), 117.

17. Geyikdaği, *Political Parties in Turkey*, 88.

18. Geyikdaği, *Political Parties in Turkey*, 90.

19. Feroz Ahmad, *The Turkish Experiment in Democracy: 1950–1975* (London: C. Hurst, 1977), 64–65.

20. George S. Harris, *Turkey: Coping with Crisis* (Boulder, Colo.: Westview Press, 1985), 96.

21. Geyikdaği, *Political Parties in Turkey*, 102.

22. Harris, *Turkey: Coping with Crisis*, 130–131.

23. Zurcher, *Turkey: A Modern History*, 268.

24. Zurcher, *Turkey: A Modern History*, 270.

25. Ahmad, *The Turkish Experiment in Democracy*, 2.

26. Arthur S. Banks, Alan J. Day, and Thomas C. Muller, eds., *Political Handbook of the World: 1995–1996* (Binghamton, N.Y.: CSA Publications, State University of New York, 1997), 959.

27. Zurcher, *Turkey: A Modern History*, 276.

28. Ali L. Karaosmanoğlu, "The Limits of International Influence for Democratization," in *Politics in the Third Turkish Republic*, ed. Metin Heper (Boulder, Colo.: Westview Press, 1994), 121.

29. Geyikdaği, *Political Parties in Turkey*, 133–135.

30. Zurcher, *Turkey: A Modern History*, 282.

31. Geyikdaği, *Political Parties in Turkey*, 123. See also Çetin Özek, *Devlet ve Din* (Istanbul: Ada Yayinlari, 1982), 572.

32. Schneider, "'Rambo' and Reality: Having It Both Ways," 50.

33. Schneider, "'Rambo' and Reality: Having It Both Ways," 50.

34. Alexander Dallin and Gail W. Lapidus, "Reagan and the Russians: American Policy Toward the Soviet Union," in *Eagle Resurgent? The Reagan Era in American Foreign Policy*, 210.

35. Duygu Bazoğlu Sezer, "Turkey and the Western Alliance," *Political and Socioeconomic Transformation of Turkey*, eds. Atila Eralp, Muharrem Tunay, and Birol A. Yeşilada (Westport, Conn.: Praeger, 1993), 222.

36. Steinbach, "The European Community, the United States, the Middle East, and Turkey," 105.

37. Sezer, "Turkey and the Western Alliance," 220.

38. Sezer, "Turkey and the Western Alliance," 222.

39. Sezer, "Turkey and the Western Alliance," 223.

40. Richard Ned Lebow and Janice Gross Stein, *We All Lost the Cold War* (Princeton, N.J.: Princeton University Press, 1994), 370.

41. Dallin and Lapidus, "Reagan and the Russians: American Policy Toward the Soviet Union," 235.

42. Lebow and Stein, *We All Lost the Cold War,* 371.

43. Steinbach, "The European Community, the United States, the Middle East, and Turkey," 108.

44. Steinbach, "The European Community, the United States, the Middle East, and Turkey," 108.

45. Stephen Kinzer, "Turkey Finds European Union Door Slow to Open," *New York Times* (23 February 1997): A3.

46. Zurcher, *Turkey: A Modern History*, 317.

47. Ahmad, *The Turkish Experiment in Democracy*, 183.

48. Zurcher, *Turkey: A Modern History*, 293.

49. Geyikdaği, *Political Parties in Turkey*, 142.

50. Andrew Mango, *Turkey: Challenge of a New Role* (Westport, Conn.: Praeger, published with The Center for Strategic and International Studies, Washington, D.C., 1994), 25.

51. Ahmad, *The Turkish Experiment in Democracy*, 186.

52. Geyikdaği, *Political Parties in Turkey*, 144.

53. Ahmad, *The Turkish Experiment in Democracy*, 186.

54. Geyikdaği, *Political Parties in Turkey*, 147.

55. Mango, *Turkey: Challenge of a New Role*, 26.

56. Ahmad, *The Turkish Experiment in Democracy*, 190.

57. *Political Handbook of the World: 1995–1996*, 960.

58. Zurcher, *Turkey: A Modern History*, 312.

59. "Turkey and Ancient Anatolia: Political Developments since 1971," *Britannica Online & Book of the Year*, 1997 <http://eb.com:180/help/index.htm>.

60. Metin Heper, "Trials and Tribulations of Democracy in the Third Turkish Republic," *Politics in the Third Turkish Republic*, 233.

61. Sencer Ayata, "The Rise of Islamic Fundamentalism and Its Institutional Framework," *Political and Socioeconomic Transformation of Turkey*, eds. Atila Eralp, Muharrem Tunay, and Birol A. Yesilada (Westport, Conn.: Praeger, 1993), 64.

62. Ahmet Evin, "Demilitarization and Civilianization of the Regime," *Politics in the Third Turkish Republic*, 29.

63. Ayata, "The Rise of Islamic Fundamentalism and Its Institutional Framework," 64.

64. Heper, "Trials and Tribulations of Democracy in the Third Turkish Republic," 234.

65. C. H. Dodd, "Kenan Evren as President: From Conflict to Compromise," in *Politics in the Third Turkish Republic*, 175.

66. Dankwart A. Rustow, "Turkish Democracy in Historical and Comparative Perspective," in *Politics in the Third Turkish Republic*, 3–12.

Chapter 4 ————————————————————————————

A New Era in Relations with the United States

The Western foreign policy orientation adopted by Turkey in the aftermath of World War II had remained stable for much of the cold war. Throughout this era, Turkish foreign policy was characterized by Ankara's close alliance with Washington, and Turkey's role as the southeastern flank of the North Atlantic Treaty Organization (NATO) in containing Soviet expansionism. American installations in Turkey facilitated the detection and interception of Soviet airpower into the eastern Mediterranean; Turkish control of the straits of Bosporus and Dardanelles blocked Soviet power from entering the Aegean; and Turkey's land mass and bases deterred Soviet designs on the Persian Gulf.[1] In exchange, Turkey received the promise of protection from Soviet threats as well as significant amounts of military and economic aid to bolster its defenses. Although there were some fluctuations in Turkish foreign policy behavior toward the United States, these basic parameters of Turkey's foreign policy remained constant during the cold war.

The end of the 1980s, however, saw major changes in the structure of the international system. The Soviet Union's pledge of nonintervention in Eastern Europe in 1989 (and German reunification in 1990) brought an end to the cold war that had dominated the world arena since 1945. The subsequent disintegration of the Soviet Union in 1991 led to the warming of relations between the Russian Federation and the United States. Because the removal of the Soviet threat rendered Turkey's role as a bulwark against the communist threat on NATO's eastern flank defunct, Turkey had to question, and alter, some of its foreign policy strategies. Many of these changes brought a significant degree of uncertainty, unpredictability, and instability to Turkish foreign policy—characteristics that were not associated with it in previous periods.

1990–1998: THE POST–COLD WAR PERIOD

Foreign Policy Objectives and Strategies

At the beginning of this new era, many Turkish leaders proclaimed that their country's foreign policy goals remained unchanged in the face of the tremendous alterations in the international system in the aftermath of the cold war. Contrary to these announcements, however, there were some considerable shifts in Ankara's foreign policy strategies in the year immediately following the breakdown of the Soviet Union. One such shift was due to Turkey's involvement in the politics of the Middle East. Turkey had consistently stayed out of the turbulent conflicts of the Middle East for most of its existence, pursuing politics of neutrality in disputes among Muslim countries. President Turgut Özal, however, realized that Turkey had lost some of its strategic significance as a front-line state against the Soviet Union. In order to "reaffirm Ankara's commitment to U.S.-Turkish bilateral relations and to highlight Turkey's importance to U.S. strategic interests and concerns in the Middle East," Özal used the emergency powers given to him to deal with the Persian Gulf War to make Turkey one of the first countries to ally with the United States and to join the United Nations coalition against Iraq in August 1990.[2] In fact, Turkey became "the first nation in the region to denounce the invasion of Kuwait, first to support the UN sanctions and first to make the blockade count by shutting down Iraq's pipeline."[3] In addition, nearly one hundred thousand Turkish troops were mobilized on the Turkish-Iraqi border before the government requested and received permission from the assembly in September to send troops to the Persian Gulf and to allow foreign troops on Turkish soil. Turkey also allowed the Americans to use their major military installations at Incirlik Air Base to bomb Iraq. By giving Turkey such a central role in the crisis, Özal clearly wanted to demonstrate Turkey's allegiance to its Western allies (as Prime Minister Menderes had done decades earlier by sending Turkish troops to Korea) as well as highlight the country's strategic importance as the only democratic, pro-American, Islamic country in the Middle East. But Özal's decisions, which made Turkey extremely vulnerable to an Iraqi attack, were harshly criticized by opposition parties and by the public. Most of Turkey's NATO allies had not offered to bolster the Turkish military to prepare it for the possibility of an Iraqi attack. While only the Dutch had sent units of modern Patriot ground-to-air missiles, for example, Belgium, Italy, and Germany merely sent outdated and lightly armed warplanes that were already ear-marked for retirement.

Although Özal's actions in the war constituted a change in Turkey's policy of nonintervention in the Middle East, they did not reflect a change in behavior toward the United States. Özal argued that Turkey's role in the allied coalition against Iraq would not only carve out an important role for Turkey in the new international system but also consolidate its "status as a western stronghold in the Middle East."[4] The close cooperation between the United States and Turkey during the Gulf War succeeded in strengthening relations between the two countries in the aftermath of the crisis. In acknowledgment of the important role Ankara played in the war, for example, Washington increased the amount of security assistance and extended additional trade benefits to Turkey, doubling the value of its textile quota and granting the Turkish government $282 million in additional military and economic assistance for 1991.[5] Furthermore, the United States tried to help Turkey get back some of the billions of dollars it had lost because of the war (due to the shutting off of the pipeline, lost cross-border trade revenue, and the high cost of mobilizing the army). Washington persuaded Egypt to purchase forty Turkish-manufactured F-16s, and the European Community to expand the value of the Turkish textile quota. Moreover, the United States was instrumental in the Gulf Crisis Financial Coordinating Group's promise to provide Turkey with $4 billion in assistance and in the gulf allies' pledge to contribute $2.5 billion to the Turkish Defense Fund.[6] Meanwhile, Turkey also aspired to be more compliant to the United States's position on such issues as its hard-line stance in the Cyprus conflict; and Özal even proposed a quadripartite conference to resolve the issue. Turkey's role in the Gulf War emphasized its strategic location and "underscored the value of Turkish alliance to the United States and corroborated estimates within both governments of Turkey's continuing—albeit, changing—geopolitical importance."[7] Furthermore, as Eric Rouleau states:

Far from losing its usefulness after the collapse of the Soviet Union, as many predicted, NATO's policeman in the Eastern Mediterranean during the cold war—as perceived by the Europeans—managed to transform itself into an indispensable partner in a particularly sensitive region. Some senior policymakers at the State Department and White House [believed] that Turkey's importance for the United States [grew] given the new configuration of the post–cold war era.[8]

Turkish and American policymakers cooperated in a multiplicity of issues in the post–cold war era. For example, they shared the same views on the need to defend Bosnia-Herzegovina during the war in the former Yugoslavia. Although neither country was willing to take unilateral action in the region, they both called on the international community to help the Bosnian Muslims during the various stages of the crisis. Moreover, even though Russia was no longer an outright enemy as the Soviet Union had been in the past, it remained a potential adversary of both the United States and Turkey. Both countries, therefore, wanted to remain on friendly terms with Moscow while making sure that Moscow did not try to expand its influence in the former Soviet republics. Accordingly, the United States applauded Turkey's efforts to find new avenues of cooperation with Russia and supported the formation of the Black Sea Economic Cooperation Project (BSECP) to "create favorable conditions and establish institutional arrangements among the Black Sea countries for the development and diversification of their economic relations by making efficient use of advantages arising from geographical proximity and the complementary nature of their economies."⁹ Washington was hoping that, through the BSECP, Turkey would be able to affect the political and economic development of the former Soviet countries in the Black Sea region in such a way as to foster democratic political systems and capitalist economies in these newly independent states. Both Turkey and the United States feared Iranian influence in the region, and the United States saw Turkey as its best chance of preventing such an outcome. As such, Turkey was to act as a bridge between the former Soviet republics and the West.

Turkish and American interests also converged in the issues of the Middle East—a region stewing with potential conflicts. During most of the post–cold war period, Washington counted on Ankara to "stand up to 'rogue states' such as Iran, Iraq, and Syria; to support moderate regimes in the region; and to help consolidate the coming Israeli-Arab peace, notably by supplying water to the former belligerents."¹⁰ It was only for a brief period in 1996–1997 when Erbakan's pro-Islamic Welfare Party became the senior member of the governing coalition that the Americans doubted Turkey's ability and willingness to fulfill this role in the Middle East. Even during this period of uncertainty, however, Turkish-American cooperation in the region continued, with Ankara allowing access to the Americans to make use of several military air bases in successfully carrying out the relief operations for the autonomous Kurdish provinces in northern Iraq. In return, the United States supported the Turkish struggle against the separatist PKK, accepting (and thus bolstering) the Turkish argument that the PKK was a terrorist organization. In addition, despite criticisms from human rights organizations, such as Amnesty International and Human Rights Watch, that torture and other human rights abuses occurred in Turkey on a regular basis, Washington concurred with the Turkish government's claims that human rights violations were not systematic or government sanctioned but the result of police officers taking the law into their own hands. Washington also praised the small steps toward further democratization in Turkey—even though these steps were criticized as being inadequate by many European countries, international human rights organizations, and local opposition groups. Finally, the United States waged a campaign to convince members of the European Union to accept Turkey not only into the Customs Union (which they eventually did in December 1995) but also to the European Union as a full member.[11] Such support from the United States on issues of extreme importance to Turkey strengthened the belief in Turkey that Washington was a close ally that could be trusted to protect Turkish interests.

Despite this close cooperation between the United States and Turkey in the post–cold war period, there still remained some issues that raised tensions between the two allies. These sources of contention became exacerbated, and Turkish-American relations cooled off, during Erbakan's rule. Until this time, the most serious problems between Ankara and Washington occurred as a result of the intense lobbying of Congress by such anti-Turkish groups as the Greek-Americans and Armenian-Americans. These groups pressured Washington either to decrease American aid to Turkey or to make American assistance to Turkey contingent on some concessions from Ankara. On a couple of occasions, the Armenian-Americans, for instance, tried to get bills passed that would require Ankara to admit (and thus apologize for) the genocide of Armenians during World War I and the War of Independence in order to continue receiving American aid. Congress failed to pass legislation that would attach such a contingency to aid for Turkey once Turkish leaders made it clear that they would never make such an admittance, and that rather, they would turn down all aid offered by the United States.

The Gulf War and its aftermath, however, also created some problems for the country. One major issue Turkey faced after the war concerned the Kurdish security zone in northern Iraq. During the war, the Americans had encouraged Kurdish leaders in Iraq, namely Masoud Barzani and Jalal Talabani, to revolt against Saddam Hussein's regime because of the regime's incessant repression of the Kurds. Together, these two Kurdish leaders launched an insurrection in northern Iraq and were met by the wrath of the Iraqi army, which embarked on an effort to eliminate the country's Kurdish population once the Americans halted their offensive against them. As thousands of Kurdish refugees fled to Iran and prepared to flee to Turkey, Turkey closed its southeastern border knowing that it did not have the resources to provide food, shelter, and health care to the refugees. Instead of accepting the refugees, Ankara proposed a plan to establish a security zone in northern Iraq, where the Kurds would be protected and a no-fly zone would be established. The United Nations would provide relief operations, and an intervention force made up of American, British, and French troops would ward off Iraqi attempts to further suppress the Kurds (called "Poised Hammer," and later, "Provide Comfort II"). The implementation of this proposal, however, did not prevent the Iraqi Kurds' problems from burdening Turkey. In fact, the security zone in northern Iraq—a virtual no-man's land over which no central authority governed—became a hotbed of anti-Turkish, Kurdish guerrilla activity and a base for the PKK to launch attacks into Turkey. Another problem Turkey faced after the Persian Gulf War was an economic one; because Iraq had been one of its major trading partners, Turkey lost millions of dollars in trade revenues because of the comprehensive sanctions imposed on Iraq by the United Nations' Security Council.

While Turkey's foray into the Middle East was one shift in its foreign policy strategy, another change consisted of the country's involvement in the former Soviet republics. During the reign of the Soviet Union, Turkey did not have relations with the Soviet republics, many of which share with Turkey religious, ethnic, and linguistic ties, because it feared repercussions from Moscow, which actively discouraged them from forming bilateral relations that excluded the Moscow government. With the dissolution of the Soviet Union and the independence of the Soviet republics, however, "the sudden rediscovery of almost forgotten peoples of Turkic origin led to inflated hopes and unrealistic expectations on the part of some Turkish officials."[12] Ankara's eagerness for developing close relations with these newly emerging states, and its hope that they would adopt its political and economic model—a Muslim country with a pluralist democracy and capitalist economy—was encouraged by its Western allies who were weary of increased Iranian influence in the region. The first years of the post–cold war period, therefore, were characterized by Turkish politicians engaging in strong rhetoric that celebrated the "brotherhood" between Turkey and many of the former Soviet republics as a feeling of euphoria swept across the country that Turks were not alone in the world. Both Turkish leaders and the public discussed the possibility that its newfound role in the region would elevate Turkey's status in the international arena and perhaps raise it to the level of a regional superpower. Ankara thus focused on forming close economic and political ties with the countries of the Caucasus and Central Asia. In March 1991, for example, President Özal launched the Black Sea Economic Cooperation Zone—an initiative aimed at gradually establishing free trade among the countries that surround the Black Sea. In addition, by the end of 1991, the presidents of many of the Central Asian republics, such as Uzbekistan, Turkmenistan, and Kyrgystan, had traveled to Turkey on official visits as Ankara pledged to support their development efforts. The burst of enthusiasm about the role

Turkey would play in the former Soviet republics in the first years of the post–cold war era, however, was replaced by a more pragmatist approach by the mid-1990s. Turkish officials realized that they had "overestimated their capability to affect political, social, and economic developments in the newly independent Turkic states" because not only did these states not wish to alienate Moscow, but they also wanted to cultivate relations with other countries that were also prepared to assist them.[13] By 1995, therefore, Ankara had shifted its ambitions in the region to the institutionalization of economic and political ties without aiming to form a union or a commonwealth. (Although the desire for the establishment of such organizations were never officially announced, the rhetoric of Turkish leaders in the early years of the post–cold war era indicated that Ankara was optimistic about such possibilities for the future.)[14]

Another shift in Turkish foreign policy in the post–cold war period consisted of Turkey's improving its relations with a number of countries in the Balkans, which became independent after the removal of Soviet influence from their political systems. The government that came to power in Bulgaria after the fall of the communist regime had to rely on the support of the Turkish minority in winning office, and thus had to mend Bulgaria's often troubled relations with Turkey. The removal of Soviet influence from the Balkans, however, did not remove all of Turkey's difficulties in the region. The war in former Yugoslavia among the Bosnians, Serbs, and Croats, for example, presented some significant problems for Ankara. Because Turks share ethnic ties with the Bosnians, there was considerable pressure on Ankara from the Turkish public to intervene on behalf of Bosnia-Herzegovina. The various governments in power during this time, however, followed cautious and pragmatic policies. Prime Minister Çiller, for example, was very vocal and persistent in calling on the West to intervene in the conflict and made such symbolic gestures as visiting the war-torn country along with her Pakistani counterpart Prime Minister Benazir Bhutto. Ankara, however, did not take any unilateral actions to assist the Bosnian Muslims.

These shifts in Turkey's foreign policy strategies, although rather significant, did not signify a change in the country's foreign policy orientation because Turkey's relations with the United States remained excellent and continued to constitute the most important element of its foreign policy in the post–cold war era. Furthermore, during this time, successive governments stressed the importance of the EU and asserted Turkey's strong desire to become a full member in this organization. Turkish leaders, in other words, emphasized that Turkey was diversifying its foreign policy to complement, not supersede, its relations with its Western allies. Another alteration in Turkey's foreign policy strategy, one that led to questions about the direction of the country's foreign policy orientation, however, occurred with the rise to power of Prime Minister Necmettin Erbakan in June 1996. Erbakan's Islamist party, the Welfare Party (RP), received a plurality of 21.6 percent in the national elections of December 1995. The bitter personal rivalry between Tansu Çiller, leader of the True Path Party (DYP), and Mesut Yilmaz, leader of the Motherland Party (ANAP)—both moderate, right-of-center parties—prevented them from forming a lasting coalition. Although Çiller had severely criticized Erbakan's pro-Islamic policies and pledged to never join forces with the Islamists, the possibility of an investigation into her and her husband's suspicious financial dealings led her to form a coalition government with the Welfare Party. Although Çiller was deputy prime minister as well as foreign minister in this coalition, Erbakan did not relegate himself to dealing only with domestic issues.

Erbakan's anti-Western discourse and some of his foreign policy decisions and actions created a major schism with the interests of the West. Erbakan had risen to power by engaging in extremist rhetoric. He had declared, for example, that he wanted to withdraw Turkey from NATO, end military ties with Israel, and cancel the agreement that allowed Americans to operate relief missions from the Turkish bases to assist the Kurdish enclaves in northern Iraq. He had expressed his desire to form an "Islamic NATO," and "Islamic common market," as well as an organization of eight important Muslim countries resembling the Group of Seven called the D-8 (the "D" would stand for developing countries). In his campaign speeches, Erbakan had even called for an end to interest rates and for a jihad (holy war) against Jerusalem. His ascent to the post of prime minister was thus extremely troubling to many in the United States. In August 1996, for example, Morton Abramowitz, a former American ambassador to Turkey and president of the Carnegie Endowment at that time, asked, "How do you deal with a NATO ally led by a man who is fundamentally anti-NATO, fundamentally anti-Semitic and fundamentally pro-Islamist, even when he's largely behaving himself?"[15] As prime minister, Erbakan was a lot less radical and a lot more status quo–oriented than Erbakan, the opposition leader and campaigner. He toned down much of his anti-Western rhetoric and did not implement many of the changes that he had pledged to make. One of his close associates, State Minister Abdullah Gul, even admitted that "(in) Turkey, politicians sometimes exaggerate, and not just Erbakan."[16] Furthermore, even though he had said that he would terminate the American forces flying surveillance missions over Iraq, he extended the security and defense agreements with the United States. He withdrew his demands for military and industrial cooperation with

Iran after the objections from Turkey's military leaders. Perhaps most contrary to his rhetoric of the past (when he vigorously condemned Israel as being the enemy of Islam), Israel's security cooperation agreements with Turkey remained untouched, leading Israeli warplanes to "practice maneuvers in Turkish airspace while military technicians upgrade[d] Turkish fighters."[17] During the fall 1996 convention of the Welfare Party, in a hall that was decorated with Turkish flags and a portrait of Atatürk rather than "banners honoring radical Muslim movements, Hamas martyrs and Iranian ayatollahs" as had been the case in the past, Erbakan avowed Turkey's friendship for the United States and Europe, asserting that Turkish foreign policy was "not changing direction or anything like that."[18]

Prime Minister Erbakan's government, however, did take steps that challenged some of the basic tenets of Turkish foreign policy. In addition, some of the actions and speeches of the prime minister drew harsh criticisms from Turkey's Western allies. Less than a week after taking office, in a meeting with Under Secretary of State Peter Tarnoff on July 2, 1996, Erbakan announced that he believed that "as a first step to secure peace in the Middle East, [Israel] must withdraw from the territories it invaded, including the Golan Heights" and that his government intended to form closer ties with "all the brotherly Muslim countries in the region."[19] These statements were particularly disturbing to the Americans because Turkey had been one of Washington's crucial allies in the Middle East peace process, and Washington needed continued support from Ankara on this issue. Even more disturbing, however, was Erbakan's first official foreign visit in August 1996 during which he traveled to Iran (as the first stop in a tour of such Muslim countries as Pakistan, Malaysia, and Indonesia), a staunch U.S. adversary. This visit was particularly alarming because it led to the signing of a $20 billion agreement for Turkey to buy natural gas from Iran. Coming less than a week after the passing of a law by the U.S. Congress (on August 5, 1997) intended to isolate sponsors of international terrorism (mainly Iran and Libya) by barring other countries from trading with them, Erbakan's deal with Iran openly flouted the wishes of the United States.

The prime minister's next foreign visit was even more controversial—a trip to Libya in October 1996. Erbakan became one of the few world leaders to extend a friendly hand to Colonel Muammar al-Qaddafi, and referring to the American bombing of Tripoli in 1986, he declared that Libya, instead of being a terrorist state, was in fact a victim of terrorism.[20] The trip, however, was a public-relations fiasco because the Libyan leader berated Turkey for being a puppet of the West and for not giving the Kurds a homeland. The fact that Erbakan did not respond to this diatribe and allowed Turkey to be denigrated caused a political crisis in Turkey. As leading politicians called for Erbakan's resignation, yet another foreign trip (which also included Nigeria, another country not favored by the United States, and Egypt, which was not particularly welcoming toward the Turkish prime minister due to his public gestures of support for the Islamic brotherhood) contributed to the growing schism between Ankara and Washington.

Another source of contention between the United States and Turkey (one that did not necessarily result from the Welfare Party's anti-Western stance, but which may have been handled more diplomatically by a different government) arose out of Washington's hard-line stance against Iraq. A few years after the end of the Gulf War, Ankara became increasingly eager to normalize relations with Iraq. Meanwhile, the Americans wanted to maintain intact the comprehensive sanctions against Iraq until Baghdad fully complied with the conditions set forth by the United Nations. Turkey had had cordial political and close economic relations with Iraq prior to the Gulf War and had suffered tremendously as a result of the sanctions. Prior to the war, the pipeline in Turkey that carried Iraqi oil from northern Iraq to the Mediterranean earned Turkey rental revenue worth up to $1.2 billion annually.[21] By the mid-1990s, therefore, Ankara wanted the pipeline to be reopened to lessen some of its economic problems. Iraq and Turkey had also traded significantly with each other, especially in the form of cross-border exchanges, prior to the Gulf War. In 1987, for example, Iraq was the second-largest recipient (after Germany) of Turkish goods, receiving 9.3 percent of total exports.[22] The fact that this amount had dropped to 0.9 percent by 1991 made Ankara anxious for the UN to lift the sanctions so that it could resume trade with Iraq.

An additional cause for concern among Turks was that the establishment of the autonomous Kurdish region in northern Iraq created a political vacuum in the area. The absence of an effective political authority in the region complicated Turkey's struggle with the PKK because the Kurdish terrorists often used this no-man's-land as a training ground for their military operations into Turkey. Consequently, Ankara openly opposed the United States in September 1996 and urged President Saddam Hussein to impose his authority in northern Iraq. Only three weeks after the United States staged cruise missile attacks on military installations in southern Iraq to protest Hussein's attempts to assert authority in northern Iraq, Foreign Minister Çiller announced that the guerrilla operations of the PKK from camps in northern Iraq could no longer be tolerated by Ankara. She declared that the government had sent a delegation to Hussein to tell him that "if he can establish a degree of rule [in northern Iraq] that puts an end to terrorist infiltration, that would be fine by us. If not, we will take measures to see that terrorists do not operate on our borders. We defend the territorial integrity of Iraq, but the lack of authority there has been tragic for us."[23] Although Çiller's remarks were not followed by concrete actions to urge Iraq to reestablish authority in the region (and Turkey sought to deal with the problem by conducting bombing raids into the areas in the region populated by PKK guerrillas), they were criticized by State Department officials in Washington who were concerned about Ankara's efforts to undermine U.S. operations and ambitions in the region.

Although Erbakan claimed to have a new vision for Turkey as a "nationalist democracy, a society that tolerates secular voices but is at heart religious, conscious of history and infused with a God-given sense of earthly mission," as well as a new vision for the world in which Turkey would play a greater role in battling prejudice against Islam and injustice in the world, he did not have a free hand in implementing his policies.[24] On the one hand, the Welfare Party's coalition partner—a secular party—worked to balance Erbakan's Islamist tendencies. On the other hand, Turkey's military establishment prevented him from taking any actions that strayed from Turkey's secular and Western-oriented principles. On February 29, 1997, for example, the meeting of the National Security Council resulted in a severe public warning by the military to Erbakan's government. The communiqué stated that "no steps away from the contemporary values of the Turkish Republic would be tolerated," and that "it has been decided that in Turkey, secularism is not only a form of government but a way of life and the guarantee of democracy and social peace."[25]

The Decision-Making Process

The reforms that were implemented in the former Soviet bloc countries after 1989 coincided with the launching of a gradual process of political liberalization in Turkey. In April 1989, for example, the Turkish government announced a reduction in the time people could remain in custody without being charged from fifteen days to twenty-four hours—an important development that restricted the time when most torture took place.[26] An antiterrorism law passed in the same month, however, was a setback to the democratization process, for it gave the authorities extraordinary powers to deal with whatever they chose to designate as terrorism. The political reform process gathered more momentum a few years later with more significant changes introduced in March and April 1991. At this time, the cabinet introduced a number of constitutional amendments that not only brought changes to the political system, such as the enlargement of the Grand National Assembly, direct presidential elections, and the lowering of the voting age to eighteen, but also made some improvements in the country's human rights provisions. In January 1991, under the guidance of President Özal, the cabinet abolished the law "restricting the use of languages other than Turkish."[27] In addition, the assembly approved the deletion from the penal code of three articles that had banned politics on the basis of class or religion. The use of terrorism to further political ideals was left as an offense, with the concept of terrorism still defined rather broadly. These political reforms occurred at this time because Turgut Özal was the first president willing to make concessions to the Kurds. His presidency also removed some of the influence of the military, not only because Özal himself was a civilian but also because he was willing to challenge openly the power of the military.

The Persian Gulf crisis showed Özal's willingness to take foreign policy decision-making away from the military establishment. In the face of significant dissent from opposition parties as well as the Motherland Party, Özal bypassed the government and the assembly to give full Turkish support to the United States. He engaged in personal, secret diplomacy, mostly in the form of direct telephone conversations with U.S. President George Bush. It was Özal's eagerness to give Turkey a central position in the coalition against Iraq that led to the alteration of the long-standing policy of neutrality in Middle Eastern affairs. While Özal claimed that the central role Turkey had assumed in the Persian Gulf crisis increased its strategic importance to the West and its standing in the world, many prominent politicians were extremely dissatisfied with the country's gulf policies. Foreign Minister Ali Bozer and Defense Minister Sefa Giray resigned from their cabinet positions in protest in October 1990. It was the resignation of Chief of Staff Necip Torumtay on December 3, 1990, however, that shocked the country. Torumtay disagreed with the way Özal was dealing with the crisis as well as his personalized way of policymaking and wanted Turkey to pursue a more moderate policy. He stated in his letter of resignation, "I am resigning because I cannot continue to do my duty with the principles I hold and with my understanding of state affairs."[28] Özal's defiance of Torumtay was interpreted by the public and politicians as an attempt to reestablish the primacy of civilian politics over the military. When rumors circulated that Torumtay's resignation might lead the High Command to stage another military intervention if Özal did not start acting more prudently in the conduct of foreign policy, Özal declared that he was not afraid of anyone. The military, which had been at the forefront of Turkish foreign policy since the 1960 intervention, had thus been relegated to the background with Özal's gulf policies.

The president's aggressive handling of the Gulf crisis did not, however, increase the Motherland Party's popularity in Turkey. Its standing in the polls had diminished significantly after a political crisis that erupted in April 1991 over the installation of Özal's wife, Semra, as chair of ANAP's Istanbul branch. Prime Minister Mesut Yilmaz wanted to increase people's confidence in the governing Motherland Party and called for early elections to be held on October 20, 1991. The result was a defeat for the Motherland Party as Demirel's True Path Party won a plurality with 27 percent of the vote.[29] The Motherland Party with Mesut Yilmaz as its new leader came in a close second with 24 percent, and the left-of-center Social Democratic Populist Party (*Sosyal Demokrat Halkci Parti*, SHP), third with 20 percent. Another party that did well in these elections was the Welfare Party, which received 16.9 percent of the vote. This percentage, however, was rather deceiving because the Welfare Party had joined together with the neo-fascist Nationalist Labor Party and the Islamic Democratic Party. Although none of these three parties would have been able to win the 10 percent necessary to enter into the assembly, they were able to attain seats by forging this alliance. Their coalition did not last long, and soon after the assembly convened, Nationalist Labor Party deputies left the coalition to become independents. With these election results, the most logical coalition would have been between the center-right Motherland and True Path Parties, but the animosity between their leaders prevented such a coalition from being formed and led Demirel to form a government with the Social Democratic Party.

This new government intended to further the political liberalization reforms started in 1989 and pledged more constitutional change, more academic and press freedom, more democratization, and an expansion of human rights. Although it succeeded in closing down the Eskişehir Prison, infamous for its treatment of political prisoners, the government was not able to carry out subsequent political liberalization measures. Its inability to adopt democratic reforms stemmed from the vehement opposition to them by the right-wing faction of the True Path Party, which argued that the political violence still prevalent in Turkey made it imperative that the government not relax any of its policies of control. Meanwhile, the Kurdish insurgency continued to wreak havoc in the southeastern region of the country, and Turkish politicians could not reach a consensus on how to deal with this extremely sensitive and volatile problem. President Özal started entertaining the idea of finding a political solution to the crisis. He held talks with Iraqi Kurdish leaders Barzani and Talabani who had been given jurisdiction of an area in northern Iraq that was to be a haven for Iraqi Kurds. Naturally, this virtual no-man's-land (due to the lack of an effective government, police force, etc.) that bordered Turkey also became a hotbed for the PKK terrorists. Özal's meeting with Barzani and Talabani yielded some positive results as both men ordered the PKK out of the area.

After President Özal's death on April 17, 1993, Prime Minister Demirel became president. The leadership of the True Path Party went to Tansu Çiller, and the new DYP-SHP coalition government was accorded a vote of confidence by the assembly, making Çiller Turkey's first female prime minister. The program of the coalition included goals for further democratization, secularization, and privatization. An important problem for the government was the increased guerrilla activity by the PKK in southeastern Anatolia. Abandoning Özal's forays into finding a political solution, Çiller's government focused on a military response to deal with the situation and launched a major offensive against the PKK's camps in northern Iraq in March 1995. Meanwhile, under considerable pressure from the West to further its democratization in order to be admitted to the European Union, the Grand National Assembly amended sixteen articles of the constitution on July 23, 1995. These amendments were to "dramatically expand and strengthen Turkey's democracy, provide greater freedom of association, and . . . remove some of the last vestiges of the 1980 military rule."[30] The amendments included lowering the voting age to eighteen, allowing certain civil service unions to enter into collective bargaining agreements, and lifting bans against associations from participating in the political process. The governing coalition broke down, however, when a revived CHP (which had become the junior coalition partner after merging with SHP in February 1995) withdrew its support from the government in September 1995. The collapse of the government resulted from the unwillingness of the leader of the CHP, Deniz Baykal, to make concessions on his party's left-wing principles. As a result of the inability of Çiller and Yilmaz to form a coalition, new elections had to be scheduled for December 1995.

While the Kurdish insurgency and unstable governments were two issues that dominated the 1980s, another problem was the wide, and rapidly increasing, gap between the rich and the poor. The economic liberalization policies pursued since 1980 led to a situation in which the rich got richer and the poor got poorer. A new class of extremely wealthy entrepreneurs emerged from successes in the import-export and construction sectors. The wealth of these groups was reflected in the store shelves that were filled with luxury goods imported from around the world, goods that the majority of the population could not afford. There were more Mercedes-Benzes and BMWs on the streets than domestically manufactured cars, and the wealthy found additional avenues to showcase their fortunes. The purchasing power of the middle and lower-middle classes in the country, however, had diminished significantly, and reports of the World Bank stated that Turkey was among the seven countries with the worst figures for income disparity.[31] The extremely high inflation rate, as well as the high unemployment rate, made life very difficult for the majority of the population.

The rather inconclusive results of the December 1995 elections and eventual agreement between the True Path Party and the Welfare Party brought the Islamists to power. As discussed above, the entry of the Welfare Party into the government as the senior partner in the coalition and the role of Erbakan as Turkey's prime minister clearly brought a new dimension to Turkish foreign policy decision-making. Erbakan clearly used religion for political purposes and even declared that people who did not vote for the Welfare Party would be punished by God. Whereas it would have been impossible for such a politician to become a major policymaker in Turkey during previous eras, certain factors facilitated his rise to power in the post–cold war period. First, Islam had become an increasingly important force in Turkish society and Turkish politics since the strictly secular single-party era. The military had grown more tolerant of religion and had even accepted its ability to contribute to peace and stability in society. Second, the military was much less eager to intervene in politics to halt the growing power of the Welfare Party in the post–cold war era because it believed that Turkey needed to stay on the path of democracy in order to be accepted as an equal partner by the West. The value of democracy had increased tremendously during this time because of the disintegration of the world's major authoritarian power, the Soviet Union. Military leaders understood the importance of letting democracy work if Turkey wanted to achieve such goals as entry into the European Union. Third, the Welfare Party was able to capitalize on the ineffectiveness of the other parties, which were embroiled in political squabbles and corruption scandals, in providing basic services to the people. Different branches of the party set up an efficient system of grassroots organizations to provide cheap bread, health services, and education (including religious education) to the poor. Erbakan also presented the Welfare Party as the only party that was not corrupt and which worked for the benefit of the people.

The foreign policy decision-making arena in Turkey in 1996 thus looked quite different from that of previous times. An Islamic party was in power with a prime minister who had made statements that indicated that he wanted to change the direction of Turkish foreign policy. His first international trip to Iran, Libya, Egypt, and Nigeria showed that he was clearly a new type of prime minister, one who was more concerned with improving

Turkey's relations with these Muslim countries than with upsetting its long-time ally, the United States (which had condemned Iran and Libya as countries that harbored terrorists). Although Erbakan toned down some of his anti-Western rhetoric after this controversial trip, he continued to call for pro-Islamic changes in the domestic arena (such as building mosques in prominent Istanbul locations, lifting bans on the wearing of religious head wear, etc.). Meanwhile, although the National Security Council had been somewhat tolerant of Erbakan's radical forays into the foreign policy arena, it finally demonstrated that it was not ready to give up its role in the decision-making process. In a meeting on February 28, 1997, for example, it ordered Erbakan to accept the enforcement of secularist laws and ideology. In a memorandum issued after this meeting, the NSC participants "declared loyalty to the secular and modern nature of the state, reaffirmed a goal to make Turkey a full member of the European Union and declared that 'secularism in Turkey is not only the state but is also the guarantor of social peace, democracy and a way of life.' "[32]

Even before Erbakan's rise to power in Turkey, the foreign policy decision-making arena of the post-war period looked somewhat different than it had in previous eras. The way that Özal secured a central place for Turkey in the Persian Gulf crisis was the first time a president had taken the reigns of foreign policy decision-making and refused to be influenced by the military officers. As a result, Turkey's extensive involvement in a Middle Eastern conflict was a clear break from its previous policy of nonintervention in the affairs of this turbulent region. Although Erbakan did not attempt to change the basic tenets of Turkish foreign policy after becoming prime minister, some of his actions and rhetoric led many to question the stability that had prevailed in Turkish foreign policy for so long. As a result of these developments, the post–cold war foreign policy decision-making arena in Turkey looked much more diverse than it had in previous eras. There were members of the cabinet from the Welfare Party interested in creating a more Islamic state and society, and from the True Path Party who were secular but relegated to the background. Additionally, the cabinet contained military officers making sure the country did not stray from such principles as the secularism embodied in its constitution. Many of these changes in the foreign policy decision-making arena resulted from the economic policies Turkey had pursued throughout its history. In particular, it was the economic liberalization reforms of the 1980s that contributed to the disfranchisement of large sectors of the population who lent their support to such alternative movements as the Kurdish separatists and Islamists.

Foreign Policy Behavior

This brief shift in Turkish foreign policy behavior toward the United States once again occurred as a result of a number of sources of foreign policy. One important factor was the alteration of domestic structures. The changes in Turkish economic policy that introduced drastic economic liberalization measures in the 1980s worsened the distribution of income. The poor got poorer and the rich not only got richer but also found new ways to flaunt their wealth. As a result, the poorer sectors of society grew increasingly dissatisfied by the mainstream political process and lent their support to alternative movements, such as the PKK and the Islamists. Soon afterward, the Welfare Party capitalized on this dissatisfaction to increase its popularity by working at a grassroots level to provide such basic necessities as cheap bread and health clinics. Meanwhile, the policies of the 1980 military regime allowed for the growing influence of Islam as a force to counter left-wing tendencies in Turkish society. This new permissive attitude toward religion continued and expanded during the Özal years. Consequently, by the mid-1990s, the Welfare Party was a force to be reckoned with in Turkish politics.

The second factor contributing to the shift in foreign policy behavior was the change in the structure of the international system. As the world went from a system of clearly defined bipolarity to something not as easily understood, Turkey experienced an identity crisis. As scholars and politicians questioned the role Turkey would play in the new international order, Erbakan and the Welfare Party took advantage of the conflicts that had sprung up all over the world in the aftermath of the cold war (such as Bosnia to Nagorno-Karabakh) by arguing that these ethnic wars were being tolerated by the West because Muslims, not Christians, were the victims. He asserted that Turkey would be able to realize its rightful place as a powerful regional leader in the new international order only if it aligned itself with the Islamic world. Because the end of the cold war was a time in which many questioned the role Turkey would assume in the post–cold war era, and because new avenues for Turkish foreign policy had finally opened up in the former Soviet republics, people were more willing to lend an ear to Erbakan's arguments.

The third factor to contribute to the shift in foreign policy behavior involved the actions of other governments. Although the United States maintained close ties with Turkey after the end of the cold war, Ankara faced rejection from the Europeans during this time. As will be discussed in the following chapter, not only was Turkey's 1987 application for membership in the European Union rejected, but the Europeans made clear that Turkish accession would not even be considered in the near future. This alienation from Europe made many Turks more open to Erbakan's beliefs and rhetoric that Turkey's rightful place was with the countries of the Islamic world and not the West. As a result of these three factors, the Welfare Party won a narrow plurality in the December 1995 elections and proceeded to bring about some changes to Turkish foreign policy behavior. It is important to note that despite his campaign promises to the contrary, however, Erbakan was not able to shift Turkey foreign policy orientation. Not only was he in office for too brief a period of time, but he also had the military apparatus constraining his behavior. He was able to make anti-Western foreign policy decisions and take actions only during the first few months of his tenure in office.

It was the power of the Turkish military that prompted Erbakan to tone down his anti-Western stance. The military establishment, the guarantors of not only Turkey's secular character but also its Western foreign policy orientation, made it very clear to Erbakan that they would not be reluctant to intervene if they felt the actions of the Welfare Party threatened Turkey's stability and security. In response to a political rally in Sincan, in which the Iranian ambassador called for the implementation of Islamic law, *sharia*, in Turkey in February 1997, for instance, the armed forces showed their strength when they sent a fleet of tanks to roll through the streets of the town (twenty-five miles from the capital).[33] The Welfare government became more moderate in its foreign policy views soon after the military leaders made clear their intention to keep Turkey's long-standing alliance with the West intact. They were not as not willing to compromise on domestic issues and government leaders clashed with the National Security Council (NSC, the political arm of Turkey's military establishment) over a number of issues. Some areas of contention regarded the laws that governed the running of religious institutions, the laws that prevented women from wearing religious headdresses in government buildings, and the building of mosques in prominent neighborhoods in Istanbul. Although a few of the NSC's warnings to Erbakan that unless he implemented certain measures, he would be forced out of office, went unheeded, Erbakan finally yielded to the pressure from the military and resigned on June 18, 1997.

NOTES

1. Bruce R. Kuniholm, "Turkey and the West Since World War II," *Turkey Between East and West: New Challenges for a Rising Regional Power*, eds. Vojtech Mastny and R. Craig Nation (Boulder, Colo.: Westview Press, 1996), 60.

2. Sabri Sayari, "Turkey: The Changing European Security Environment and the Gulf Crisis," *Middle East Journal* 46.1 (Winter 1992): 14.

3. William Safire, "The Second Front," *New York Times* (1 November 1990): A29.

4. Erik J. Zurcher, *Turkey: A Modern History* (London: I. B. Tauris, 1993), 318.

5. Sayari, "Turkey: The Changing European Security Environment and the Gulf Crisis," 19.

6. Sayari, "Turkey: The Changing European Security Environment and the Gulf Crisis," 19.

7. Kuniholm, "Turkey and the West Since World War II," 62.

8. Eric Rouleau, "Turkey: Beyond Ataturk," *Foreign Policy* (Summer 1996): 84.

9. Sükrü Elekdağ, "Black Sea Cooperation Region Project," Turkish Ministry of Foreign Affairs, May 9, 1991 (unpublished) as quoted in J. F. Brown, "Turkey: Back to the Balkans?" *Turkey's New Geopolitics*, eds. Graham E. Fuller and Ian O. Lesser with Paul B. Henze and J. F. Brown (Boulder, Colo.: Westview Press, 1993), 156.

10. Rouleau, "Turkey: Beyond Ataturk," 84.

11. Rouleau, "Turkey: Beyond Ataturk," 85.

12. Gareth Winrow, *Turkey in Post-Soviet Central Asia* (London: Royal Institute of International Affairs, 1995), 3.

13. Winrow, *Turkey in Post-Soviet Central Asia*, 14.

14. Winrow, *Turkey in Post-Soviet Central Asia*, 51.

15. Steven Erlanger, "New Turkish Chief's Muslim Tour Stirs U.S. Worry," *New York Times* (10 August 1996): A2.

16. Celestine Bohlen, "Islamic Party Walking a Tightrope in Turkey," *New York Times* (12 July 1996): A8.

17. Stephen Kinzer, "The Islamist Who Runs Turkey, Delicately," *New York Times Magazine* (23 February 1997): 30.

18. Kinzer, "The Islamist Who Runs Turkey, Delicately," 30.

19. Stephen Kinzer, "Meeting U.S. Envoy, Turkish Premier Takes Pro-Arab Stance," *New York Times* (3 July 1996): A13.

20. Kinzer, "The Islamist Who Runs Turkey, Delicately," 31.

21. Phebe Marr, "Turkey and Iraq," *Reluctant Neighbor: Turkey's Role in the Middle East*, ed. Henri J. Barkey (Washington, D.C.: U.S. Institute of Peace Press, 1996), 45.

22. Marr, "Turkey and Iraq," 52.

23. Stephen Kinzer, "Turks, Opposing U.S., Urge Iraq to Take Control of Kurdish Area," *New York Times* (21 September 1997): A1.

24. Kinzer, "The Islamist Who Runs Turkey, Delicately," 30.

25. Stephen Kinzer, "In Defense of Secularism, Turkish Army Warns Rulers," *New York Times* (2 March 1997): A10.

26. Zurcher, *Turkey: A Modern History*, 304.

27. Philip Robins, "The Overlord State: Turkish Policy and the Kurdish Issue," *International Affairs* 69.4 (1993): 665.

28. Feroz Ahmad, *The Making of Modern Turkey* (London: Routledge, 1993), 201.

29. Arthur S. Banks, Alan J. Day, and Thomas C. Muller, eds., *Political Handbook of the World: 1995–1996* (Binghamton, N.Y.: CSA Publications, State University of New York, 1997), 961.

30. "Turkish Parliament Passes Sweeping Democratic Reforms," Press Release of the Turkish Embassy, Washington, D.C., July 24, 1995.

31. Ahmad, *The Making of Modern Turkey*, 204.

32. Hugh Pope, "Turkey's Military Orders Erbakan to Curb Islamists," *Wall Street Journal* (3 March 1997): A1.

33. Kinzer, "The Islamist Who Runs Turkey, Delicately," 31.

Chapter 5 ————————————————————————

Relations with the European Union

Turkey's relations with Western Europe, its connections with both individual European countries as well as with European organizations, have been crucial in Ankara's pursuit of a Western-oriented foreign policy since the inception of the Turkish Republic in 1923. The cold war era, in particular, was defined by Ankara's efforts to become an integral part of various European institutions. Although Turkey succeeded in joining Western Europe's political alliance—the North Atlantic Treaty Organization (NATO)—in 1952, Turkish-European relations have been shaped by its attempts to be accepted into the European Union (EU). Membership in this organization was seen by Turks as "the culmination of a process that has been going on for 150 years," from the days in which Turkey was a member of the Concert of Europe, to the time that it was described as "the sick man of Europe."[1] This chapter, therefore, focuses on the ups and downs of Turkey's relationship with the European Union and the repercussions of this relationship for Turkish foreign policy.

Although Turkey's Western foreign policy orientation has remained stable since 1923, its foreign policy behavior toward Western Europe experienced some shifts. The first of these alterations occurred in 1978 when Ankara abruptly suspended the negotiations for the establishment of a customs union with the European Community after fifteen years of actively pursuing this goal. The second shift occurred in 1987 when the Turkish government applied for full membership in the organization. At this time, Turkey had not achieved a customs union with the EC and was just emerging from a period in which Turkish-European relations were significantly strained. The most important reason for these alterations stemmed from the domestic environment in Turkey, especially in the economic arena. In fact, the importance of its economic relations with Western Europe prompted Ankara to tolerate constant criticisms and successive rejections from the Europeans. In addition, Turkish policymakers consistently maintained that Turkey's relations with Western Europe were among its most important because Western Europe constituted its most important trading partner, its source of foreign investment and foreign exchange. Turkey's relationship with Western Europe, in other words, was much more economically oriented than its relationship with the United States. Consequently, Ankara's foreign policy behavior toward this region was greatly influenced by the economic conditions prevalent in Turkey at various times. The single-minded pursuit (except for a brief period in the late 1970s) of EU membership is one example that demonstrates the importance of economic motivations in the conduct of Turkish foreign policy.

SHIFTS IN FOREIGN POLICY BEHAVIOR

The Turkish relationship with the European Union, formerly known as the European Economic Community (EEC) and the European Community (EC), began when Turkey applied for associate membership in the organization on July 31, 1959. It became an associate member after the signing of the Ankara Agreement in 1963 (which defined the terms, conditions and the timetable for Turkey's admission into the EC). Although Ankara's foreign policy behavior toward the organization was unwavering for the next fifteen years, a major shift occurred when Prime Minister Bülent Ecevit suspended Turkey's relations with the European Community in October 1978. The most important reason for this marked departure from policies of the past resulted from the fact that the Turkish economy was facing a serious crisis situation during this time, and a number of influential businessmen, members of the media, and politicians believed that implementing the necessary steps for EC membership would have detrimental effects on the economy. As a result of this economic crisis, Prime Minister Ecevit's political stability was rather fragile, preventing him from undertaking a controversial endeavor that could further damage his position.

The second shift occurred almost a decade later when Prime Minister Turgut Özal's government applied for membership in the organization in 1987. Many in Turkey as well as in Europe felt that the application was premature because Turkish-European relations had been particularly strained following the 1980 coup d'état in Turkey. The Europeans had been harshly critical of the military regime's suspension of democratic institutions as well as its human rights violations. Furthermore, Ankara had not achieved many of the prerequisites (either implicit or explicit) for full membership—the establishment of a customs union, a certain level of economic development, and a well-functioning democracy. The 1987 application was thus submitted at a time in which Turkey was not quite ready for EC membership, and in

which the EC was not ready for Turkey. The main reasons for this change
in policy once again stemmed from the domestic arena. Ankara wanted to
capitalize on the economic liberalization and the subsequent economic
growth in Turkey by increasing trade with European countries. Furthermore,
at a time of growing uncertainty about the direction of Turkish foreign policy
(as a result of improving relations with the Islamic world as well as the
strength of Islamist forces in Turkish society), the government wanted to
reaffirm its allegiance to the Western world. The prevalent belief among
policymakers was that only by becoming a full member of the European
Community would Turkey be able to consolidate its rightful place in the
Western world.

1945–1978: Associate Membership in the European Union—
Stage 1

As discussed earlier, the leaders of the Turkish Republic had followed a
policy of westernization since the inauguration of the republic in 1923, but
a number of circumstances in the world arena—such as the Great Depression
and World War II—had hindered their efforts to be integrated into the
Western world. The conditions that emerged in the international system in
the aftermath of World War II, however, provided Turkish officials with an
opportunity to forge binding ties with the West.[2] It was during this time
that Ankara forged a close association with the United States based on Turkey's strategic position in the emerging East-West conflict. Turkey's new role
as an ally of the United States led to a natural alignment with the Americans'
European allies in the cold war. As such, Turkey was included in Europe's
post-war economic recovery program, the Marshall Plan, in 1947 and subsequently joined the Council of Europe. Turkey joined NATO as a full
member in 1952.

The next important organization formed in Europe was the European Coal
and Steel Community in 1951. This was augmented by the European Community, which was launched with the signing of the Treaty of Rome on
March 25, 1957. As Atila Eralp asserts, "According to Turkish policymakers,
membership in the new European Community was a logical extension of
Turkey's inclusion in the other western organizations since the Community
provided an economic dimension supplementing and cementing the western
alliance."[3] On March 25, 1957, therefore, Turkey submitted its application
for associate membership in this organization. Its application was prompted
by two major political considerations. First, Turkey desperately wanted to
consolidate its position as an integral part of the Western world and Turkish

policymakers believed that EC membership would fulfill this goal. Second, Ankara was concerned that its exclusion, and Greece's inclusion (a distinct possibility at the time because Greece had applied for membership two months earlier) in Western institutions would be detrimental to the country's various international goals.[4] There were also economic incentives behind the decision to apply for membership as Turkey stood to reap significant benefits from an association with this successful organization. While Turkish politicians were enthusiastic about Turkish membership in the EC, however, European officials approached Ankara's application rather cautiously. They were concerned that Turkey's economic problems as well as its low level of economic development would harm the association and impede its efforts at economic integration. Their desire to be impartial in their relations with Greece and Turkey because of the two countries' strategic positions in the cold war (and the fact that Greece had already been admitted as an associate member), however, finally led them to dismiss their objections to Turkey's application.

The Association Agreement (also known as the Ankara Agreement) outlining the terms and conditions of Turkey's association with the European Community was signed on September 12, 1963, and came into effect on December 1, 1964. The stated objectives of the agreement were as follows:

1. the formation of a customs union;
2. a three stage (preparatory, transitional, and final) alignment of the economic and social policies of Turkey and the EC, including the eventual achievement of freedom of movement of workers;
3. financial cooperation to further Turkey's economic development.[5]

In addition, Article 28 of the agreement specified that ultimately, the full membership of Turkey in the EC was anticipated. The preparatory stage of the agreement was launched with the granting of financial assistance to Turkey in order to facilitate its integration into Europe. The European Investment Bank extended $175 billion worth of loans for infrastructure projects while the EC agreed to preferential treatment for Turkish agricultural exports.[6] This first stage of the association moved forward without any problems and Turkish and European officials launched the transitional stage of the Ankara Agreement in May 1967. Disagreements soon emerged, however, when the two sides had to decide on the terms and conditions for establishing a timetable toward the formation of a customs union between Turkey and Europe. Both the Europeans and the Turks were reluctant to make the type of commitment required by a customs union. The turmoil in Turkey immediately before and after the military intervention of 1971 also impeded the swift adoption of the timetable. As a result, a timetable did not come into effect until January 1973. At that time, the European Community abolished customs duties and nontariff barriers on most products from Turkey. Some exceptions were made in textiles; and restrictions remained on cotton, yarn, cotton textiles, and machine-woven carpets. After the accession to the next stage in 1973, Turkey agreed to lift duties on some commodities imported from Europe over a twelve to twenty-two-year time frame. Meanwhile, the EC was to continue providing Turkey with financial assistance, and all restrictions on the free movement in Europe by Turkish workers would be lifted (after a phased process leading up to it) by December 1, 1986.[7]

Although 1973 was the year in which Turkey acceded to the second stage of the Association Agreement, it was also the year in which the German government issued a ban on the recruitment of migrant workers from countries that were not members of the EC.[8] Not only was this ban followed by similar measures in other European countries but it was also augmented by visa requirements that allowed only family members of legally settled workers to immigrate to Germany and other EC countries. These restrictions on the free movement of labor were imposed because the Germans felt that their economy, which was facing a number of problems, could no longer handle the steady stream of low-skilled workers pouring into the country. Although Germany may have been justified in this line of thinking, its actions openly defied the Ankara Agreement by preventing the gradual move toward the lifting of all restrictions on the free movement of Turkish workers. The issue of the so-called guest workers (the name given to migrant workers in Germany) became a considerable source of tension between Ankara and the European capitals, creating the most tension with Germany—Turkey's largest trading partner in Europe and the home of about four-fifths of all Turkish migrants in the EC.[9] It also led the Turkish public to question the European commitment to integrating Turkey into Western Europe.

Although EC members had been the first party to not comply with the terms of the Association Agreement, the Turks were even more delinquent in taking the necessary steps for the next phase of the agreement—the establishment of the customs union. By the early 1970s, opposition to a customs union with Europe had started to build up among a diverse group of people in Turkey. Turkish politicians, who had viewed membership in the EC as an integral part of their foreign policy, began to question its value in the period of détente in Soviet-American relations that had emerged in the 1970s.

Big businessmen worried about the effects increased imports from Europe would have on Turkey's own industrialization and economic development, and both groups felt dissatisfied by the amount of financial assistance provided by the EC to prepare Turkey for the customs union. They also realized that "the gradual opening of their economy to European competition ran contrary to the established policy of planned national economic development by way of import substitution" that Ankara had adopted as its development program and was not quite ready to abandon.[10] In addition, the oil crisis of 1973–1974 and the three-year U.S. arms embargo on Turkey instituted in 1974 (in response to the Turkish invasion of northern Cyprus) led to serious economic problems for Turkey during the second half of the 1970s. As a result, the Turkish government felt that it could not afford to implement the provisions of the Ankara Agreement. It adopted only two small tariff reductions, did not begin the process of adjustment to the EC's common external tariff, and stopped the measures to reduce quantitative restrictions on imports from the EC. Meanwhile, numerous discussions about the harmful effects of the customs union led to the government's conclusion that taking the necessary steps to accede to the next stage of the Ankara Agreement would be detrimental to the Turkish economy. Consequently, in October 1978, the government of Bülent Ecevit, the leader of the left-of-center Republican People's Party, suspended some of its earlier commitments under the agreement and suspended its ongoing relations with the EC. In so doing, Ecevit was trying to gain time to formulate a policy that would not only be acceptable to more people in Turkey but that would also protect the Turkish economy from the potentially harmful effects of the customs union.

It is important to note that while Turkey was immersed in this economic and ideological crisis, Greece had applied for full membership in the European Community in 1975. At the time, Greek and Turkish officials shared many of the same concerns about the effects of the customs union on their weak economies but took vastly different approaches in dealing with the problem: Ankara halted relations with the EC while Athens pushed for further integration and full membership. As a result, Greece became a full member of the EC in January 1981. In retrospect, Turkey's actions during this time have been criticized by many as a missed opportunity. Although the Turkish economy had not been ready for EC membership in the late 1970s, applying with Greece would have bolstered the Turkish application. Many scholars have argued that the EC's eagerness about being even-handed in its relations with Turkey and Greece (because of their strategic significance as NATO allies in the ongoing cold war) would have prompted the organization either to admit both countries or to delay both applications. In other words, the worst-case scenario of Athens' inclusion and Ankara's exclusion from the organization may have been averted.

Ecevit's halting of relations with the EC was the first shift in Turkish foreign policy behavior toward Western Europe. Ankara abruptly steered off course in 1978 after years of pursuing closer ties with the European Community and European countries. The most important factor contributing to this significant change in Turkish foreign policy behavior was the domestic structure of Turkey at the time. As discussed previously, Turkey was facing a severe economic crisis during the 1970s. Oil prices had soared as a result of the oil shocks of 1973–1974, and Turkey had to pay enormous amounts for oil imports (on which it was becoming increasingly dependent). Stagflation in industrialized countries had depressed the demand for Turkish exports, reducing the country's export earnings, and remittances from Turkish workers abroad were diminished due to the weakening of labor markets in European countries. Furthermore, the current account of the balance of payments deficit was $3 billion and external debt was $11 billion (1977).[11] In such an unstable economic environment, many policymakers as well as influential businessmen saw the accession to the next stage of the Ankara Agreement as an economic gamble that had the potential to do great harm to an economy already in shambles. Adoption of the customs union would mean that Turkish goods would no longer be protected against European competition, Turkish workers producing import-substituting goods would lose their jobs, and the Turkish economy would be significantly affected by the swings in European markets. The government was thus not willing to risk making a decision that could exacerbate the troubles of the Turkish economy. Furthermore, the EC policies of free-market economics contradicted the principles of import-substituting industrialization (ISI) that was being pursued in Turkey during this time. In the political sphere, on the other hand, the 1970s in Turkey were characterized by a series of unstable coalitions that were too weak to carry out the reforms necessary to make the customs union a success. The political system was extremely polarized, and supporters of extremist parties on both sides of the spectrum were increasingly becoming engaged in terrorist violence that threatened to engulf the country. As a result of the political and economic crises in Turkey at the time, therefore, Ankara was not prepared to undertake an endeavor as potentially risky as the customs union, leading to the shift in Turkish foreign policy toward the European Community. Although Prime Minister Ecevit suspended the negotiations for the implementation of the customs union with the EC, however, Western Europe remained Turkey's most important trading partner. Just a year after the freezing of the customs union negotiations, for example, Turkish imports from the EC were 38.3 percent of total imports; and Turkish exports to the EC were 50 percent of total exports.[12]

1978–1986: Associate Membership in the European Union—Stage 2

The problems that arose in the transitional stage of EC membership (and the fact that both sides failed to fulfill their commitments) did considerable damage to Turkish-European relations. There was significant distrust on both sides. The fact that Greece had succeeded in becoming a full member of the organization in 1981 created more difficulties in Ankara's relationship with Brussels. Despite these obstacles to improving relations with the Europeans, however, Turkish policymakers were optimistic that the drastic economic liberalization measures adopted on January 24, 1980 (which included the devaluation of the Turkish lira, the adoption of flexible exchange rates, the liberalization of interest rates, and the lifting of controls and subsidies on most goods) would lead to increased cooperation. Turgut Özal even claimed that "the aim of the economic liberalization programme and our reforms was to facilitate our integration into the European Community as a full member."[13] The reforms to open the Turkish economy to international competition, however, were adopted without taking into consideration Turkish obligations under the Ankara Agreement.[14] While Turkish officials maintained that there was no reason to do so because the EC had not complied with provisions of the agreement concerning financial aid to Turkey, free movement of labor, and trade restrictions on textiles and clothing, the Europeans were distressed that Ankara had discounted the agreement so easily. There was no opportunity to see if the two sides could reach a consensus over this issue to enhance economic cooperation, however, because the January 24 reforms were soon followed by the coup d'état of September 12, 1980. At this time, the military seized power and suspended all democratic institutions to restore order in a society that was dominated by the terrorist activities of extremist groups. Although the EC had not been particularly disapproving of the 1971 military coup, Brussels reacted very negatively to the 1980 intervention. As Michael Cendrowicz says, "The severity of the military repression, as well as the prolonged suspension of normal democratic procedures, shocked and alienated a wide swath of public opinion in many Member States, which had not been the case in either 1960 or 1971."[15] Members of the European Parliament who were elected through direct elections after 1979 "considered themselves much more strongly as representatives of public opinion and indeed as spokesmen for the European political and moral conscience."[16] As such, they expected a higher degree of compliance with European standards of behavior from countries that had such unique connections with them as Turkey, an associate member of the EC. Community members condemned the suspension of Turkey's democratic institutions and the human rights abuses—which included the banning of political parties, systematic torture of political prisoners, mass arrests, and the suspension of civil liberties—committed in the aftermath of the coup. They suspended most provisions of the Ankara Agreement and maintained only a few commercial linkages between the EC and Turkey.

Meanwhile, during the early 1980s, many West European economies were facing a range of economic problems and could not afford to open up their markets to increased competition from Turkey. At this time, "greater integration with world markets bypassed Europe as the volume of Turkey's trade with Europe [as well as financial assistance from there] began to dwindle dramatically."[17] The Turkish government, therefore, had to look for new markets in order to implement its export-promotion strategies and turned toward the Middle East (especially Iran, Iraq, and Saudi Arabia) and North Africa. The share of trade with Middle Eastern and North African countries thus increased from 20.2 percent in 1979–1980 to 41.8 percent in 1982–1986. The Iran-Iraq war increased these countries' demand for Turkish products; Turkish exports to the Middle East and North Africa surpassed those to the European Community between 1982 and 1985; and Iran became the single biggest market during this time. As capital from these countries poured into Turkey, Ankara had to improve its traditionally distant political relations with them, allowing them to exert a greater degree of influence not only on the Turkish economy but also on Turkish society.

A combination of their objections to the military coup and their own economic situations prompted the Europeans to impose restrictions on the import of Turkish goods in 1981. At this time, Turkish imports from the EC only constituted 28.4 percent of total imports, and exports to the EC, only 33.3 percent of total exports.[18] Only five years earlier, Turkish imports from the EC had made up 47 percent of total imports, and exports to the EC had been 51.9 percent of total exports.[19] In October 1981, the EC failed to authorize disbursement to Turkey of funds already committed in a $600 million assistance program known as the fourth financial protocol. For the first time in the history of the Turkish Republic, therefore, Turkey's trade with the Middle East and North Africa surpassed that with Europe. Turkish-European relations in the political arena also deteriorated. The Europeans saw no reason to rein in their denunciation of the military regime and its means of exerting control. The European institution concerned with issues of democracy and human rights—the Council of Europe—thus suspended the credentials of Turkish delegates to its parliamentary assembly.[20] In November 1981, West German Foreign Minister Hans Dietrich Genscher visited Ankara and issued a warning that the authoritarian nature of the military regime could lead to Turkey's expulsion from the Council of Europe as well as to the total suspension of economic aid from the EC. In January 1982, the European Parliament passed a resolution that suspended the joint EC-Turkey parliamentary committee. Another blow to Turkish-European relations came in March 1982, when, as the president in office of the Council of Ministers, Belgian Foreign Minister Leo Tindemans visited Turkey and was particularly disparaging in his assessment of Turkey's human rights record. The threats by the Europeans that unless the military regime staged a swift return to democracy, Turkish-European relations would be irrevocably damaged was one factor that prompted the National Security Council to hold elections in November 1983.

Not even Turkey's return to elected government normalized relations with Western Europe, however, because the Europeans were still dissatisfied with the level of democratization in Turkey. They argued that the 1983 elections could not be considered democratic because a number of important parties and politicians were not allowed to participate in them. Furthermore, many European organizations continued to criticize Turkey's human rights record in their reports. Naturally, the harsh stance toward Turkey taken by the Europeans during and after the military coup was not appreciated by the Turks, who saw it as an infringement on their country's sovereignty.[21] Turkish policymakers viewed the issues of democracy and human rights as domestic problems, while the Europeans believed that Turkey's establishment of effective and efficient democratic institutions was a prerequisite to its full inclusion in Europe. The first step in mending relations with Ankara finally came from the Council of Europe, which resumed relations with the Turkish parliament in May 1984, noting that enough progress had been made toward restoring democracy, providing a basic level of human rights, and reestablishing full freedom of action for all political parties. In October 1986, Turkey even assumed the Council presidency (a largely ceremonial office) for a six-month term.

In addition to these political and ideological disagreements over human rights and democracy, there were also several sources of contention between Ankara and Brussels over a variety of economic issues in the 1980s. Some of these included "the volume of Turkish textile exports to the Community, the resumption of the financial aid blocked in 1981, and the free circulation of Turkish workers in Community countries as of December 1986."[22] Negotiations to reach an understanding on these issues were complicated by the fact that Turkey's longtime adversary, Greece, now a full member of the organization, was working to keep the differences between the EC and Turkey in the limelight. Nonetheless, the EC finally responded to Turkey's call for resumption of relations by announcing that a special meeting of the EC-Turkey Association meeting was to be held on September 16, 1986. Normalization of relations between Brussels and Ankara resumed after this meeting, from which the Greek delegation was conspicuously absent. One event that fostered this normalization (and prompted five countries to drop their charges against Turkey for violation of human rights) was Turkey's concession to the Council of Europe during the organization's annual meeting in early 1987 that it would grant its citizens the right to petition.

1987–1990: Application for Full Membership

Soon afterward, at a time when Turkish-European relations were showing signs of steady improvement but had not reached particularly high levels, the government of Prime Minister Turgut Özal astonished both Turks and Europeans by submitting Turkey's application for full membership in the European Community on April 14, 1987. This decision constituted another shift in Turkish foreign policy behavior toward the EC. Ankara had been following a cautious policy toward the EC, gradually mending relations in a variety of areas, and the sudden application for full membership was not expected by the Europeans at this time. There were several reasons that prompted this alteration in foreign policy behavior. Although some involved the changing nature of the international political arena, the most important reasons stemmed from developments in the domestic economic environment. The application was submitted at a time when one of the main pillars of Turkish foreign policy—the policy of westernization—was coming under attack by the rising Islamic forces in Turkish society. The alienation of the Turkish economy from the EC during the 1980s had led to the establishment of close economic ties with countries of the Middle East for the first time in the history of the Turkish Republic. The newly established economic ties with the countries of the Middle East had been accompanied by increased cooperation in the political arena: Turkey had become an active member of the Islamic conference; remained neutral during the Iran-Iraq war; and became one of the first countries to recognize the self-proclaimed independent Palestine.[23] Meanwhile, more permissive attitudes by the governments in power during the 1980s (both the military regime and Özal's government) had increased the visibility of Islam in Turkish society. Consequently, some influential sectors of Turkish society (i.e., the intelligentsia and media) promulgated that these developments threatened Turkey's long-standing Western foreign policy orientation. The desire to allay these fears was one reason for the Özal government's application for EC membership. At a time when even the Soviet Union seemed to be opening up to the West through Gorbachev's policies of perestroika and glasnost, Özal was eager to reassert Turkey's commitment to the West for political as well as economic reasons.

Furthermore, by the late 1980s, Turkish officials had realized the mistake their predecessors had made in not joining the EC at the same time as Greece, and they were eager to rectify this colossal mistake. Greece had furthered its economic and political interests as a result of its membership in the EC. Being a full member of the EC had provided Greek policymakers with a legitimate forum to make their case to the rest of the organization on the Cyprus issue as well as other disputes with Turkey. It received large amounts of economic assistance from the EC to bring its economy up to par with the rest of the member countries and obtained significant trade concessions. In addition, Greek, Spanish, and Portuguese membership in the EC gave these countries an edge in trading with the rest of Europe and left Turkey (which exported a similar assortment of products) at a disadvantage. Consequently, Turkish officials believed that EC membership would provide Turkey with the same benefits.

In addition, Turkey had just undergone several years of intense economic liberalization reforms. Many of the reforms were adopted with the objective of overcoming the structural disparities between the European and Turkish economies. The role of the state in the economy had been reduced, a number of state economic enterprises had been dismantled, and many of the restrictions on imports were lifted. Export promotion had replaced import substitution as the development plan. As a result, businessmen and economists were eager to have greater access to the European market (especially because the Middle Eastern markets had turned out to be much more fickle and unreliable than the European markets). Prime Minister Özal was especially eager to increase trade with the European Community because his government was facing an increasing array of problems that could be offset if the country experienced tremendous economic growth.

High inflation and unemployment, a climbing foreign debt, and an increasing gap between the rich and the poor plagued Turkey at this time; and the popularity of the Motherland Party was plummeting. Özal thus saw EC membership as a way to fix the country's economic problems as well as his party's own political difficulties. He was also facing pressure from the business community, which was convinced that membership in the organization would lead to increased opportunities for Turkey in the new environment of economic liberalization. Because EC membership "implied the acceptance of laws, rules, and practices necessary for the successful operation of a market economy, [it] would encourage foreign capital to invest in Turkey."[24] Özal believed, therefore, that membership in the EC would not only facilitate Turkey's full integration into the liberal world economy but would also provide Turkey with the funds to expedite that integration. In addition, contrary to the situation in the 1970s, once they got used to the idea of applying for full membership in 1987, all major political parties supported Özal's pro-EC stance, albeit for different reasons. The left-of-center Social Democratic Populist Party, for example, lent its support to Özal's policies because it believed that EC membership would further democratization and stability in Turkey. Meanwhile, many Turks believed that Turkey had earned its chance to become an equal member of the European Community. It had been a loyal ally of many European institutions over the years, liberalized its previously closed economy, started to experience substantial rates of growth and development, and was in a relatively stable political situation. As such, there was a feeling of optimism that the long-desired goal of EC membership would finally be realized.

On December 18, 1989, however, the Commission of the European Community announced that "opening negotiations [for membership] would serve no useful purpose as the EC was not ready to enlarge nor was Turkey ready for membership," and that rather, "links between the two sides should be strengthened in the framework of the treaty of association that they had concluded in 1963."[25] This news was received in Turkey "not just as a disappointment, but as a shock for which [the] Turkish public was very little prepared."[26] Although the EC had not precluded the possibility of Turkish membership at a future date, member countries were consistent in their conviction that Turkey's application for membership was premature. The EC had been undergoing some major changes shortly before and during the discussions surrounding Turkish membership: it had just incorporated Greece (1981), and Spain and Portugal (1986) as members; it had recently started recovering from a long period of internal stagnation by launching a common internal market by the end of 1992; and had just adopted some changes in its decision-making procedures by adopting the Single European Act in 1986.[27] Furthermore, the accession of Greece to full membership had been particularly costly to Western Europe because of the transfers and credits granted to Greece to bring its economy up to par with other EC members.[28] Meanwhile, Turkey's population was six times as large as Greece's; its economy was much less developed and more agriculturally oriented; and its population significantly poorer. As a result, the European Community was not even ready to consider Turkish membership in the organization. Despite the considerable efforts of the Turkish government, therefore, on February 5, 1990, on the advice of the Commission, the Council of Ministers announced the rejection of Turkey's application for membership.

The European's reasons for rejecting Turkey's application were articulated in the Commission's "Opinion" published on December 18, 1989. Although the opinion commended Turkey for the progress achieved in the economic arena during the past decade, it argued that the Turkish economy had to overcome "structural disparities in both agriculture and industry, macro-economic imbalances, high levels of industrial protectionism, and a low level of social protection."[29] This assessment was based on a number of factors: Turkey's per capita GDP was about half that of the EC's poorest members; its annual population growth rate of 2.5 percent was ten times the EC average; Turkey's long-term foreign debt of $38 billion was the seventh highest in the world; and despite recent efforts at privatization, the state-owned sector was responsible for 40 percent of manufacturing output.[30] In addition, the inflation rate in Turkey consistently hovered around 70 to 100 percent. The Commission, however, did not limit itself to commenting on Turkey's economic readiness for accession to the EC. Rather, it included in the opinion observations about a number of social and political issues as well. It asserted, for example, that neither the level of human rights nor the treatment of minorities in Turkey was at a level necessary in a democracy; and that Turkey's unresolved conflict with Greece over Cyprus (as well as over other issues) had a negative impact on its application for membership.[31]

Turkish officials, businessmen, and the public were not only discontented with the rejection from the EC but were also indignant at the reasons cited in the opinion. Minister of Foreign Affairs Ali Bozer expressed the Turkish outrage by arguing that "the opinion reflects a static approach vis-à-vis Turkey's dynamic structural, economic, industrial, and social evolution, and it fails to present the country's overall posture in perspective."[32] He maintained that the disparities between the Turkish and European economies cited in the opinion had lessened over the years, and would continue to do so. Furthermore, such differences also existed with the economies of Greece, Spain, and Portugal at the time that these countries were accepted into the EC. Foreign Minister Bozer was even more critical of the opinion's discussion of the political situation in Turkey, calling it "an exercise in ambiguity." He asserted that Ankara's conflicts with Athens as well as Turkey's so-called minorities problem were "matters which lack any direct bearing on the commonality of interests between the EC and Turkey."[33] He added that, "fully cognizant of the excuse that these references were inserted into the opinion text upon the insistence of a single EC member, Turkey nevertheless cannot accept nor silently tolerate such unwarranted discrimination."[34] In these rather harsh words, Bozer reflected the public opinion prevalent in Turkey at the time. Most Turks were very upset by the EC's rejection because they felt unsure of the role their country would play in the emerging world order. The EC opinion was published at the end of 1989—a year of immense uncertainty in Turkish foreign policy because of the imminent end of the cold war. Turks also felt personally insulted by the EC rejection, arguing that their country was rebuffed because the growing prejudice and xenophobia in Western Europe could not handle Turkey's cultural and religious differences. Many questioned whether, as Lesser said, "the fundamental issue for many Europeans [was] whether Europe can or should embrace an Islamic country of 57 million."[35]

Despite the rejection of the Turkish application for membership in 1989, however, Turkish-EC relations became more normalized during this time. In September 1988, the European Parliament finally approved the Walter Report, which recommended that even though the EC should not fully endorse the political regime in Turkey at the time, it should recognize the recent progress made.[36] Consequently, the Joint Committee with the Turkish Grand National Assembly was reconstituted and started meeting regularly (three times a year) to discuss the various issues that affected relations between Ankara and Brussels.

1990–1997: Relations with the European Union During the Post–Cold War Era

The end of the cold war ushered in a degree of uncertainty to Turkish-European relations. Because Turkey's relationship with Western Europe had been built on the circumstances of the cold war era, the breakdown of the bipolar system and the disintegration of the Soviet Union led to the questioning of Turkey's strategic value for Western Europe as well as its role in the European alliance. As the continuing relevance of NATO in the post–cold war world order was debated in Turkey and in the West, Turkish policymakers as well as scholars feared an erosion of the links between Ankara and its European allies. Moves by the Europeans to "improve the coordination and cooperation of their security policies in institutions and channels outside the Alliance" in organizations such as the West European Union (WEU) and in EC bodies such as the European Political Cooperation (EPC) added to these fears.[37] The perceived tendency toward the "Europeanization of Europe's defense" was troubling for Turkey, which did not want to witness European countries allied with one another in a sort of "Fortress Europe" created around the EU and the WEU, but without Turkey.[38] In addressing the organization on June 5, 1991, President Özal voiced his discontent at Turkey's exclusion from the attempts to build a European defense system around the WEU (in which Turkey had observer status). He declared, "Turkey cannot be expected to play its traditionally strong role in defense of the continent if it's unable to 'participate fully in the making of the new Europe.' "[39] Ankara was especially anxious about the possibility that a new defense alliance in Europe would include Greece but not Turkey, thus threatening the fragile stability in the Aegean.

Turkey entered the post–cold war era in a quandary about the state of its relations with Western Europe. One of the main reasons for Özal's assumption of a central role for Turkey in the Persian Gulf crisis was the belief that a show of loyalty to its allies would bolster Turkey's strategic importance for the United States and Western Europe. As discussed in the previous chapter, Turkey's position in the Gulf War did prompt Washington to view Turkey as a crucial strategic ally even in the face of the diminished Soviet threat. It did not, however, have the same effect on the Europeans. In fact, some events during the Gulf War exacerbated friction in Turkish-European relations. For example, Germany was rather negligent in providing Turkey with the assistance and reinforcement it requested from its NATO allies during the crisis. Although the Germans eventually deployed eighteen Alpha Jets to Erhac and Diyarbakir as part of the Allied Mobile Force air reinforcements, the slowness of the response led many in Turkey to believe that the Germans were reluctant to commit forces on Ankara's behalf. Contrary to Özal's expectations, therefore, Turkey's position in the Gulf War did not prompt an immediate convergence of Turkish and European interests. Some scholars such as Ian Lesser even argued that by assuming such a central role in the Persian Gulf crisis, Turkey had shown its Middle Eastern nature to the European policy elites who were "increasingly unwilling to accept the additional burden of a direct exposure in the Middle East" as they formulated new defense and security policies for the post–cold war era.[40]

Despite occasional setbacks, however, relations between Ankara and Brussels did see some improvements in the aftermath of the Gulf War. Turkey signed a free trade and cooperation agreement with the European Free Trade Association (EFTA) in October 1991 with the goal of being incorporated into the European Economic Area and increasing trade with EC and EFTA members. Although this positive development was dampened by Greece's blockage of a package of measures to release credits aimed at improving

Turkish-European relations, another event furthering the normalization of relations occurred at the summit meeting of the EC's heads of state and government in June 1992.[41] A declaration of the European Council stated that "the Turkish role in the present European political situation is of the greatest importance."[42] As a result, the implementation of the provisions of the Ankara Agreement was restarted on November 9, 1992. At this time, Turkey pledged to execute the necessary steps for the establishment of a customs union by 1995, and the EC agreed to reopen discussions on political issues and work to enhance economic and industrial cooperation.[43] A month later, Turkey became an associate member of the WEU.

Turkish-European economic relations reached their highest point since the Association Agreement with the establishment in December 1995 of the much-anticipated customs union between Turkey and the EU. At this time, Turkey became the first country to form a customs union with the EU without being a member of the organization first. The customs union stipulated that the following provisions would eventually be established:

- free circulation of goods, abolition of all existing customs duties, removal of quantitative restrictions and provisions applying to processed agricultural products as well as products under the legal jurisdiction of the European Coal and Steel Community;
- implementation of the [EU's] common external tariff on goods from third countries and cooperation between customs authorities [as well as the adoption of a] common trade policy . . . ;
- cooperation on the harmonization of agricultural policy and provisions for reciprocal preferential market access;
- mutual minimization of restrictions on trade in services . . . ;
- harmonization of commercial legislation regarding competition policy, state aid, anti-dumping legislation [etc.][44]

Although the conditions of the Ankara Agreement had stated that the establishment of the customs union would coincide with the free circulation of labor, the EC had withdrawn this provision from its negotiations with Turkey. Furthermore, the visas that most European countries imposed on Turkish travelers in earlier times also remained in place. As a result, not even the establishment of the customs union could prevent the Turkish public from feeling that they were being excluded from Europe and that they would always remain outsiders. The policies of many European governments (i.e., the strict requirements in granting citizenship, light punishments for people accused of hate crimes against Turkish immigrants, etc.) toward the millions of Turkish immigrants in the continent furthered this perception. Although it was mainly economic and social concerns that drove the German government, for example, to adopt restrictions on the free movement of labor in the 1970s, "the issue of free movement of labor for Turks [had] increasingly become intermingled with European domestic political issues such as policy towards asylum-seekers and the resurgence of racist xenophobia in Germany and elsewhere" in the post–cold war era.[45] As debates about the threat to European civilization from Islam and foreign cultures became commonplace in Europe, Turks increasingly felt that perhaps it was their culture, religion, and ethnicity that kept them out of the EU. Politicians such as Necmettin Erbakan capitalized on the European rejection and did their utmost to convince the Turkish public that they would never be embraced by Christian Europe. Millions of people believed Erbakan's claims and voted for his Welfare Party, which promised a position for Turkey as a leader in the East rather than a reject in the West.

Despite a gradual improvement of Turkish-European relations in the post–cold war era, therefore, a number of issues of contention still remained. Disputes surrounding the Cyprus conflict became more pronounced, for example, when the Republic of Cyprus applied for full membership in the EC in July 1990. The government of northern Cyprus and Ankara ardently objected to this application. They asserted that it was illegal according to both Cypriot constitutional law and international law. An "Opinion" of the European Commission, however, maintained that not only was Cypriot membership in the EC possible but also "that Cyprus's integration with the Community implies a peaceful, balanced and lasting settlement of the Cyprus question" to "create the appropriate conditions for Cyprus to participate normally in the decision-making process of the European Community and in the correct application of Community law throughout the island."[46] The possibility of Cypriot membership in the EU with Turkey's continued exclusion was particularly disturbing to Ankara for political as well as economic reasons. Membership of the Republic of Cyprus in the EU would mean that it would reap the economic benefits of membership, exacerbating the disparity with northern Cyprus. It would also have an additional venue in which it could make its case in bringing a political settlement to the unresolved Cyprus conflict. In addition, Cypriot membership would cement the belief already prevalent among Turks that the Europeans were biased in their treatment of Greek-Turkish relations, always leaving Turkey at a disadvantage.

Another source of conflict in Turkish-EU relations concerned democracy and human rights in Turkey. As discussed previously, the Europeans were extremely critical of the 1980 coup d'état and the brutal rule of the subsequent military regime. Criticism of the insufficiency of human rights and democratic institutions subsided to a certain degree after 1992 in light of the pro-democracy reforms adopted by Ankara. The Europeans maintained, however, that additional improvements needed to be made, especially with regard to the treatment of Turkey's Kurdish minority. First and foremost, the Europeans were disturbed by the fact that the Kurds of Turkey were not recognized as a minority (as only religious minorities in Turkey are given minority status). The Europeans also condemned certain activities of the Turkish military in fighting Kurdish separatist terrorism. The army often used rather unconventional methods, such as searches of entire villages to look for PKK terrorists or supporters, and the imprisonment of people considered to be PKK sympathizers. The Europeans insisted that these methods, which invariably harmed the Kurdish civilian population in the southeast region of the country, constituted human rights violations that were unacceptable for a country that defined itself as not only democratic but European as well.

Although such significant issues between Ankara and Brussels remained unsolved, both sides worked to enhance their areas of cooperation in the post–cold war period. Even after the removal of the Soviet threat, EU members were influenced by strategic considerations in formulating relations with Turkey. During this time, the threat of Soviet expansionism as a determinant of European-Turkish relations "[was] replaced by a more diffuse idea of European strategic interests and a related Turkish role with regard to the situation in the Middle East and possible developments in Central Asia."[47] Turkey's role as the southeastern flank of NATO in preventing Soviet expansionism was replaced by its capacity to act as a stabilizing force in a inherently tumultuous region. In the post–cold war era, Europeans valued Ankara for its perceived ability to influence emerging Islamic countries in Central Asia into adopting secular, democratic systems (thereby facilitating trade with these potentially tremendous markets) and curbing the influence of Islamist states like Iran. Consequently, Turkey's role in the post–cold war period was often described as a "bridge" between the East and the West by European as well as American policymakers.

Turkish foreign policy behavior toward the European Union, like Turkish foreign policy behavior toward the United States, showed that it was susceptible to shifts. The first change in behavior was characterized by the sudden halting of negotiations toward the implementation of a customs union with the EC in 1978, after years of seeking fuller integration to as many European institutions as possible. The second involved an abrupt application for full membership in the EC in 1987, coming soon after a difficult period in

Turkish-European relations. Both these alterations in behavior occurred in spite of an unchanging foreign policy orientation as Ankara followed a strictly Western foreign policy orientation for most of the cold war and post–cold war periods. Ankara was not reluctant to alter its patterns of behavior, however, when policymakers felt that change was in the best interest of the country.

A number of scholars and politicians thus expected that the end of the cold war would bring another shift in Turkish foreign policy behavior toward Western Europe. Some predicted that the end of the cold war and the subsequent changes in the international system would lead Ankara to replace its close ties with Europe with relations with Central Asian republics, Middle Eastern neighbors, and Balkan countries. Lesser argued, for example, that "frustration with Turkey's limited role in Europe has encouraged Turks to turn to alternative outlets for international activism in the republics of the former Soviet Union, the Balkans and . . . the Middle East."[48] In the first years of the post–cold war period, numerous Turkish politicians engaged in strong rhetoric that celebrated the "brotherhood" between Turkey and many of the former Soviet republics, suggesting that Turkey's future lay with these newly emerging states. Ankara worked on forming close economic and political ties with the countries of the Caucasus and Central Asia in such forums as the Black Sea Economic Cooperation Zone (an initiative aimed at gradually establishing free trade among the countries that surround the Black Sea). Despite the initial outpouring of enthusiasm for Turkey's enhanced role in regional affairs, however, Turkish officials soon realized that it was in the country's best interest to use its ties to the East to supplement its ties to the West. The United States was too important a political ally, and Western Europe too important an economic ally, to replace. Because maintaining strong political ties with the Europeans made it easier to cooperate with them in the economic sphere, successive governments worked to enhance relations. Even the Islamist Prime Minister Erbakan did not take any actions to alienate EU members.

Europe's economic importance for Turkey, in other words, prompted Ankara to keep relations with Western Europe in the forefront of its foreign policy agenda in the post–cold war era. This occurred despite the fact that the Europeans consistently berated Turkey about the inadequacy of its democracy, its poor human rights record, its stance in the Cyprus conflict, and its problems in the Aegean. They offered nothing concrete in exchange and relegated Turkey to a "black sheep" status.[49] Turkey had to endure such treatment because Western Europe was Turkey's most important economic partner. In 1990, 53.1 percent of Turkish exports went to EC countries, while 14.8 percent went to other OECD countries, 19.3 percent went to Islamic countries, and 7.6 percent went to East European countries.[50] By 1993, almost 45 percent of Turkish foreign trade (47.2 percent of exports and 41.8 percent of imports) was still with EU members.[51] Most direct foreign investment in Turkey originated in European countries. In 1991, for example, the United Kingdom, Germany, Netherlands, France, and Italy combined accounted for half of the total foreign investment in Turkey.[52] Europeans comprised the majority of tourists who visited Turkey, contributing to the country's burgeoning tourism sector. In addition, 2.5 million Turkish workers and their dependents lived in such countries as Germany, France, Holland, Belgium, and Sweden. The significant remittances from these workers were an invaluable source of foreign exchange for the Turkish economy. As a result of these multifaceted economic ties, Turkey could not afford to replace its relations with the prosperous Europe with unreliable economic partners in Central Asia, the Middle East, or the Balkans.

Ultimately, Turkish-European relations in the post–cold war period were characterized by the same dynamics as those of earlier periods: by Turkey's consistent efforts (except for the brief period in the late 1970s) to become fully integrated into all European institutions, and the Europeans' insistence that it needed to accomplish more—in both the economic and political fields—to reach that objective. Furthermore, Turkey seemed doomed to remain on the fringes of Europe in the post–cold war period. In fact, the likelihood of Turkey's being accepted as a European country appeared quite remote in 1998, and the differences between Turks and Europeans were more magnified than ever. The possibility of Turkish membership in the European Union—viewed as the ultimate European club—was harshly renounced in March 1997 when Foreign Minister Klaus Kinkel of Germany announced that "it is clear that Turkey will not become a member of the European Union in the foreseeable future."[53] Turkey tolerated a constant barrage of criticism and various rejections from the Europeans, however, because of Western Europe's tremendously important role in the Turkish economy.

NOTES

1. Michael Cendrowicz, "The European Community and Turkey: Looking Backwards, Looking Forwards," in *Turkish Foreign Policy: New Prospects*, ed. C. H. Dodd (Huntingdon, United Kingdom: Eothen Press, 1992), 17.

2. Atila Eralp, "Turkey and the European Community: Prospects for a New Relationship," in *The Political and Socioeconomic Transformation of Turkey*, eds. Atila Eralp, Muharrem Tunay, and Birol Yeşilada (Westport, Conn.: Praeger, 1993), 194.

3. Eralp, "Turkey and the European Community," 195.

4. Eralp, "Turkey and the European Community," 194.

5. Cendrowicz, "The European Community and Turkey," 10.

6. Eralp, "Turkey and the European Community," 197.

7. Eralp, "Turkey and the European Community," 197.

8. Heinz Kramer, "Turkey and the European Union: A Multi-Dimensional Relationship," in *Turkey Between East and West: New Challenges for a Rising Regional Power*, eds. Vojtech Mastny and R. Craig Nation (Boulder, Colo.: Westview Press, 1996), 206.

9. Kramer, "Turkey and the European Union," 206.

10. Kramer, "Turkey and the European Union," 207.

11. Rusdu Saracoğlu, "Liberalization of the Economy," in *Politics in the Third Turkish Republic*, ed. Metin Heper (Boulder: Westview Press, 1994), 65.

12. Canan Balkir, "Turkey and the European Community: Foreign Trade and Direct Foreign Investment in the 1980s," in *Turkey and Europe*, eds. Canan Balkir and Allan M. Williams (London: Pinter Publishers, 1993), 137 (Statistical Appendix, Table G).

13. Meltem Müftüler, "Turkish Economic Liberalization and European Integration," *Middle Eastern Studies* 31.1 (January 1995): 89.

14. Kramer, "Turkey and the European Union," 208.

15. Cendrowicz, "The European Community and Turkey," 14.

16. Cendrowicz, "The European Community and Turkey," 14.

17. Eralp, "Turkey and the European Community," 200.

18. Müftüler, "Turkish Economic Liberalization and European Integration," 89.

19. Balkir, "Turkey and the European Community," 137 (Statistical Appendix, Table G).

20. Mehmet Ali Birand, *Turkiye'nin Ortak Pazar Macerasi, 1959–85* (Istanbul: Milliyet Yayinlari, 1985), 434.

21. Eralp, "Turkey and the European Community," 201.

22. Eralp, "Turkey and the European Community," 202.

23. Eralp, "Turkey and the European Community," 203.

24. Andrew Mango, *Turkey: The Challenge of a New Role* (Westport, Conn.: Praeger, 1994; published with The Center for Strategic and International Studies, Washington, D.C.), 90.

25. Mango, *Turkey: The Challenge of a New Role*, 86.

26. Cendrowicz, "The European Community and Turkey," 19.

27. Kramer, "Turkey and the European Union," 209.

28. Mango, *Turkey: The Challenge of a New Role*, 91.

29. Ali Bozer, "Turkish Foreign Policy in the Changing World," *Mediterranean Quarterly* (Summer 1990): 16.

30. Ian O. Lesser, "Bridge or Barrier? Turkey and the West After the Cold War," in *Turkey's New Geopolitics*, eds. Graham E. Fuller and Ian O. Lesser with Paul B. Henze and J. F. Brown (Boulder, Colo.: Westview Press, 1993), 104.

31. "Commission Opinion on Turkey's Request for Accession to the Community" (Brussels: Commission of the European Communities, December 1989).

32. Bozer, "Turkish Foreign Policy in the Changing World," 17.

33. Bozer, "Turkish Foreign Policy in the Changing World," 18.

34. Bozer, "Turkish Foreign Policy in the Changing World," 18.

35. Lesser, "Bridge or Barrier?" 105.

36. Cendrowicz, "The European Community and Turkey," 15.

37. Duygu Bazoğlu Sezer, "Turkey and the Western Alliance," in *Political and Socioeconomic Transformation of Turkey*, eds. Atila Eralp, Muharrem Tunay, and Birol A. Yeşilada (Westport, Conn.: Praeger, 1993), 226.

38. Sezer, "Turkey and the Western Alliance," 226.

39. Lesser, "Bridge or Barrier?" 107.

40. Lesser, "Bridge or Barrier?" 104.

41. Mango, *Turkey: The Challenge of a New Role*, 86.

42. "Conclusions of the Presidency," *Agence Europe* No. 5760 (28 June 1992): 5.

43. Kramer, "Turkey and the European Union," 211.

44. Kramer, "Turkey and the European Union," 211.

45. Kramer, "Turkey and the European Union," 206.

46. Commission Opinion on the Application by the Republic of Cyprus for Membership, Brussels, 30 June 1993, Doc. COM (93) 313 fin. Also, Kramer, "Turkey and the European Union," 218.

47. Kramer, "Turkey and the European Union," 222–223.

48. Lesser, "Bridge or Barrier?" 99.

49. Edward Mortimer, "The Black Sheep," *Financial Times* (11 November 1997).

50. Balkir, "Turkey and the European Community," 137 (Statistical Appendix, Table G).

51. Müftüler, "Turkish Economic Liberalization and European Integration," 89.

52. Balkir, "Turkey and the European Community," 125.

53. Stephen Kinzer, "Europeans Shut the Door on Turkey's Membership in Union," *New York Times* (27 March 1997): A13.

New Foreign Policy Partners

Many people had conjectured that the end of the cold war and the removal of the Soviet threat would diminish Turkey's strategic value for the United States and Western Europe. Because these entities were Ankara's most important foreign policy partners during the cold war, marginalization from them would mean that Turkish policymakers would have to look for new foreign policy partners in the newly independent republics of the former Soviet Union. The restructuring of the bipolar system, however, did not change Turkey's foreign policy orientation. Despite some ups and downs in Turkey's relationship with its Western allies, ties to the United States remained strong in the post–cold war era as the Persian Gulf War provided the context for enhanced Turkish-American cooperation. Although Ankara's relations with Western Europe were more troubled in the 1990s than its ties with the United States, cooperation continued and was even enhanced in the economic sphere with the establishment of a customs union with the European Union (EU) in 1995. In addition, Turkey's strategic position as a "bridge" between the East and West contributed to its continuing relevance for the European Union. Although there were no changes in Turkey's Western foreign policy orientation in the post–cold war era, however, Turkish policymakers worked on establishing relations with the former Soviet republics and searched for new foreign policy partners in the Middle East.

RELATIONS WITH THE FORMER SOVIET REPUBLICS

Despite considerable rhetoric by Turkish politicians at the outset of the post–cold war era that Turkey would form close political and cultural alliances with the former Soviet republics, in the long run, most of the ties have fostered cooperation in the economic arena. Political relations have consisted mostly of symbolic gestures, but economic relations have been significant and substantial.

Turkey had not attempted to establish ties with the Turkic-speaking republics in the Soviet Union prior to the disintegration of this superpower because it did not want to endanger its relations with Moscow. Kemalism (the state ideology based on the ideas of Mustafa Kemal Atatürk espousing nationalism, secularism, and modernization), and thus the Republic of Turkey, rejected pan-Turkism—an expansionist doctrine that called for bringing all Turkish and Turkic peoples under one nation-state—as dangerous because it could bring on the wrath of the Soviet Union. In fact, in March 1921, even before the foundation of the Republic, Atatürk had signed a Treaty of Friendship with the Soviets. According to this treaty, both sides agreed to "forbid the formation or presence on their territory of organizations or groups claiming to be the government of the other country or part of the territory and also the presence of groups that have hostile intentions with regard to the other country."[1] The few ultra-nationalists in Turkey who espoused pan-Turkist ideologies were regarded as radicals, and possible alliances with the Turkic-speaking populations of the Soviet Union were not discussed by mainstream politicians or members of the citizenry during the cold war. Meanwhile, although the Soviet Turkic peoples were cognizant of the fact that they shared a cultural bond with the Turks of Turkey, they had not sought to define themselves as a type of Turk or Muslim because religion and nationality were to be subordinate to the Marxist Soviet state.[2]

The end of the cold war and the dissolution of the Soviet Union thus meant that for the first time in over a century, Turkey was free to forge relationships with the fifty million people of Turkic origin living in Central Asia and the Caucasus with whom the Turks of Turkey shared strong ethnic, religious, cultural, and linguistic ties. The possibility of forming alliances with these countries was strongly supported by the Turkish public, especially by the millions of people in Turkey who had descended from Caucasians, Abkhazians, Chechens, Kabardans, Karachays, Nogays, Kumyks, Lezgins, Avars, and Azeris.[3] Although these various groups, many of which came to Turkey in the 1850s and 1860s, had assimilated to Turkish culture long ago, they mobilized to support their brethren who had come under attack (such as the Abkhazians in Georgia and the Azeris in Nagorno-Karabakh) and were eager to form a dialogue with their counterparts in the Soviet Union. The opening up of Central Asia and the Caucasus as potential foreign policy partners after the disintegration of the Soviet Union thus meant that Turkey could overcome "its perennial sense of isolation and dependence left over from the slippery triangular pattern of the cold war, when Turkey, peripheral to the European Community and a distant associate of the Arab Middle East, had relied heavily on the United States."[4]

Consequently, the beginning of the post–cold war era was characterized by a feeling of elation in Turkey. The overwhelming sentiment that Turks were not alone in the world was celebrated by Turkish policymakers and the public, and the possibilities for the future were eagerly discussed. Many conjectured that cooperation in a number of fields with these newly independent states would lead to further growth and development in Turkey. A number of politicians as well as scholars even suggested that Ankara would be able to assume a regional leadership position in the emerging international system.[5] As the Turkic-speaking republics joined the United Nations, there was even talk (mostly among Turkish politicians) of adding Turkish to the list of the six official languages of the United Nations.[6] In February 1992, Prime Minister Süleyman Demirel (a generally cautions politician) announced that, with the dissolution of the Soviet Union a "gigantic 'Turkish' world" was being shaped, stretching from the Adriatic Sea to China.[7]

Turkey's hopes for the future were bolstered by the leaders of the Turkic-speaking republics in Central Asia and the Caucasus who turned to Ankara in the early 1990s to form relationships that would fulfill mutual political and economic needs. As such, Turkey formalized its relationships with many Commonwealth of Independent States (CIS) countries by signing countless protocols that called for political, cultural, and economic cooperation. It also "pledged more than $886 million in Eximbank credits to the region and worked to build infrastructural ties in transport and telecommunications, to extend financial and business contacts, and to reinforce cultural relations by developing scholarship and student exchange programs."[8] Turkish policymakers traveled to many of the newly independent states and made sweeping statements about the "brotherhood" that existed between the Turks and the people of these nations. They were often accompanied by large groups of businessmen who were eager to play a significant role in modernizing the states of the former Soviet Union. Meanwhile, the leaders of the newly independent republics lavished extensive praise on Turkey. The Uzbek president Islam Karimov, for example, stated in December 1991 that he admired Turkey as one would admire an older brother and that Uzbekistan had much to learn from Ankara. Similarly, the president of Kyrgyzstan "likened Turkey to the morning star which was guiding the paths of the Turkic republics."[9] Consequently, Turkey had very ambitious goals in the region at the beginning of the post–cold war period. Soon afterward, however, due to a number of domestic and international constraints, Turkish politicians had to rein in those formidable aspirations.

Foreign Policy Goals in the Region

The most important long-term objective of Turkish politicians on both sides of the political spectrum was to secure a central position for Ankara in the political, cultural, and economic development of the newly independent republics of the former Soviet Union. The goal was for Turkey to serve as a model—a predominantly Muslim country that was secular, democratic, free-market oriented, and aligned with the West—for the states of Central Asia and the Caucasus. In the early days of the post–cold war era, Ankara believed that exporting its own Western-oriented ideology and regime to the former Soviet republics would have several important repercussions: (1) increased standing in world affairs due to its position as a bridge between the East and the West; (2) heightened security because of the emergence of allies with which it shared political, economic, and cultural characteristics; and (3) enhanced economic well-being due to cooperation with the resource-rich states. It is important to note that despite such grandiose objectives in its relations with the former Soviet republics, and—contrary to allegations by Moscow, Athens, Belgrade, and Teheran—Ankara did not have hegemonic aspirations in the region. In order to allay the suspicious underlying such accusations, Prime Minister Demirel explained the nature of the relationship with the newly independent states of Central Asia and the Caucasus as one among equals by saying that "our cooperation with those republics does not mean we will put our mortgage in their economic and political policies. If we do that, they would move further away from us. Respect for their identity should be the main principle of Turkey."[10] Pan-Turkism was thus rejected once again as state policy.

Several considerations prompted Ankara to assume these rather elevated goals regarding the Soviet Union's successor republics. The most important factor stemmed from the changes in the structure of the international system. The breakdown of the Soviet Union had led many politicians in Turkey to question the continued relevance of the North Atlantic Treaty Organization (NATO) in the new international arena as well as Turkey's position in the alliance. What role would Turkey play in the organization now that its long-standing one as a bulwark against communism no longer existed? Turkish fears about the post–cold war era were reinforced by the European Community's 1989 rejection of the Turkish application for full membership, which indicated that Turkey was not going to be integrated into Europe in the near future. Ankara was thus eager to define a new role for itself in the post–cold war period. As such, it viewed the former Soviet republics as entities with which it could develop new foreign policy relationships and avert being isolated in the newly emerging international system. Its efforts to become involved in the Soviet successor states were commended by the United States and Western Europe, which desperately wanted to prevent Iran (another, vastly different "model" for the Central Asian republics) from expanding its influence in the region. In February 1992, for example, NATO Secretary General Manfred Worner announced that NATO was counting on Turkey to uphold the interests of the West in Central Asia and to prevent the spread of radical Islam there, as espoused by Iran.[11] Accordingly, it seemed that Turkey's position as a front-line state against communism would be replaced by its role as a bulwark against Islamic fundamentalism in the post–cold war era.

Another factor that contributed to Turkey's desire to export its ideology and regime to the Turkic-speaking republics was its desire to form alliances in a particularly unstable region of the world. Turkey had not enjoyed close ties with any of its neighbors for much of its history (and in fact, had difficult relationships with many) and was eager to find allies. As Duygu Bazoğlu Sezer said, "Given the deteriorating regional climate over the last decade, the adoption of the 'Turkish model' by the former southern Soviet republics would offer Turkey security by expanding the liberal, democratic, and secular belt to the border of China."[12] Furthermore, many Turkish policymakers expected that an active role in the region would enhance Turkey's international status, perhaps even elevating the country to the position of a regional leader. An improved standing in the international arena could, in turn, improve its chances of gaining admission into the European Union.

Although Ankara's foreign policy objectives were quite lofty in the early days of the post–cold war era, they were soon constrained by the fact that the end of the cold war was accompanied by the rise of numerous ethnic and national conflicts, leading to significant instability and insecurity in the region. It seemed that Ankara had overestimated its abilities to play a political, cultural, and economic role in the development of the newly independent republics. The Central Asian states were much closer to (and more dependent on) the Russian Federation than originally anticipated, and the linkages with Moscow remaining from Soviet days were hard to break. The fact that the Central Asian republics had no history of democracy or free market economics made it difficult for them to adopt the "Turkish model." Furthermore, Turkey was competing not only with Russia but also with Iran for influence in the former Soviet Union. Eager to reap the benefits of cooperation with all three countries, the Soviet successor states were not willing to favor relations with one over the others. As a result of these various developments, Turkey had to scale back many of its aspirations in the region. A few years into the post–cold war era, although economic cooperation between Turkey and the Turkic republics was still strong and growing, the cultural exchanges and political alliances promised in the early 1990s had not materialized.

Political and Cultural Relations with the Former Soviet Republics

Turkey's fear of jeopardizing relations with Moscow prevented it from establishing ties with the Soviet republics until Mikhail Gorbachev assumed power in the Soviet Union and started instituting reforms in the country's internal and external affairs. A part of Gorbachev's reforms was giving individual Soviet republics "limited freedom to conduct a foreign policy of sorts."[13] In late 1990, the Central Asian republics (as well as other Soviet republics) declared their sovereignty. Although Moscow was still in charge of making the important decisions at this point, for the first time in the history of the Soviet Union, low-level delegations from the various republics were allowed to exchange visits with Turkish diplomats. The talks among culture ministers or mayors soon gave way to meetings between higher level officials. In March 1991, for example, the Turkish president Turgut Özal traveled to Russia, Azerbaijan, Kazakhstan, and the Ukraine. A few months later, the prime minister of Kyrgyzstan (May 1991) and the president of Tajikistan (June 1991) visited Ankara. During these various exchanges, agreements on cultural, scientific, technological, and economic cooperation were signed as Turkish policymakers sought to establish relations with the Soviet republics in areas that were not threatening to Moscow. In August 1991, however, the failure of the hardliners' coup attempt against Gorbachev hastened the disintegration of the Soviet Union. Soon afterward, most of the Central Asian republics declared their independence from Moscow, and Ankara became more willing to abandon its Moscow-centered policy. Because Turkish policymakers were still cautious, however, it was not until the fall of 1991 that they started considering the republics of Central Asia and the Caucasus a new arena for Turkish foreign policy.

Once Ankara decided to become involved in the Soviet successor states, it moved rather quickly; Turkey became the first country to recognize the independence of Azerbaijan (November 9, 1991). Its decision to do so was prompted by the desire to prevent Iran from becoming the first country to recognize this newly emerging state as well as by the pressure from the Turkish public, which favored close ties with the Azeris.[14] Turkey announced its readiness to recognize the independence of all the independent republics a week after the formation of the Commonwealth of Independent States on December 8, 1991 (which indicated the official breakup of the Soviet Union). Turkish policymakers were soon involved in a whirlwind of diplomatic activity to establish relations with the former Soviet republics. Treaties of Friendship and Cooperation were signed with Kyrgyzstan (December 1991) and Azerbaijan (January 1992). In February and March 1992, Turkish foreign minister Hikmet Çetin embarked on an extensive tour of Central Asia and the Ukraine. Less than two months later, Prime Minister Demirel visited four Central Asian republics and pledged to contribute $1.2 billion for their economic development.[15] During this trip, Demirel also announced Turkey's pledge to admit ten thousand students from the Soviet successor states into Turkish universities.

These various exchanges culminated in the first Turkic summit, which was held in Ankara in October 1992 to expand and formalize the avenues of cooperation among the Turkic republics. The meeting was attended by the presidents of Turkey, Uzbekistan, Turkmenistan, Kyrgyzstan, Kazakhstan, and Azerbaijan. Tajikistan (not really a Turkic state because it is mostly Farsi-speaking) was also invited to attend but was unable to do so because of its ongoing civil war. Turkey entered the summit with rather grandiose expectations, such as the establishment of a Turkic Common Market and a Turkic Development and Investment Bank and a firm commitment from Kazakhstan, Uzbekistan, and Turkmenistan to build oil and gas pipelines to Europe via Turkey.[16] The meeting, however, only produced one document—the Ankara Declaration—which failed to fulfill Turkey's ambitions in the region. This declaration discussed the need to develop cooperation in such arenas as culture, education, language, security, and economics. It called for the establishment of working groups to explore the best ways in which collaboration could be developed, as well as for the need to hold similar meetings on a regular basis. In addition, Turkey and Turkmenistan signed a protocol to build a natural gas pipeline from Turkmenistan to Turkey, and for Turkey to build a new airport in Ashgabat.

The summit, however, did not result in the creation of a Turkic Common Market, Bank, or Commonwealth. No firm pledges to build new oil pipelines were made. Not even a press communiqué was issued because President Nazabaev of Kazakhstan "refused to sign a statement implying the recognition of the Turkish Republic of Northern Cyprus as an independent state [because he was] concerned that parallels could be drawn between the position of the Russian minority in Kazakhstan and that of the Turks in Cyprus."[17] Furthermore, despite concerted efforts by Azerbaijan and Turkey, the other states showed their unwillingness to oppose Moscow and refused to make any statements condemning Armenia's actions in Nagorno-Karabakh, the mostly Armenian enclave within Azerbaijan over which Armenia and Azerbaijan were fighting.

The summit was thus a huge disappointment for Ankara. Participants had demonstrated that, despite independence, they were not willing to stray too far from the policies of Moscow. Meanwhile, Russia had made it clear that, although it had largely ignored Central Asia and the Caucasus in the first years of the post–cold war era, it was unwilling totally to divest from the region. In fact, its involvement in the civil war in Tajikistan in 1992 and in the internal power struggle in Azerbaijan in 1993 demonstrated that Russia would spend considerable resources on the problems of the "near abroad." Furthermore, the ravages of the civil war in Tajikistan as well as the general feeling of instability in the region made the former Soviet republics eager to remain a part of the Russian security umbrella. Turkic policymakers also realized that continuing to be a part of the ruble zone would ensure an indirect Russian subsidization of their economies.[18] In addition, they recognized the fact that Turkey simply did not have the resources to provide the kind of assistance that was needed for economic growth and development and that they needed to foster relationships with other countries as well. The summit was thus a turning point in Turkish foreign policy behavior toward the former Soviet Union and prompted Turkish officials to realize that they needed to reevaluate and retrench some of their objectives in the region.

Soon afterward, Turkish policy toward the former Soviet republics became less based on "fanciful notions of ethnic solidarity" and more on self-interest.[19] As Ankara struggled to define the scope of its relationship with the former Soviet republics, foreign policy objectives toward the region were scaled back to focus on cultural and economic relations rather than political ones. Accordingly, Turkey continued to provide assistance to these newly independent states in a wide variety of ways that fostered the expansion of such ties. Turkish officials hoped that, even with the absence of political cooperation, Turkey's economic and cultural role in Central Asia and Azerbaijan would enhance its international status and lead to economic gains. Because feelings of nationalism and brotherhood with the Turkic-speaking states were still strong among the Turkish citizenry, Ankara continued to engage in high-level exchanges and emphasized multilateral as well as bilateral economic cooperation with the republics. In early 1992, for example, the long inoperative Economic Cooperation Organization (ECO) was revived and expanded to include Azerbaijan, Kazakhstan, Kyrgyzstan, Tajikistan, Turkmenistan, and Uzbekistan. The ECO was described as "a first step towards a potential common market for [over] three hundred million people."[20] These people were spread over almost eight million square kilometers and shared a cultural cohesion because the organization incorporated all of the non-Arab countries of western and central Asia.[21] Furthermore, on June 25, 1992, Armenia, Azerbaijan, Bulgaria, Georgia, Greece, Moldova, Romania, Russia, Turkey, and Ukraine signed a treaty in Istanbul to launch the

Black Sea Economic Cooperation (BSEC) zone. Turkey continued to foster bilateral economic ties with the former Soviet republics as well. In April 1993, for example (shortly before his death) President Özal went on an official tour of Uzbekistan, Turkmenistan, Kyrgyzstan, Kazakhstan, and Azerbaijan. During this trip, Özal traveled with a larger-than-usual entourage of businessmen who were exploring the opportunities for Turkish companies to develop infrastructure, telecommunications, and transportation mechanisms in the region. In addition, the Turkish Agency for Technical and Economic Cooperation (TIKA) was established in 1992 to train personnel to work in a market economy, institute computer linkages between research centers in the former Soviet republics and Turkey, and establish a Eurasian Union of Chambers of Commerce. Turkish companies were active in installing telephone systems, and Turkish Airlines scheduled regular flights between Ankara and the Central Asian capitals. On a cultural level, the Turkish government provided two thousand students from each Turkic state with scholarships to attend a university in Turkey during the 1992–1993 academic year. The Turkish Ministry of Education worked on preparing history textbooks to be used in the Central Asian republics as well as in Azerbaijan. A Turkish television station (*Avrasya*) was even broadcast to the region to familiarize Turkic speakers with Turkish.[22] As Ankara focused on the cultural and economic fields, military cooperation was touched upon but not fully explored because of Moscow's stated mistrust of it. The military agreements that were signed did not amount to much more than small numbers of cadets from Central Asia coming to Turkey to receive training. The military ties between Russia and the former Soviet republics, on the other hand, were much closer than those with Turkey.

Another forum in which Turkic states met to explore avenues for cooperation was the first General Assembly of the Turkic States and Turkic People's Friendship and Cooperation Group in Antalya in March 1993. This meeting, which focused on Turkic solidarity, was also attended by nongovernmental groups from non-Turkic states such as the Russian Federation. Its slogan, "*Dilde, fikirde, iste birlik*" (Unity in language, thought and action), however, was particularly alarming to those concerned with pan-Turkist tendencies in Turkey. Moscow was especially harsh in its criticisms of the conference and voiced concerns about its pan-Turkist overtones. By the time the second Turkic summit was held, therefore, policymakers in the former Soviet republics in Central Asia were extremely careful not to antagonize the Russians further.

The environment surrounding the second Turkic summit (held in Istanbul in October 1994 after a series of delays) was quite different from that during the first summit. Not only had Turkey's ambitious goals in the region deflated, but Moscow was openly critical of the summit. The Russian spokesman for the Ministry of Foreign Affairs said that it was "unthinkable that a summit based on the principle of nationality will not disturb Russia."[23] Furthermore, Ankara approached the second summit with much more modest expectations. As a result, it was considerably more satisfied with the outcome. The Istanbul Declaration resulting from the summit was more precise about the construction of oil and natural gas pipelines. An article of the declaration stated that the oil and gas "ought to be exploited and transported to the world via the most economic route and in the shortest time, and . . . 'welcomed the work being carried out among interested countries on natural gas and oil pipelines to be built extending to Europe and the Mediterranean via Turkey.' "[24] The Istanbul summit also commended the cooperation among the ministers of culture and education and decided to hold regular meetings among the foreign ministers of the six Turkic states. Political cooperation, however, remained weak. Although an article stating the importance of abiding by the Security Council resolutions regarding the conflict between Azerbaijan and Armenia in Nagorno-Karabakh was included in the final declaration, both the Turks and the Azeris were disappointed that it had not been worded in a way that condemned the Armenian occupation of Azerbaijan.

As was the case after the first Turkic summit, the Second General Assembly of Turkic Peoples was held shortly after the second summit. Although pan-Turkic sentiments were once again expressed during this meeting, Prime Minister Tansu Çiller tried to focus the meeting on developing new avenues of economic cooperation between the Turkic countries. During her speech, for example, she discussed the possibility of establishing an organization like the North American Free Trade Agreement (NAFTA) or the European Union among the Turkic states. Once again, however, pan-Turkic sentiments were expressed by some nongovernmental participants. Although Prime Minister Çiller and President Süleyman Demirel had been cautious in not partaking in such rhetoric, the fact that they attended an event in which pan-Turkic feelings were expressed prompted Russia to question Turkey's goals in the region.

Bilateral Relations

Turkish policymakers did not limit themselves to forming multilateral relations with the former Soviet republics but also worked on establishing close bilateral ties. Ankara's relationship with Azerbaijan—the closest of its foreign policy partners in the region—demonstrates, however, the opportunities as well as constraints Turkish officials faced in these endeavors. Turkish-Azeri relations were the most important, for a number of reasons: the Turkic dialect of the Azeris was the closest to the Turkish spoken in contemporary Turkey; the two countries shared a twelve-kilometer common border; and a significant number of Azeris and Azeri descendants lived in northeastern Turkey. Azerbaijan's former President Abullfaz Elcibey was an enthusiastic admirer of Turkey's political, economic, and cultural organizations and often expressed his desire to develop similar institutions in Azerbaijan. In November 1993, Turkish Foreign Minister Hikmet Çetin even described the Turkish-Azeri relationship as one between "one nation but two states."[25] Ankara had a number of ambitious policy goals toward Azerbaijan during the post–cold war era. These included: "Azerbaijani sovereignty over Nagorno-Karabakh, the mostly Armenian enclave within Azerbaijan; a friendly, but not necessarily pan-Turkic, Azerbaijani administration; preventing or at least limiting Russian return to Transcaucasia; and participating in Azerbaijani oil production and the export of a significant portion of Azerbaijani oil through Turkish territory."[26]

In order to achieve these goals, Turkish policymakers signed a number of protocols and agreements with Baku. Consequently, there was substantial bilateral trade between the two countries and Turkey accepted barter arrangements as the form of payment by the Azeris (who were unable to pay their $20 million debt to Turkey via other means because of the difficulties faced by their economy). Cultural links were maintained through state-run and private Turkish television channels in Azerbaijan, scholarships for Azeri students in Turkish universities, and military academies as well as other activities. Furthermore, to Turkey's satisfaction, Baku rejected Moscow's attempts to reintroduce Russian troops into Azerbaijan, either as border guards or as peacekeepers in Nagorno-Karabakh despite the favorable disposition of Azeri President Aliev to Moscow.[27]

Despite the establishment of such close links, however, Turkey also faced some difficulties in its relationship with Azerbaijan. Ankara's desire not to become directly involved in the conflict in Nagorno-Karabakh was one source of tension with Baku. After the Armenian capture of the Azeri town of Kelbejar on April 4, 1993, for example, Azeri President Elchibey requested Turkish helicopters to evacuate civilians from the region. Despite significant pressure from the Turkish public to supply the helicopters and its support of the Azeri position in principle, Ankara refused to provide direct military assistance to Azerbaijan. Instead, it suspended Western relief flights to Yerevan by closing its airspace to them and consistently pushed for a negotiated settlement.[28] Ankara did not want to anger the traditionally hostile Armenians, give ammunition to the strong anti-Turkish Armenian lobbies in the United States and France, or enter into a possible confrontation with Russia. Turkey's desire to stay out of a conflict that could have negative repercussions was thus stronger than its aspiration to show its allegiance to Azerbaijan or to act as a regional leader on this issue. Ankara's long-standing foreign policy principle of nonintervention in regional affairs, which had only been violated on a few occasions, thus prevailed even in the face of significant changes in the foreign policy arena.

While Turkey's relationship with even this closest ally among the former Soviet republics was far from perfect, its other bilateral relations were even more complicated. Although many of the newly independent states were friendly and wanted to establish close ties with Ankara, the end of the cold war also led to the rise of some antagonistic regimes in the region. The independence of Armenia, for example, was rather troubling for Turkish policymakers because of uncertainty about how hostile it would be toward its traditional enemy, Turkey. The animosities with Armenia stemmed from the fact that "the Armenians in Armenia and those in the diaspora hold Ankara responsible for the 1915 hostilities during which, they claim, the Ottoman army carried out a genocide of the Armenian population in eastern Turkey."[29] In order to prevent having to deal with another belligerent neighbor in the future, Ankara worked on establishing cordial relations from the outset. In the first years of the post–cold war period, it invited Armenia to join the Black Sea Economic Cooperation zone, granted humanitarian assistance (wheat deliveries), and allowed the transport of international aid across Turkish territory (until the ban mentioned above).[30] Despite these efforts, Turkish-Armenian relations were troubled by the middle of the decade, mostly as a result of the strife in Nagorno-Karabakh. Even after the signing of a cease-fire agreement in the conflict in July 1994, Turkey maintained the road and rail embargo on humanitarian and other goods bound for Armenia until April 1995 and finally lifted the ban only because of American pressure. The reports by the Turkish press that Armenia was preparing to purchase ground-to-air missiles from Russia to be stationed along the Turkish border added to the tensions.[31] Additional impediments to Ankara's efforts to establish close ties with the republics of the Caucasus and Central Asia emanated from two powerful states in the region that also desired to wield influence over these newly independent countries, Russia and Iran.

Constraints in the Region: Russia

Russian leaders failed to pay much attention to Central Asia for a brief period in the early post–cold war period while they were trying to deal with the breakup of the Soviet Union and concentrating on the task of forging relations with the United States and Europe. Soon afterward, however, Moscow started refocusing on its relations within the Commonwealth of Independent States (CIS). In February 1993, President Yeltsin declared that Russia would assume a special peacekeeping role in the former Soviet republics.[32] In April 1995, furthermore, Russia announced that it would bypass the Caucasus section of the 1990 Conventional Forces in Europe (CFE) Treaty, which limited the presence of troops and heavy weaponry throughout European Russia and the Caucasus.[33] As part of these reengagement efforts in Central Asia and Azerbaijan, Moscow challenged the active role that Turkey was attempting to play in the region. As such, the historic Turkish-Russian rivalry was refueled as fears of Pan-Turkism grew in Russia. Disdain for what was perceived as Ankara's pan-Turkic tendencies was voiced not only by extreme nationalists such as Vladimir Zhirinovsky but also by well-respected scholars such as Alexei Arbatov (the chairman of the Department of the Institute of World Economy and International Relations of the Russian Academy of Sciences).[34] The Russians were afraid, for example, that Tatarstan and Bashkortostan, encouraged by Turkish leaders' rhetoric about the importance of independence for the former Soviet republics, might want to secede from Russia. They were also dissatisfied with Turkey's subtle pro-Chechen stance in the conflict in Chechnya. Soon after President Demirel met with rebel Chechen leader Dzhokhar Dudayev in October 1993, for instance, the Turkish ambassador in Moscow was called in by Russian government officials to assure them that such a meeting would not be repeated in the future.[35] Despite overwhelming public opinion in Turkey calling for a condemnation of Russia after its armed intervention in Chechnya (as well as some demands for intervention on behalf of the Chechens), Ankara did not condemn Moscow but merely advocated finding a peaceful solution to the crisis.

One arena in which the Turkish-Russian rivalry was played out was Azerbaijan. Moscow's covert support for Armenia in its conflict with Azerbaijan in Nagorno-Karabakh contributed to the ouster of strongly pro-Turkish Azeri president Abufaz Elcibey. Elcibey had alienated the Russians when he accused them of aiding the Armenians and when he refused Azeri membership in the CIS in October 1992. Instead, Elcibey had espoused a pan-Turkic ideology and envisioned Azerbaijan as part of an emerging Turkish sphere of influence.

Due to a number of factors, which included corruption in the government, failure to hold promised elections, and economic decline, however, Elcibey was overthrown by the rebel warlord Suret Huseinov in June 1993. After assuming control of the capital, Huseinov invited Gaidar Aliyev (first secretary of the Communist Party in Azerbaijan from 1969 to 1987) to become president.[36] One reason for Huseinov's success was the support his forces received from the Russian military command in Azerbaijan. Consequently, Elcibey was replaced by a leader who had better ties with Moscow. Despite protests in Turkey, the Turkish government did not criticize the events that led to Elcibey's ouster. Prime Minister Tansu Çiller even visited Moscow in September 1993 to demonstrate that Turkish-Russian relations would be undisturbed by these developments in the Caucasus. Furthermore, Turkish-Azeri relations remained strong and Aliyev was eager to maintain the strong relationship with the Turks.

Another source of competition in Russian-Turkish relations centered around the development of the Chrirag, Gunashly, and Azeri oil reserves in the Caspian Sea containing an estimated four billion barrels of oil. President Elcibey had "agreed, in the spring of 1993, with the Azerbaijan Oil Consortium (AIOC)—consisting of a number of Western oil companies, and Turkey's state oil company Turkish Petroleum Joint Stock Company (TPAO)—to develop these fields."[37] Russia was vehemently opposed to this agreement. Meanwhile, Elcibey was overthrown before he signed the contract with the AIOC, and his successor, President Aliyev, canceled the agreement. Presuming that Russia's involvement in the project would lessen its opposition to Baku's exploration of Azeri shores on the Caspian Sea, Aliyev renegotiated the agreement in March 1994. As such, Russia was also included in the AIOC, and 10 percent of Baku's own shares were transferred to Moscow. Meanwhile, Russia and Turkey also competed over the prospective pipeline routes for Azeri oil. Ankara wanted Azeri oil to be transported through pipelines going across Turkish territory (through a pipeline to carry this oil to the Mediterranean port of Ceyhan via the so-called Baku-Ceyhan pipeline) while Moscow insisted that the existing pipelines to the Russian Black Sea port of Novorossisk be expanded.

While challenging Ankara's leadership role in the former Soviet Union, Russia also provided a range of incentives to the republics to maintain close relations with Moscow. Those that remained in the ruble zone, for example, received economic benefits, and countries that continued to be allied with Moscow obtained assurance of external and internal security they could not get from Turkey. Consequently, the former Soviet republics were unwilling to stray too far from the wishes of the Russians and were cautious in their relations with Turkey.

Although Moscow's demands and desires, and the former Soviet republics' continued dependence on Russia acted as a constraint for Turkey's developing ties with Central Asia and the Caucasus, it is important to note that Russia and Turkey succeeded in supplementing their rivalry in the region with close bilateral relations. The two countries signed a Treaty of Friendship, Good-Neighborliness and Cooperation in March 1991 that described Russia and Turkey as two friendly states resolved to enhance cooperation in a variety of areas. Accordingly, they pledged to "maintain their common borders, refrain from the use [or threat] of force against each other, disallow their territories to be used for similar purposes, to consult at every level at regular intervals and to cooperate against terrorist activities in all their forms."[38] The two countries signed another agreement for economic, scientific, and technical cooperation on the same day, which sought to increase bilateral trade. In November 1992, with the signing of a $75 million protocol, Turkey became the first NATO member to purchase military equipment from Russia.[39] Consequently, by 1997, Russia was Turkey's second-largest trading partner, with bilateral trade amounting to $14 billion annually.[40] In addition, natural gas from Russia was one of Turkey's most important energy sources; thirty thousand Turkish workers operated in Russia; and Turkish construction companies invested $6 billion there.[41] Furthermore, the two countries shared similar interests in that they both wanted to see stability and security in the region.

Constraints in the Region: Iran

Another constraint on Turkish foreign policy behavior emanated from one of Ankara's hostile neighbors, Iran. Iran also shared ethnic and linguistic ties with the region, especially with Tajikistan (whose language is much closer to Farsi than Turkish) and Azerbaijan (which is composed mostly of Shi'ite Muslims like Iran rather than Sunni Muslims like Turkey). It has a common border with Azerbaijan and Turkmenistan, providing access to the Indian Ocean to these landlocked states. Most important, Teheran had reasons to become involved in the region—it wanted to "[overcome] international isolation and . . . preempt potential threats to its territorial integrity."[42] As a result, Teheran challenged the role that Turkey wanted to pursue as a secular, democratic role model for the Muslim former Soviet republics and offered its vastly different political and social system as an alternative model. It sent religious leaders to all the Central Asian republics as well as Azerbaijan and invited hundreds of students to study Islam in Iran.[43] The rivalry between Iran and Turkey manifested itself when each country attempted to sway the Muslim former Soviet republics to adopt its alphabet. The Central Asian countries and Azerbaijan had been using the Cyrillic alphabet since the 1860s (the time of their absorption by the Russian Empire) and the choice they had to make between the Latin and Arabic scripts reflected the path they would choose for themselves as independent states. Adopting the Latin script, as Turkey proposed, would mean that they were deciding on a secular future, whereas embracing the Arabic script, as Iran suggested, would mean that they were aligning themselves with Islamic countries. Although Iran was supported by the Arab world in promoting the Arabic script, most of the Central Asian countries as well as Azerbaijan adopted the Latin alphabet. Only Tajikistan decided on the Arabic one.

There was competition between Turkey and Iran as to which country would have more economic influence in the region. Both countries wanted their ports to be used by the Central Asians and their companies to work on the construction of roads, railways, and oil pipelines there. Ankara launched the Black Sea Economic Cooperation (BSEC) project to play a greater economic role in the successor states in 1991. Similarly (and perhaps to counter the power of the BSEC), in 1992 Iran established the Caspian Sea Cooperation Scheme with Russia, Azerbaijan, Kazakhstan, Turkmenistan, and itself as members. Contrary to some beliefs, however, the competition between Ankara and Teheran in the region was not particularly hostile. In fact, the rivalry was somewhat offset by cooperation in that both countries were members of the Economic Cooperation Organization, were important trading partners, and shared common interests in solving the Kurdish issue.[44]

Russia and Iran did not pose the only constraints on Ankara's developing political relations with the Central Asian states and Azerbaijan. Another major constraint was that there were so many other issues in Turkey's international agenda that were of more vital interest. Because its most important "challenges [were] still the familiar dilemmas of relating to Europe, managing friction with regional neighbors, overcoming the pattern of confrontation with Greece including the unresolved Cyprus problem, and most of all handling the escalating rebellion in Kurdistan," Turkish policymakers did not have the time or the resources to focus entirely on the former Soviet republics.[45]

Economic Relations

Ankara's actions and decisions in the former Soviet republics demonstrate the close relationship between a state's foreign policy and its economic policy; that economic means are often employed to reach political objectives and vice versa. In the post–cold war era, Turkish officials used economic incentives to further their political goals and political incentives to further their economic objectives in the region. Just as offering its political system as a model for the newly independent states had been one of Ankara's major foreign policy goals in the former Soviet Union, presenting its economic system as such was another one. Policymakers and scholars believed that the Turkish economic model would be appropriate for the former Soviet republics because it had recently undergone a successful transformation from being a closed, protectionist economy to an open, free-market economy. Ankara's aspirations in the economic arena, like its political goals, however, were also inflated in the early days of the post–cold war period. It had wanted to be the main provider of credit and aid to the Turkic-speaking states, the most important source in the development of their markets, and their major link to Western capital. Ankara's conviction that it would be able to fulfill these roles led the government to make considerable, and rather unrealistic, promises to the Central Asian states and Azerbaijan. Policymakers, however, had to adjust Turkey's goals in the region once the realities of the post–cold war era set in. They realized that Turkey did not have the necessary resources to provide the republics with the kind of assistance needed for their economic growth and development (such as advancements in technology, infrastructure, training, etc.). Furthermore, the financial crisis of 1994 in Turkey led to the recognition of the fact that the Turkish economy was still unstable, underdeveloped, and itself dependent on foreign assistance.

Despite these constraints, however, Turkey extended economic assistance packages to the former Soviet republics. It granted over $78 million of humanitarian assistance to the five Central Asian states by the end of 1994.[46] It also contributed more than 24,000 tons of wheat (costing $2.6 million) to Kyrgyzstan, and 624,000 tons of wheat and 216,000 tons of sugar (worth $70.3 million) to Uzbekistan.[47] In addition, the Turkish Eximbank provided millions of dollars of credit to pay for other products from Turkey and to finance the work of construction companies in the region. The main areas of cooperation with Uzbekistan, for example, were the "production and transportation of agricultural products, building of light industrial complexes, the search for and extraction of minerals, the manufacture of textile goods, constructing infrastructure for tourism, cooperation in transport and communications and operating food industries."[48]

Another economic role Turkey played in the former Soviet republics was to act as a conduit between the Turkic states and Western private firms. Although some multinational companies preferred to operate out of Moscow rather than Ankara or Istanbul (in order to gain access to the huge Russian market as well) while doing business with the members of the CIS, many others opted to work through Turkey. The Turkish firm Alarko, for example, formed a partnership with an Austrian (Rosh Credit) and an American (HovSons) company to expand the Black Sea port of Trabzon to facilitate Armenian trade with the West. Moreover, while Turkey could not match the economic assistance offered by other countries or the financial incentives provided by Western companies, Turkish entrepreneurs' familiarity with the culture and the language of the region gave them an advantage in doing business with the Turkic republics. Many Turkish companies thus worked in cooperation with multinationals as subcontractors and middlemen. In addition, a number of Turkish businesses (such as banks, construction, mining, and leather companies) formed joint ventures with their counterparts in Central Asia and the Caucasus. In Kazakhstan alone, for example, there were over a hundred joint ventures in the energy, transportation, mining, and maritime transportation sectors.[49] In addition, a Turkish company (BMB) and its Turkmen counterpart decided to build a natural gas pipeline to reach Europe via Turkey.[50]

It was not just the desire to assist their brethren that prompted the Turkish government and businessmen to become widely involved with the economic development of the region. Turkey benefited significantly from the increased trade, and Turkish policymakers were hopeful that the countries dependence on Middle Eastern oil would be offset in the future by increased Central Asian oil supplies. The expectation was that Central Asia would become Turkey's main source of energy once the infrastructure to extract and transport additional oil was developed. Ankara was also hoping to benefit from the expansion of the region's natural gas and oil industry through "transit fees; investment in pipelines, terminals and refineries; oil service industry benefits; and shipping and finance."[51]

Even after many of Turkey's political goals in the region had to be scaled back, economic involvement in the former Soviet Union remained strong. Politicians traveling to the region were often accompanied by large groups of businessmen (sometimes around a hundred) who signed lucrative agreements with the governments of the republics. In addition, "Turkey's diplomatic missions [were] virtually competing with each other to increase the volume of trade with the countries to which they [were] accredited. Turkish companies [had] also become the country's commercial and investment representatives abroad. The old image of the 'warrior Turk' [was] giving place to the figure of the contemporary businessman.[52] In fact, Turkey's professed role as a "bridge" between the East and the West, especially in the economic arena, was one of the cornerstones of its foreign policy in the post–cold war period. Ankara did not limit itself to forming economic alliances with the Turkic republics in the CIS but sought to establish avenues of cooperation with other former Soviet republics as well as with the Balkan states. One of Turkey's most important foreign policy initiatives during this time was the launching of the BSEC zone in 1991.

On June 25, 1992, Albania, Armenia, Azerbaijan, Bulgaria, Georgia, Greece, Moldova, Romania, Russia, Turkey, and Ukraine signed the first formal agreement establishing the BSEC zone, thus "committing themselves to multilateral cooperation in the region based on the principles of a market economy."[53] The main goal of the BSEC was to take advantage of the geographical proximity and similar economic structures of member countries to strengthen economic cooperation among them, gradually working toward the free circulation of capital, services, goods, and labor. Member countries were to work together to revitalize the neglected economy of the Black Sea region and collaborate in such areas as transportation, telecommunications, energy, and environmental protections. The organization also aspired to establish a regional bank that would finance development projects and regional joint ventures. One of Turkey's main roles in the organization was to impart its knowledge (based on its own recent experience) of the transformation from a closed economy to an open-market one to member countries.[54] Turkey expected to reap significant benefits from the BSEC zone. The successful establishment of the regime would mean the opening up of a formerly closed (or at least restricted) market of more than 350 million people. In addition, the "natural complementarity between the economic structures of Turkey and some of the key members of the Black Sea Economic Union, e.g., Russia, [would] likely contribute to a very rapid expansion of trade and investment in the future."[55] Turkey was able to capitalize on this complementarity by exporting consumer goods and construction services and importing raw materials and energy resources from the former Soviet republics. Although the BSEC was, above all, an economic organization, it had political objectives as well. The expectation was that enhanced collaboration in the economic sphere would not only lead to better living conditions in member states but also political stability in a region rife with bilateral conflicts (even among member states such as Turkey and Greece, Armenia and Azerbaijan, and

Russia and Georgia). Because of its tremendous potential for economic as well as political gains, the Black Sea Economic Cooperation scheme "emerged as the centerpiece of Ankara's efforts to develop a more active external policy after the cold war."[56] It also helped diversify Turkey's foreign policy agenda because Ankara's position in the organization was not dependent on its relations with Western Europe or with the United States.

Despite the optimism surrounding the BSEC, the successful implementation of various aspirations of the organization was constrained by several factors. The most important of these was the shortage of economic wealth. Unlike similar organizations (such as the EU) that have extensive capital resources at their disposal to achieve integration and equality among member states, the BSEC did not have adequate funds. In fact, most of its members were developing countries that depended extensively on foreign aid. Another constraint stemmed from the fact that many of the BSEC members were "confronted with tremendous problems of short-term stabilization in an effort to engineer the transition from a totally state-regulated system to a market-oriented system."[57] These economic pressures were compounded by political ones. The fact that many of the member states were run by unstable governments, for example, brought into question the issue of implementation. Would these countries' often fragile administrations, in other words, be able to carry out the necessary reforms to transform their economies to free-market systems? Furthermore, the Black Sea region was dominated by bilateral conflicts, many among countries that were members of the BSEC. The unresolved issues between Greece and Turkey (Cyprus, water rights in the Aegean, etc.), for example, led to tensions between their governments and hostility among their people. Similarly, Armenia and Azerbaijan were fighting over Nagorno-Karabakh, and Russia and Georgia clashing over Abkhazia. Despite these significant obstacles to the success of the BSEC in fostering economic cooperation and political stability in the region, however, there was great hope for the organization. As Ziya Öniş wrote, neither the economic nor the political problems should be exaggerated:

The countries involved, given the depth of their economic development, the quality of their technological infrastructure and labor force, plus raw material and energy reserves, embody enormous long-term economic potential, once the problems of transition are overcome. . . . [Furthermore], the project itself could provide a powerful impetus for regional cooperation to help resolve these bilateral tensions.[58]

The disappearance of the Soviet threat had led to a period of uncertainty in Turkish foreign policy decision-making as Turkish policymakers questioned the role of NATO in the post–cold war era and its commitment to Turkish security in the emerging international arena. As such, "the opportunity to assert a leadership role in a major world region which was also the birthplace of the Turkish nation seemed irresistible."[59] Ankara thus entered the post–cold war era with exaggerated enthusiasm and inflated goals in the region that had been the Soviet Union. These included forging close ties in the political, economic, and cultural spheres, acting as a model for the Turkic republics' economic and political development, and assuming a regional leadership position. Several major impediments, both internal and external, however, constrained Turkish foreign policy behavior: its economy was too weak to be the major supplier of foreign assistance; its actions and decisions in the region were challenged by Moscow and Teheran; and its foreign policy agenda was already filled with issues that were of greater importance for national security. Furthermore, the former Soviet republics realized that they would gain the most if they did not limit themselves to forging ties with one regional power but if they played these states against one another.

Despite these constraints, Turkey succeeded in becoming involved in the region. Seven years after the end of the cold war, the biggest part of this involvement was in the economic arena: Turkish companies were very active in a variety of sectors in the former Soviet republics; joint ventures flourished; Central Asia and the Caucasus became an important source of energy for Turkey; and the Black Sea Economic Cooperation zone was one of the centerpieces of Turkish policy in the region. This rather intense emphasis on developing close economic relations with a region outside of Turkey's traditional foreign policy partners marked a departure from earlier times in which Ankara focused its foreign relations entirely on the United States and Western Europe and in which security issues dominated the foreign policy agenda. As Duygu Sezer observed,

[Turks] no longer confine foreign and security policy thinking to political-military matters but reach out to include a variety of economic and community dimensions. Political, social, and economic change within Turkey as well as the dynamics of the new geopolitical environment have allowed the Turkish leaders who were at the helm when the cold war ended, particularly former prime ministers Turgut Özal and Süleyman Demirel, to reinterpret the vitality of the formative concepts underlying Turkish foreign policy in larger, international terms.[60]

RELATIONS WITH THE MIDDLE EAST

One area of foreign policy that developed in a rather unexpected fashion in the post–cold war period was Turkey's relations with the Middle East.

Ankara's international commitments had determined its foreign policy behavior toward the Middle East and prevented it from getting involved in the turbulent affairs of this region for much of the cold war period. Although there were some shifts in behavior, one of the main pillars of Turkish foreign policy during the cold war was nonintervention in regional affairs. As Andrew Mango remarked, "the founding fathers of the Turkish Republic believed that, in its last phase, the Ottoman Empire had expended to no good purpose the human and material resources of Anatolia in the lands inhabited by the Arabs. They were determined not to repeat [this] mistake."[61] In addition, Turkish foreign policy toward the Middle East was formulated according to Ankara's commitments to its Western allies and its actions and decisions in the region often angered and alienated the Arabs. In the post–cold war period, however, there were some significant alterations in Turkish foreign policy behavior toward the Middle East. Turkey became directly involved in the Persian Gulf War in the early 1990s and focused on forging close military ties with Israel in the later part of the decade. As such, Ankara showed that it was no longer willing to sit on the sidelines of this important region.

The first fifteen years of the cold war era had been characterized by Turkey's desire to show its allegiance to the Western world in order to be incorporated into as many Western institutions as possible. Although Turkey voted against the partition of Palestine when it was being voted on in the United Nations, for example, it recognized the newly created state of Israel on March 29, 1949. In 1959, Altemur Kiliç, an assistant to the Turkish representative to the United Nations, explained this decision by saying that it was made "to emphasize Turkey's Westernness and objective attitude in the [Middle East]."[62] During the 1950s, Turkish policymakers felt that they would best be able to demonstrate Turkey's strategic value to their Western allies if they pursued an activist policy in the Middle East. Consequently, Ankara worked to prevent the newly independent states in the region from succumbing to Soviet influence and thereby threatening Turkish security. It signed a pact of mutual cooperation with the Western-oriented regime in Iraq in February 1955. Later in the same year, this alliance—called the Baghdad Pact—was enlarged to include the United Kingdom, Iran, and Pakistan. For the next five years, Ankara worked to counterbalance the growing Soviet influence in the region, pushing for a Western intervention in Syria (in response to the growing military and economic relationship between this country and the Soviet Union) and in Iraq (in response to the republican overthrow of the pro-Western monarchy in 1958).[63] It seemed that every decision made and action taken by Turkish policymakers was to demonstrate

Turkey's pro-Western position. As a result, Turkey was seen as an instrument of the West and resented by the Arab states.

Turkey's activist role in the Middle East came to an end with the downfall of the Democratic Party in 1960. As Philip Robins said, "for the next three decades Turkish policy toward the region was markedly more cautions, even to the point of meekness."[64] For the remainder of the cold war period, Turkish foreign policy in the region was guided by the principles of nonintervention in the domestic affairs of the Middle East and noninterference in conflicts between Middle Eastern states. Ankara also tried to be more even-handed in its relations in the region. Eager to shed its image of a Western tool, it attempted to improve relations with the Arab states in the 1960s. Ankara was particularly disturbed by the Arabs' pro-Greek position during the Cyprus crisis of 1963 and saw the cooling off of relations with the United States in the aftermath of the crisis as an opportunity to develop better ties with Middle Eastern states. In an attempt to separate Turkish interests in the region from American and NATO interests, for example, Ankara did not permit the United States to use the military bases in Turkey for refueling and supply activities during the 1967 Arab-Israeli War. It opposed the Israeli occupation of Arab territories and reduced diplomatic relations with Israel in December 1980, withdrawing its entire embassy staff from Tel Aviv, leaving only a second secretary to serve as chargé d'affaires. Ankara also worked on developing closer economic ties with countries in the Middle East. As a result, in the 1980s, capital from the region—especially Saudi Arabia and other oil-rich Arab states—became a major source of foreign exchange for the Turkish economy.[65] Furthermore, President Kenan Evren's election as the chairman of the Islamic Standing Committee for Economic and Commercial Cooperation in 1981 formed the basis for closer financial and political relations with a number of Middle Eastern countries. Despite such efforts, however, Turkey's relations with its Middle Eastern neighbors—Syria, Iran, and Iraq—were distant; cordial at best and openly hostile at worst.

Turkish-Syrian relations were the most antagonistic as historical animosities between the two countries were exacerbated by East-West tensions. One contentious issue was the *sancak* (district) of Alexandretta, or Hatay to the Turks. France, which controlled this region, had allowed the inhabitants of Hatay to choose their nationality in 1939. Although they chose to be incorporated into the Turkish Republic, Syria refused to concede the loss of this territory for years to come. Turkey and Syria also clashed over Turkey's control over the Euphrates River (one of Syria's major water sources) and over Syria's support of violent anti-Turkish groups, such as the Armenian

Secret Army for the Liberation of Armenia (ASALA) in the 1970s, and the Kurdish Workers Party (PKK) in the 1980s and 1990s. Turkish-Iranian relations, on the other hand, were more cordial for much of the cold war because both countries were members of the Northern Tier security organization's Baghdad Pact and the succeeding Central Treaty Organization (CENTO) against the Soviet Union. After the Iranian revolution of 1979, however, relations deteriorated abruptly as Ayatollah Khomeini chastised Turkey's secularism and Teheran became a major supporter of Islamist forces within Turkey that worked to undermine the secular nature of the state. Meanwhile, Turkey's relations with Iraq were the best of all three until the very end of the cold war. The Turkish-Iraqi relationship was based on Baghdad's dependence on Ankara for the security of its communications and supply lines and Iraq's importance as a major trading partner for Turkey. The two countries also shared common problems such as the presence of large Kurdish minorities. The relatively affable Turkish-Iraqi relationship ended with the end of the cold war, however, as Turkey became one of the first countries to support the United States's position against Baghdad in the Persian Gulf War.

After its brief experiment with an activist policy in the Middle East during the 1950s, Turkey maintained a cautious and consistent foreign policy toward the region during much of the cold war. It remained, in other words, "a diffident and tentative actor in the Middle East."[66] Consequently, despite its geographical position and its historic role in the region, it was not considered a major actor in Middle Eastern affairs. Also during this time, Ankara aspired to remain neutral in the frequent conflicts of the region, maintaining its policy of nonintervention in the domestic affairs of the Middle Eastern states. According to Robins,

by 1989 and the end of the cold war, Turkish policy toward the Middle East was routine and well understood. In substance, it was materially oriented and politically non-interventionist. In style, it was low key and predominantly incremental. In essence, it was Kemalist; that is to say, intrinsically uninterested in and comparatively aloof from the Middle East, while studiously concerned not to appear to be projecting power beyond its borders.[67]

The changes that occurred in the structure of the international system and in the Middle East as a result of the end of the cold war, however, prompted Turkey to establish a greater presence there than it had in previous times. During the cold war, the Soviet Union had been an important actor in Middle Eastern affairs, directly challenging the United States's military and ideological role in the region. After it disintegrated, therefore, the dynamics of the region changed considerably. While the United States was left as the only outsider state to wield significant power over regional affairs, incentives to offer protection, political support, and financial assistance to its allies in the region diminished with the removal of the Soviet threat. Furthermore, Russia was not willing or able to continue to support countries such as Syria, Iraq, and Libya, which had allied with the Soviet Union during the cold war. In addition, the historic signing of the Declaration of Principles by the Palestinians and Israelis on September 13, 1993, brought the region "one step closer to normalcy and to regular commercial and diplomatic relations."[68] As Henri Barkey said, therefore, "The end of the cold war may have provided Turkey with opportunities it never imagined it could have: it appears, with the exception of Russia, to be the strongest regional military power, and few in the area can compete with [its] economic dynamism."[69]

After years of pursuing a policy of nonintervention in the Middle East, Turkey entered the post–cold war era as one of the major players in the Persian Gulf crisis. It became one of the first countries to ally with the United States against the Iraqi invasion of Kuwait in August of 1990 and contributed to the successful enforcement of the United Nations sanctions on Iraq by shutting off the oil pipelines on Turkish territory. Furthermore, Ankara allowed American military aircraft to use the Incirlik Air Base for air strikes into Iraq and deployed nearly 100,000 Turkish troops along the Iraqi border (forcing Iraq to dread the possibility of a two-front war). The decision to become so involved in the crisis was made almost exclusively by President Turgut Özal who defied the wishes of the opposition parties, his own Motherland Party, the military, and the Turkish public. The main reason for Ankara's direct involvement in the Gulf War was President Özal's desire to secure a strategically important position for Turkey in the new international environment where Turkey's traditional role as a bulwark against Soviet expansionism would no longer be of great value to its Western allies. President Özal believed that by assuming a central role in the gulf crisis, Turkey would bolster its bilateral relationship with the United States. As discussed previously, this was seen as a necessity in the emerging international order.[70]

Turkey's involvement in the Persian Gulf War led to some positive as well as some negative developments. On the positive side, Washington doubled the value of its textile quota and granted the Turkish government $282 million in additional military and economic assistance for 1991.[71] Furthermore, the United States persuaded Egypt to purchase forty Turkish-manufactured F-16s, and the European Community to expand the value of the Turkish textile quota. Moreover, as Bruce Kuniholm wrote, Turkey's role in the Gulf War "underscored the value of [the] Turkish alliance to the United States and corroborated estimates within both governments of Turkey's continuing—albeit, changing—geopolitical importance."[72]

The Persian Gulf War also had several negative repercussions for Turkey. It lost the $1.2 billion in rental revenues that it had been earning annually prior to the war from the oil pipeline that carried Iraqi oil from northern Iraq to the Mediterranean.[73] Furthermore, Iraq and Turkey had been close trading partners before the war. In 1987, Iraq was the second-largest recipient (after Germany) of Turkish goods, receiving 9.3 percent of total exports.[74] This percentage dropped to 0.9 percent by 1991, and as a result of the United Nations sanctions imposed on Baghdad, did not recover. Another negative development for Turkey was the establishment of the autonomous Kurdish region in northern Iraq in the aftermath of the Gulf War. This area, in which no one wielded effective political authority, was used as a base by the PKK guerrillas to launch military operations into Turkey. Although Turkey's involvement in the Persian Gulf War had a mixed outcome, Ankara's foreign policy behavior during the crisis constituted a marked departure from its previous pattern of behavior. After four decades during which Turkish policymakers pursued a noninterventionist policy in the Middle East, Turkey became an important player in regional affairs by assuming a central role in the first serious conflict of the post–cold war era.

Another departure from the prudent policies of the cold war period occurred with Turkey's forging of close military ties with Israel in the second half of the 1990s. Ankara's relations with Israel had been friendly but cautious since Turkey's recognition of the Jewish state in March 1949. Turkey, however, had distanced slightly its foreign policy from the United States and strengthened its ties with Islamic countries in the 1970s. Consequently, Ankara reduced its diplomatic contacts with Israel to a "symbolic level" in December 1980 as a reaction to Israel's reaffirmation of the annexation of east Jerusalem and its designation of the city as the country's capital.[75] Turkey also denounced the extension of Israeli law to the Golan Heights in 1981. Despite these setbacks, however, relations were cordial and gradually improved, culminating in the July 1986 visit of Israeli Industry and Trade Minister Ariel Sharon to Turkey. Diplomatic relations were finally restored after the end of the cold war, in December 1991. Soon afterward, President Chaim Herzog became the first Israeli head of state to visit Turkey, in July 1992. After the signing of the Oslo peace agreement in 1993, the two countries embarked on an effort to develop closer bilateral relations.

The next few years were characterized by a series of high-level diplomatic exchanges between Turkish and Israeli officials who signed agreements on

such issues as security cooperation, combating terrorism, and developing agricultural projects in Central Asia. In February 1996, "Israel established its
first-ever formal military link to a predominantly Muslim country when it
signed a military training agreement permitting Israeli air force jets to fly in
Turkish air space."[76] This military agreement was followed by the signing of
a free-trade agreement in March of the same year. Because the Turkish military establishment had the ultimate say in the conduct of foreign policy and
favored closer ties with Israel, not even the rise to power of Necmettin Erbakan, the leader of the pro-Islamic Welfare Party, in July 1996 could harm
the growing cooperation between the two countries. In February 1997, Turkish Army Chief of Staff Ismail Hakki Karadayi visited Israel and recommended more high-level exchanges to build on the agreements of prior years.
Subsequently, Israeli Foreign Minister David Levy traveled to Ankara and
Turkish Defense Minister Turhan Tayan visited Israel in April, Turkish Deputy Chief of Staff Çevik Bir went to Israel in May, and Israeli Chief of the
General Staff Amnon Lipkin-Shahak visited Turkey in October of 1997.
These various exchanges resulted in the signing of several important agree-
ments between the two countries.

A number of these pertained to the military arena. For example, Israeli
Aircraft Industries was to modernize fifty-four of Turkey's Phantom F-4E
aircraft and "to clinch the deal Israel granted Turkey a line of credit nearly
equal to the entire cost of the modernization."[77] In addition, Turkey was to
upgrade its weapons technology through the purchase of other equipment
from Israel. The two countries also decided to invest $150 million in the
production of hundreds of Popeye II missiles and to engage in joint training
exercises. Turkish F-16 pilots and crews were to learn about electronic war-
fare from the Israelis while the Israeli pilots were to practice long-range flying
over mountainous land in Anatolia. The growing Turkish-Israeli military
alliance culminated in Operation Reliant Mermaid in January 1998, the first
joint military exercise between the Israeli and Turkish navies and the American Sixth Fleet.[78] Jordan was invited to observe the operation and sent the
commander of its navy. The high rank of the observer signified the importance Jordan attached to the exercise. Although the stated goal of Operation
Reliant Mermaid was exclusively to improve the coordination of search-and-
rescue operations, Syria and Egypt condemned the maneuvers as "provocative
[to the other Arab countries] and dangerous [for the region's security]."[79]
The possibility of such a close Turkish-Israeli military alliance was thus un-
settling for many of these countries' neighbors in the region.

Israel also became an important economic partner for Turkey in the post–
cold war period. The free trade agreement signed by Ankara and Jerusalem

in March 1996 came into effect in May 1997. This agreement was expected to lead to a quadrupling of annual trade between the two countries in just three years (from $450 million to $2 billion).[80] Furthermore, the continuous flow of tourists from Israel became indispensable to Turkey's burgeoning tourism sector. Just in 1997, 400,000 Israelis—8 percent of the country's population—visited Turkey and spent $3 billion.[81]

Israel and Turkey's new strategic alliance was forged as a result of shared interests. Both countries had antagonistic relations with Syria, Iraq, and Iran, as well as distant (or even hostile) relations with most Arab countries. Furthermore, they were both close allies of the United States. The end of the cold war—the removal of Soviet support from many Arab countries and the Israeli-Palestinian peace agreement—thus provided an opportunity for them to develop closer ties than they had had previously with each other and with other states in the region.

SHIFTS IN FOREIGN POLICY BEHAVIOR

The post–cold war period in Turkish foreign policy was thus characterized by several important shifts in behavior. Ankara worked on forging close relations with a previously unexplored region—the newly independent republics of Central Asia and the Caucasus, and although it suffered some setbacks and had to diminish some of its aspirations in the region, it succeeded in diversifying its foreign policy. The growing relations with the former Soviet republics prompted Turkish foreign policy to change from one that focused entirely on the country's relations with the West to one that was more regional in its orientation. Turkish policymakers, however, were careful to emphasize that these newly developed ties would not supersede Turkey's relations with its Western allies but would augment them. Several factors motivated Ankara in its efforts to become involved in Central Asia and the Caucasus. It was eager to find allies in a region of the world where it had always had enemies, especially allies with which it shared ethnic, religious, and cultural ties. In addition, Turkish policymakers believed that it was imperative for them to find a new role for Turkey in the post–cold war era now that the removal of the Soviet threat had made its position as a bulwark against Soviet expansionism obsolete. The goal was to assume a new role for Turkey as a "bridge" between the East and the West. They also wanted to use Turkey's geographic and cultural proximity to the Turkic Soviet successor states to take advantage of the significant economic opportunities in this region.

Another shift in behavior in the post-cold war period occurred with regard

to Turkish foreign policy toward the Middle East. After remaining unin-
volved in the region for most of the cold war era, Turkey changed course
rather abruptly by assuming a central position in the Persian Gulf War.
Further abandoning its long-standing policy of neutrality in the region, Ankara developed a strategic military partnership with Israel in the late 1990s.
Turkish policymakers were once again motivated by post–cold war developments. One of the most important reasons for the forging of close ties
with the Israelis was Turkey's marginalization from Western Europe. The
countries of this region no longer depended on Turkey for protection from
the Soviets and openly rejected the possibility that Turkey would be admitted
to the EU in the near future. At a EU summit in Luxembourg in December
1997, "European leaders rejected the plea that [Turkey] should at least be
given some encouragement, if it could not be admitted quickly."[82] Turkish
policymakers reacted to this rather angrily and halted political relations (i.e.,
negotiations for EU membership) with the Europeans. Ankara's objective
was to replace Turkey's close relationship with Western Europe with a strategic partnership with the United States and Israel. While the success or
failure of this new foreign policy approach still remains to be seen, it con-
stitutes a significant break from the cold war period.

NOTES

1. Basil Dmytryshyn and Frederick Cox, *The Soviet Union and the Middle East—
A Documentary Record of Afghanistan, Iran and Turkey 1917–1985* (Princeton, N.J.:
Kingston Press, 1987), 473–480.

2. Turkkaya Ataöv, "Turkey's Expanding Relations with the CIS and Eastern
Europe," *Turkish Foreign Policy: New Prospects*, ed. C. H. Dodd (Huntingdon,
United Kingdom: Eothen Press, 1992), 100.

3. Paul B. Henze, *Turkey: Toward the Twenty-First Century* (Santa Monica:
RAND Publications, 1992), 29.

4. Ziya Öniş, "Turkey in the Post–Cold War Era: In Search of Identity," *Middle
East Journal* 49.1 (Winter 1995): 57.

5. Morton Abramowitz, "Dateline Ankara: Turkey After Özal," *Foreign Policy*
91 (Summer 1993): 165.

6. Turkkaya Ataöv, "Turkey, the CIS and Eastern Europe," *Turkey and Europe*,
eds. Canan Balkir and Allan M. Williams (London: Pinter Publishers, 1993), 192.

7. *Cumhuriyet*, 23 January 1992: 1.

8. R. Craig Nation, "The Turkic and Other Muslim Peoples of Central Asia,
the Caucasus, and the Balkans," *Turkey Between East and West: New Challenges for
a Rising Regional Power*, eds. Vojtech Mastny and R. Craig Nation (Boulder, Colo.:
Westview Press, 1996), 105.

9. Gareth Winrow, *Turkey in Post-Soviet Central Asia* (London: Royal Institute of International Affairs, 1995), 15.

10. *Turkish Daily News*, 8 May 1992.

11. Winrow, *Turkey in Post-Soviet Central Asia*, 12.

12. Duygu Bazoğlu Sezer, "Turkey in the New Security Environment in the Balkan and Black Sea Region," *Turkey Between East and West: New Challenges for a Rising Regional Power*, 87.

13. Winrow, *Turkey in Post-Soviet Central Asia*, 10.

14. Winrow, *Turkey in Post-Soviet Central Asia*, 12.

15. Sezer, "Turkey in the New Security Environment in the Balkan and Black Sea Region," 85.

16. Winrow, *Turkey in Post-Soviet Central Asia*, 19.

17. Winrow, *Turkey in Post-Soviet Central Asia*, 20.

18. Winrow, *Turkey in Post-Soviet Central Asia*, 20.

19. Philip Robins, "Between Sentiment and Self-interest: Turkey's Policy Towards Azerbaijan and the Central Asian States," *Middle East Journal* 47.4 (Autumn 1993): 593–610.

20. Anthony Hyman, "Moving Out of Moscow's Orbit: The Outlook for Central Asia," *International Affairs* 2 (1993): 298.

21. Richard Pomfret, "The Economic Cooperation Organization: Current Status and Future Prospects," *Europe-Asia Studies* 49.4 (1997): 658.

22. Winrow, *Turkey in Post-Soviet Central Asia*, 25–26.

23. *Turkish Daily News*, 19 October 1994.

24. Winrow, *Turkey in Post-Soviet Central Asia*, 30.

25. Sezer, "Turkey in the New Security Environment in the Balkan and Black Sea Region," 88. See also Statement by Foreign Minister Hikmet Çetin before the TGNA's Commission on the Plan and the Budget, Meeting on the Budget for Fiscal Year 1994, 17 November 1993, p. 23.

26. Süha Bölükbaşi, "Ankara's Baku-Centered Transcaucasia Policy: Has It Failed?" *Middle East Journal* 51.1 (Winter 1997): 82.

27. Bölükbaşi, "Ankara's Baku-Centered Transcaucasia Policy," 92.

28. Bölükbaşi, "Ankara's Baku-Centered Transcaucasia Policy," 85.

29. Bölükbaşi, "Ankara's Baku-Centered Transcaucasia Policy," 82.

30. Sezer, "Turkey in the New Security Environment in the Balkan and Black Sea Region," 89.

31. Katherine A. Wilkens, "Turkey: Emerging Regional Power or State in Crisis?" *Great Decisions* (Hanover, N.H.: Dartmouth Printing Company, 1998), 78.

32. Duygu Bazoğlu Sezer, "View from Turkey: Turkey's New Security Environment, Nuclear Weapons and Proliferation," *Comparative Strategy* 14 (1995): 152.

33. Bölükbaşi, "Ankara's Baku-Centered Transcaucasia Policy," 87.

34. Alexei G. Arbatov, "Russian Policy Priorities for the 1990s," *Russian Security After the Cold War*, eds. T. P. Johnson and S. Miller (Washington: Brasseys, 1994), 26–27.

35. Winrow, *Turkey in Post-Soviet Central Asia*, 43.

36. Nation, "The Turkic and Other Muslim Peoples of Central Asia, the Caucasus, and the Balkans," 108–109.

37. Bölükbasi, "Ankara's Baku-Centered Transcaucasia Policy," 87.

38. Ataöv, "Turkey, the CIS and Eastern Europe," 197.

39. Abramowitz, "Dateline Ankara," 165.

40. Wilkens, "Turkey: Emerging Regional Power or State in Crisis?" 78.

41. Wilkens, "Turkey: Emerging Regional Power or State in Crisis?" 78.

42. Nation, "The Turkic and Other Muslim Peoples of Central Asia, the Caucasus, and the Balkans," 106.

43. Ataöv, "Turkey, the CIS and Eastern Europe," 200.

44. Winrow, *Turkey in Post-Soviet Central Asia*, 49.

45. Nation, "The Turkic and Other Muslim Peoples of Central Asia, the Caucasus, and the Balkans," 98.

46. Winrow, *Turkey in Post-Soviet Central Asia*, 34.

47. Winrow, *Turkey in Post-Soviet Central Asia*, 34.

48. Ataöv, "Turkey, the CIS and Eastern Europe," 202.

49. Winrow, *Turkey in Post-Soviet Central Asia*, 39.

50. Ataöv, "Turkey, the CIS and Eastern Europe," 202.

51. Abramowitz, "Dateline Ankara," 168.

52. Ataöv, "Turkey, the CIS and Eastern Europe," 192.

53. N. Bülent Gültekin and Ayse Mumcu, "Black Sea Economic Cooperation," *Turkey Between East and West: New Challenges for a Rising Regional Power*, 179.

54. Oral Sander, "Turkey and the Turkic World," *Central Asian Survey* 13.1 (1994): 43.

55. Önis, "Turkey in the Post-Cold War Era," 58.

56. Ian O. Lesser, "Bridge or Barrier? Turkey and the West After the Cold War," *Turkey's New Geopolitics*, eds. Graham E. Fuller and Ian O. Lesser with Paul B. Henze and J. E. Brown (Boulder, Colo.: Westview Press, 1993), 103.

57. Önis, "Turkey in the Post-Cold War Era," 59.

58. Önis, "Turkey in the Post-Cold War Era," 59–60.

59. Nation, "The Turkic and Other Muslim Peoples of Central Asia, the Caucasus, and the Balkans," 105.

60. Sezer, "Turkey in the New Security Environment in the Balkan and Black Sea Region," 80.

61. Andrew Mango, "Turkish Policy in the Middle East: Turning Danger to Profit," *Turkish Foreign Policy: New Prospects*, ed. C. H. Dodd (Huntingdon, United Kingdom: Eothen Press, 1992), 58.

62. Altemur Kiliç, *Turkey and the World* (Washington World Affairs Press, 1959), 189.

63. Philip Robins, *Turkey and the Middle East* (New York: Council on Foreign Relations Press, 1991), 26–27.

64. Robins, *Turkey and the Middle East*, 27.

65. Birol A. Yesilada, "Turkish Foreign Policy Towards the Middle East," *Polit-*

ical and Socioeconomic Transformation of Turkey, eds. Atila Eralp, Muharrem Tunay, and Birol A. Yeşilada (Westport, Conn.: Praeger, 1993), 175.

66. Philip J. Robins, "Avoiding the Question," *Reluctant Neighbor: Turkey's Role in the Middle East*, ed. Henri J. Barkey (Washington, D.C.: United States Institute of Peace Press, 1996), 179.

67. Robins, "Avoiding the Question," 180.

68. Henri J. Barkey, "Turkey and the New Middle East," *Reluctant Neighbor: Turkey's Role in the Middle East*, 31.

69. Barkey, "Turkey and the New Middle East," 31.

70. Erik J. Zurcher, *Turkey: A Modern History* (London: I. B. Tauris, 1993), 318.

71. Sabri Sayari, "Turkey: The Changing European Security Environment and the Gulf Crisis," *Middle East Journal* 46.1 (Winter 1992): 19.

72. Bruce R. Kuniholm, "Turkey and the West Since World War II," *Turkey Between East and West: New Challenges for a Rising Regional Power*, 62.

73. Phebe Marr, "Turkey and Iraq," *Reluctant Neighbor: Turkey's Role in the Middle East*, 45.

74. Marr, "Turkey and Iraq," 52.

75. Arthur S. Banks, Alan J. Day, and Thomas C. Muller, eds., *Political Handbook of the World: 1995–1996* (Binghamton, N.Y.: CSA Publications, State University of New York, 1997), 961.

76. Daniel Pipes, "A New Axis: The Emerging Turkish-Israeli Entente," *Turkish Times* (1 February 1998): 4.

77. Pipes, "A New Axis," 4.

78. Serge Schemann, "Unusual Naval Alliance Shows Off, and Arabs Glare," *New York Times* (8 January 1998): A1.

79. Schemann, "Unusual Naval Alliance Shows Off," A1.

80. Pipes, "A New Axis," 4.

81. Pipes, "A New Axis," 4.

82. Stephen Kinzer, "Turks Reinvent Their World," *New York Times* (28 December 1997): sec. 4, 6.

Conclusion

The international system experienced significant changes as the East-West conflict was eased, the cold war ended, and the Soviet Union disintegrated. Consequently, the bipolar structure that had prevailed for nearly half a century collapsed. This shift affected not only the superpowers but also states that played various supporting roles in the cold war. Turkey had been an important secondary actor in the cold war whose foreign policy orientation and behavior was greatly influenced by Ankara's position in the East-West conflict. Its role as a front-line state in containing Soviet expansionism, in other words, not only helped shape its political relations with others but also influenced its economic policy as a result of the prominent role of foreign aid. Consequently, the prevailing view among scholars of Turkish politics was that Turkey's international commitments, such as its membership in the North Atlantic Treaty Organization (NATO), determined its foreign policy regardless of what type of regime or government was in power.[1] Because the structure of the international system was such an important factor in determining Turkish foreign policy, changes in this structure were bound to alter the ways in which Turkey interacted with other states.

The structure of the international system, however, could not be the only determinant of Turkish foreign policy. In fact, "multiple meanings and explanations . . . underlie even the simplest of foreign policy actions."[2] Domestic factors—a state's geography, social structure and population, political institutions, and its economic and military capabilities—also helped shape foreign policy. Acting as constraints, opportunities, or both, they can increase a state's vulnerability or contribute to its enhanced standing in the international area. In examining Turkish foreign policy, therefore, this book adopted a framework for analysis developed by Hillal Dessouki and Bahgat Korany that incorporates the domestic environment with systemic factors. In addition to the domestic environment, Dessouki and Korany assert that a state's foreign policy orientation, its decision-making processes, and its foreign policy behavior have to be taken into account in foreign policy analysis. The

foreign policy orientation results from a state's foreign policy elites' perceptions of the world and their country's role in it. Meanwhile, the decision-
making process involves the question of how foreign policy decisions are
actually made—how leaders reach foreign policy decisions and which institutions help shape foreign policy. The foreign policy behavior is composed
of the state's concrete foreign policy decisions and actions. One reason why
this framework is particularly suited to an analysis of Turkish foreign policy
is that it operates within an international political economy perspective. Such
an approach is necessary because in the current system of interdependence
and globalization the boundaries between economics and politics have eroded
considerably and the linkages between a state's position in the global political
economy and its economic and foreign policy are more important than ever.

An examination of Turkish foreign policy during the cold war and post–
cold war periods showed that although Turkey's most important foreign
policy objective, the goal of maintaining its national security and territorial
integrity, remained stable over the years, there were shifts in the policies and
tactics used to achieve this as well as other objectives. Furthermore, there was
a significant level of continuity in Ankara's foreign policy orientation in the
cold war and post–cold war periods. For most of Turkey's post-war history,
Turkish policymakers remained staunchly pro-Western in their outlook, even
during periods in which Turkish-American relations were troubled. One
reason for this high level of stability was the institutional monism in the
foreign policy decision-making arena as the military establishment maintained a monopoly in this area. It was not until the post–cold war era that
there seemed to be a higher degree of pluralism in foreign policy decision-
making. For the first time in the history of the Turkish Republic, there were
foreign policy elites (such as high-ranking Welfare Party officials) who wanted
to change the direction of the country's foreign policy and who actually took
steps toward this goal. After a brief time in which people questioned the
direction of Turkish foreign policy, however, the armed forces once again
showed that they were the primary decision-makers in the conduct of foreign
policy in Turkey. It was only during Welfare's brief reign as the governing
party that the possibility of a shift in Turkey's long-standing pro-Western
foreign policy orientation was even entertained.

One factor that contributed to Welfare's rise in Turkey was the economic
policies pursued during the preceding sixteen years. The free-market policies
implemented at this time gave rise to extremely high rates of inflation and
unemployment, significant decreases in real wages, and a highly inequitable
distribution of income. Meanwhile, although large sectors of the population
were suffering tremendously as a result of these economic conditions, suc-

cessive governments seemed unable and unwilling to work toward alleviating these problems. Consequently, the poor, the uneducated, and the unemployed were willing to support alternative political movements such as the PKK and the Welfare Party. The Welfare Party ultimately succeeded in convincing these groups that it was the only party that would work for their benefit.

Some shifts in foreign policy behavior had occurred in Turkey prior to Welfare's rise to power, however. Although Turkey's foreign policy orientation remained stable, there were several important shifts in Ankara's foreign policy behavior toward the United States and Western Europe. These changes transpired as a result of a combination of factors—the structure of the international system, domestic factors, and the actions of other states. Furthermore, the alterations in foreign policy behavior toward Western Europe prompted Turkish policymakers to look for new foreign policy partners in the previously unexplored areas of Central Asia, the Caucasus, and parts of the Middle East.

REDUCED THREATS TO NATIONAL SECURITY

One expectation regarding Turkish foreign policy in the post–cold war era was that the end of the cold war would reduce threats to Turkey's national security and territorial integrity. Because the Soviet Union posed such a tremendous danger for Turkey during the cold war, the disintegration of this superpower would lead to a more secure environment for Turkey in the post–cold war era. Although the threats to Turkish national security emanating from the East-West conflict did decrease in the post–cold war period, however, there were other problems acting as causes of concern for Turkish policymakers.

The shifting of policies in the Soviet Union in the late 1980s removed the implicit (and sometimes explicit) threat emanating from a neighboring hostile superpower. After the Soviet Union disintegrated, the Russians, whom Turks had feared for more than three hundred years, no longer even shared a border with Turkey. Although the Russian Federation was still a formidable power, it was usually too immersed in its own affairs to pose a serious threat to the Turks. Ankara, meanwhile, succeeded in forming cordial relations with the Soviet successor states bordering Turkey—Azerbaijan, Armenia and Georgia—as well as with the other former Soviet republics. Even though relations with Armenia were often strained because of historical animosities exacerbated by current issues, the threat from this former Soviet republic did not even come close to that posed by a bordering antagonistic superpower.

Turkey's security environment to the southeast also looked better in the post–cold war period. Its Middle Eastern neighbors such as Syria, Iran, and Iraq had lost much of their financing from the Soviet Union and were considerably weakened. Iraq's military apparatus had been heavily damaged by the decade-long war with Iran and the subsequent Persian Gulf War while its economy had been ravaged by the United Nations sanctions imposed since 1991. Syria, although still hostile toward Turkey, lost the considerable amount of military and economic assistance it had received from the Soviet Union, and although Iran and Turkey competed as to which one would wield greater influence in the former Soviet republics of Central Asia, they were not particularly hostile toward each other in their rivalry.

Not all threats to security had been lifted, however. In fact, the most serious one, an internal threat, emanated from the war that the secessionist PKK was waging against the government forces in the southeastern region of the country. Furthermore, tensions with Greece often created potential threats to security; Turkey's relations with its Middle Eastern neighbors were far from friendly; and the Russian Federation was still a considerable regional power whose interests sometimes clashed with Ankara's. In the post–cold war period, however, Turkey's military concerns were less severe than they had been during the preceding seventy years. As such, the conditions prevailing at this time were conducive to shifting resources to the economic arena.

THE PROMINENCE OF ECONOMIC OBJECTIVES

Based on Kenneth Waltz's argument that a decrease in military worries allows the state to focus on its technological and economic successes and failures and replaces military competition with economic competition, another expectation was that in the post–cold war period, Turkish policymakers would have the time and resources to focus on accomplishing such economic objectives as growth and development.[3] Furthermore, in the current era of enhanced interdependence, they would increasingly employ economic instruments in achieving foreign policy goals.

During the first major international crisis of the post–cold war period, the Persian Gulf War, however, political and military considerations, not economic ones, drove Ankara's behavior. Turkey was one of the first countries to ally with the United States-led coalition against Iraq. Its most important role in the coalition was to shut off the pipeline that transported Iraqi oil through Turkish territory, thus enabling the successful implementation of the sanctions imposed on Iraq by the United Nations. Although sanctions are considered to be an economic instrument, Turkey also supported the allied coalition militarily, stationing 100,000 troops near the Iraqi border and allowing the allied forces to use the Incirlik Air Base for military operations. Ankara was motivated by political objectives in undertaking these actions. At a time of increased uncertainty about what role Turkey would play in the emerging international system, Turkish policymakers, especially President Turgut Özal, wanted to demonstrate Turkey's continued strategic importance to the United States and Western Europe. The Gulf War was thus viewed as the perfect opportunity to establish Turkey as an indispensable Western ally in the volatile Middle East.

The fact that economic considerations did not come into play can be illustrated by the significant economic losses Turkey accrued during the Persian Gulf War and its aftermath. Just the shutting off of the oil pipeline resulted in lost revenues of $500 million annually. Iraq had been one of Turkey's most important trading partners prior to the war, and the lost trade with Baghdad as well as the decreased commerce with the rest of the Middle East cost Turkey $9 billion just in the two years following the war.[4] Although the United States attempted to compensate Ankara for these losses (by, for example, increasing the amount of security assistance, extending additional trade benefits, doubling the value of its textile quota, and granting the Turkish government $282 million in additional military and economic assistance for 1991), the net result of the Persian Gulf War was a severe setback for the Turkish economy.[5]

Despite these significant economic losses, many politicians considered Turkey's behavior during the war to be a success because the Americans had seen that Turkey was an important strategic ally even in the absence of a Soviet threat. As a result, Turkish-American relations were strengthened in the post–cold war era. The most important basis of this close alliance seemed to be political as Ankara and Washington shared interests in the security arena. As such, they collaborated in such areas as the Middle East peace process and the efforts to reduce Iranian influence in the former Soviet republics in Central Asia and the Caucasus.

Meanwhile, Turkey's relationship with Western Europe focused on the economic sphere for most of the post–cold war period. This was not much of a change from earlier times because Turkish-European relations had been driven by economic considerations since Turkey became an associate member of the European Community in 1964. The announcement in December 1997 in which Prime Minister Mesut Yilmaz declared that Turkey would be halting its political relations with the European Union, however, seemed to show that Ankara would not be focusing its energies on achieving economic goals in the post–cold war era. Western Europe had constituted Turkey's most important economic partner for much of the history of the Turkish Republic. In 1990, for example, 53.1 percent of Turkish exports went to European Community (EC) members.[6] Despite Ankara's efforts to diversify its trading partners (by, for example, forming relations with the Soviet successor states), almost 45 percent of Turkish foreign trade (47.2 percent of exports and 41.8 percent of imports) was still with European Union (EU) members in 1993.[7] Half of the total investment in Turkey in 1991 came from the United Kingdom, Germany, Netherlands, France, and Italy.[8] Furthermore, the booming Turkish tourism industry depended on European tourists, and 2.5 million Turkish workers and their dependents lived in Europe, sending remittances to Turkey—an important source of foreign exchange for the economy. In addition, for most of the cold war period, Turkish policymakers sought to enhance these ties, and one of their most important foreign policy goals was gaining admission into the European Union.

Because of these close economic relations, Ankara quietly endured harsh criticisms and rejections by the Europeans for most of the post–cold war era. European policymakers consistently berated Turkey, criticizing the inadequacy of its democratic institutions, its poor human rights record, its stubborn position in the Cyprus conflict, and the weaknesses of its economy. Although the Europeans constantly demanded that Ankara work on improving these inadequacies, they did not take seriously any of the Turkish requests, which ranged from demands for a greater voice in European affairs to calls for the raising of quotas for Turkish imports into Europe.[9] The Turkish application for full membership in the EC was harshly rejected in 1989; and in March 1997 German Foreign Minister Klaus Kinkel declared that "it [was] clear that Turkey will not become a member of the European Union in the foreseeable future."[10] Because of the importance of Western Europe for the strength and stability of the Turkish economy, however, Turkey endured its black sheep status. When the European Union decided to open membership negotiations with eleven of its twelve applicants in December 1997 (including many former-Eastern bloc countries and Cyprus but excluding Turkey), however, Ankara decided to halt its political contacts with the organization. As such, Turkey announced that it would no longer engage in political discussions with EU members and that it would stop cooperating with EU representatives investigating human rights abuses in Turkey. Although Prime Minister Mesut Yilmaz emphasized that it was political relations and not economic ones that were being halted, the implication was that Turkey would be distancing itself from its longtime allies in all spheres. In announcing this shift in Turkish foreign policy, Yilmaz announced that "Turkey will not be isolated. But nobody should believe that Turkey will be forced to accept some unacceptable formulas just to enter the European Union."[11] He also declared that, rather, Turkey would pursue a "strategic partnership" with the United States.

The one area in which Turkish policymakers did emphasize the economic sphere was the former republics of the Soviet Union. Focusing on economic relations with the Soviet successor states, however, was not a conscious decision by Turkish policymakers but a decision made by default. The early days of the post–cold war period were characterized by the announcement of lofty goals for Turkey in this newly emerging foreign policy arena. In widely publicized speeches, such prominent politicians as President Süleyman Demirel announced that Turkey would act as a "model" of a secular, democratic, and free-market-oriented state for the former Soviet republics. As such, it would become an important bridge, linking these newly independent states and the West. The expectation was that this role would provide the potential for Turkey to emerge as a regional leader in the new international system.

Ankara, however, faced a number of constraints in its efforts to become actively involved in the region. The leadership role it craved was challenged by Iran (which spent considerable resources to advocate an alternative, Islamic model) and by Russia (which decided that its vital interests lay in remaining involved in the so-called near abroad). In addition, Turkey, itself being a developing country dependent on external assistance, simply did not have the material resources to be the major source of investment and foreign aid for these former Soviet republics. As a result, Turkish policymakers had to significantly scale back their grandiose political aspirations in the region and settle for developing close economic relations with the Soviet successor states. By the mid-1990s, Turkey's relations with the former Soviet republics focused on the economic arena as countless Turkish companies had operations in these countries. Furthermore, the Black Sea Economic Cooperation zone became one of the most important aspects of Turkish foreign policy in the region.

Contrary to many expectations, therefore, Turkish policymakers did not shift their emphases from political and military considerations to economic objectives. They also did not abandon political and military instruments in favor of economic ones. In fact, attempting to demonstrate Turkey's continued strategic importance in the post–cold war era, Ankara relegated economic aspirations to the background during the Persian Gulf War. Furthermore, although it had emphasized economic relations with Western Europe for decades, it took a significant risk by halting political relations with the European Union in December 1997. At this time, Prime Minister Mesut Yilmaz declared that "if the European Union persists in [religious discrimination against Turkey's Muslim population, Turkey] will have no place in such an organization" and instead, would focus its energies on forming a "strategic partnership" with the United States and Israel.[12] Although the proposed cooperation with these countries encompasses the economic, military, and political spheres, the basis for the cooperation is shared security concerns in the Middle East. Far from being relegated to the background, therefore, the security dimension still reigned supreme in the post–cold war era.

REGIONALIZATION OF TURKISH FOREIGN POLICY

A third expectation contended that the end of the cold war—the removal of the Soviet threat from the international arena and the dissolution of the Soviet Union—would lead to Turkey's marginalization from its traditional allies, the United States and Western Europe, who would no longer value it as a strategic ally in the East-West conflict. Accordingly, Turkish policymakers would be compelled to redefine their country's role in the international system and to search for alternative foreign policy partners. Hence, Ankara's foreign policy orientation would shift from one that focused on relations with the West to one that emphasized Turkey's regional alliances. The previous chapters show that there were some alterations in Turkey's foreign policy behavior toward the states in the region, especially the newly independent former Soviet republics and Israel. Furthermore, Turkish policymakers abandoned one of the long-standing pillars of Turkish foreign policy—nonintervention in Middle Eastern affairs—to become actively involved in the region during the Persian Gulf War. Despite these shifts in foreign policy behavior, however, Turkey remained resolutely pro-Western in its foreign policy orientation: the United States continued to be Ankara's most important ally, and membership in the European Union was the most important foreign policy goal for most of the post–cold war period.

Because the Turkish-American relationship had largely been defined by Turkey's role as a front-line state against Soviet expansionism, the early days of the post–cold war era were characterized by uncertainty among observers of Turkish politics as well as politicians regarding how the tremendous changes that occurred in the structure of the international system would affect Turkey's relationship with the United States. Although many Turks worried that Ankara would become a less important ally for Washington in an era of reduced East-West hostilities, the Persian Gulf War of 1990–1991 established Turkey's continued relevance for the Western alliance. In fact, Turkey's loyalty to the United States during the crisis enhanced the already close relationship between the two countries. There was only a brief period in the post–cold war period when Turkish-American relations were threatened. This occured during the year (June 1996 to July 1997) that the pro-Islamic, anti-Western Welfare Party was in office. While prime minister, the leader of the Welfare Party, Necmettin Erbakan managed to alter Turkish foreign policy behavior in such a way that Turkey's commitment to the United States was questioned by both Turkish and American scholars and politicians.

Erbakan had campaigned for an end to interest rates, called for a jihad (holy war) against Jerusalem, and had claimed that he would withdraw Turkey from NATO to form an "Islamic NATO" if he were elected. Although he did not take such drastic actions once Welfare became the leading party in the governing coalition, many of his actions and decisions as prime minister questioned the direction of Turkish foreign policy. On his first official foreign visit in August 1996, for example, Erbakan traveled to Iran, openly defying Washington's wishes to isolate Teheran, and signed a $20 billion agreement for Turkey to buy natural gas from Iran. A few months later, he visited Colonel Muammar al-Qaddafi of Libya and declared that Libya, rather than being a terrorist state, was actually a victim of terrorism. Many of Erbakan's activities during the one year he served as prime minister were not only troubling to American state officials but also to Turkey's secular military establishment.

Although Erbakan was in office for a brief period of time and was operating under a number of significant constraints, he succeeded in altering Turkish foreign policy quite drastically during this time. A variety of domestic developments, however, had led to the rise of the Welfare Party and the subsequent alterations in foreign policy. The economic liberalization reforms adopted by the Turkish government in 1980 contributed to a significant worsening of the distribution of income and resulted in the proliferation of poor and disfranchised groups who, extremely dissatisfied with the mainstream political process, were eager to support such alternative movements as the PKK and the Welfare Party. In addition, the desire of the 1980 military regime to suppress leftist tendencies in society by allowing right-wing Islamist groups to function, as well as the entry of capital from such Islamic countries as Iran and Saudi Arabia into the Turkish economy during this decade, led to the strengthening of religious forces in society. Erbakan and his followers were able to capitalize on these various tendencies to establish the Welfare Party as an honest, socially conscious alternative to the status quo. Meanwhile, systemic factors also contributed to the Welfare Party's rise to power in Turkey. The party's arguments that violence was being tolerated by the

West against Muslim populations in conflicts that had arisen in the post–cold war period (such as in Bosnia-Herzegovina and Nagorno-Karabakh) because Muslims, not Christians, were the victims in these conflicts were believed by many Turks already wary of the Western world's racist and discriminatory tendencies. Furthermore, the harsh criticisms against Turkey as well as the rejection of Ankara's desire to be accepted into the European Union prompted many to give credence to Welfare's contention that Turkey's rightful place in the world was with the countries of the Islamic world. At a time of great uncertainty in international politics, many Turks were eager to welcome a charismatic leader who was asserting that their country would become a regional leader in the new international order, even if this entailed changing course and embracing Turkey's eastern and Islamic roots.

Even though Erbakan did succeed in shifting Turkey's foreign policy behavior during the time that he was prime minister, he was not able to alter the country's foreign policy orientation. The Welfare Party was in office for too brief a period of time to bring about any long-term changes to the direction of foreign policy. More important, Turkey's staunchly secular and pro-Western military apparatus acted as a major constraint on Erbakan's behavior, making it very clear that they would not be reluctant to intervene should its leaders feel that the actions of the Welfare Party threatened Turkey's stability, security, secular character, and Western foreign policy orientation. Senior military officials criticized Erbakan's trips to Libya and Iran and made military decisions without consulting him (such as signing a military accord with Israel and staging an offensive against the Kurdish guerrillas in northern Iraq).[13] As such, they prompted Erbakan to tone down his anti-Western rhetoric and forced the party to become more moderate in its foreign policy views. The military establishment also clashed with Erbakan's government over several domestic issues. They demanded, for example, that they curb religious organizations and restrict the operation of private Koran schools. Because Erbakan refused to compromise on these issues, the generals issued strong public statements condemning the prime minister and his government. These statements "escalated to the point that they seemed to imply the threat of direct action against" the government.[14] Consequently, Erbakan yielded to the military's pressure and resigned as prime minister on June 18, 1997. At the time of his resignation, however, Erbakan was not expecting to be pushed out of the political arena. He anticipated that President Süleyman Demirel would ask Deputy Prime Minister and Foreign Minister Tansu Çiller to form a government, and that his resignation would merely lead to a reorganization of the government.[15] Erbakan also hoped that new elections would be called as early as October 1997 and that the Welfare Party would win these elections with enough votes that it would be able to form a government without a coalition partner. President Demirel, however, asked Mesut Yilmaz, the leader of the Motherland Party, to form the next government, and, after winning the support of a broad range of parties, Yilmaz became prime minister on June 30, 1997.

Prime Minister Yilmaz was quick to reestablish Turkey's credentials as a secular state and close American ally. During a trip to the United States in December 1997, he emphasized the importance Ankara was attaching to its alliance with Washington, especially in view of Turkey's determination to halt political relations with the European Union. In early 1998, forming a "strategic partnership" with the United States was Turkey's most important foreign policy objective. At this time, the United States was as important an ally for Turkey as it had been at the height of the cold war.

Meanwhile, relations with Western Europe were much more strained during the post–cold war period than they had been in earlier periods. Turkish-European relations had deteriorated considerably in the 1980s as a result of the Europeans' reproach of the 1980 military coup in Turkey and of the human rights abuses committed by the subsequent military regime. Ties had improved slightly by the time that Ankara applied for full membership in the European Union in 1987, but the 1989 rejection of this application once again hurt relations. Because the Turkish economy had achieved impressive growth rates as a result of the 1980 free-market reforms, the rejection of Turkey's application was seen as a rebuff of the country's culture and religion. Already anxious about the role their country would play in the emerging international system, many Turkish scholars, politicians, and members of the public believed that the Europeans wanted to oust Turkey from Western European institutions. Despite the often difficult state of Turkish-European relations in the post–cold war era, Western Europe remained an important part of Turkey's foreign policy agenda for most of this period. It was not until December 1997 that a major shift in orientation occurred when, as discussed earlier, Prime Minister Yilmaz announced that Turkey would be halting its political relations with the European Union and focusing its foreign policy on the United States, Israel, and the Soviet successor states in Central Asia and the Caucasus.

The shift from a strictly Western foreign policy orientation to a more regionally based one started several years before this decision was announced. Soon after the disintegration of the Soviet Union, Turkish policymakers started establishing relations with the newly independent Soviet successor states. At first, their involvement in the region was driven by rather lofty objectives, but a number of internal and external impediments constrained

Ankara's foreign policy behavior in the region. These included an economy that was too unstable to be the major supplier of foreign assistance for the Turkic republics of Central Asia and the Caucasus, and challenges by the Russians and the Iranians for dominance in the region. In addition, the former Soviet republics themselves were not willing to form alliances with Turkey to the exclusion of all others. Despite such constraints, however, Turkey became actively involved in the region. Even though the strongest relations were economic ones, Turkey's extensive engagement in the region constituted a shift in foreign policy. During the cold war period, Ankara had been very reluctant to forge relations with the peoples of Central Asia and the Caucasus (despite the prevalence of ethnic, linguistic, and cultural ties) because it feared upsetting the Soviets. This region, however, became an important foreign policy partner for Turkey after the removal of the Soviet threat. In announcing Turkey's foreign policy directives in December 1997, Prime Minister Yilmaz declared that Turkey had "very close relations with the Turkic republics of the Caucasus and Central Asia" and thus "[would] not be isolated" even if it divested from Western Europe.[16]

The development of ties with the former Soviet republics is not the only evidence that supports the contention that Turkish foreign policy behavior became more regional in the cold war era. During this period, Ankara's actions toward the Middle East also showed some changes from earlier times. One of the main pillars of Turkish foreign policy from 1960 until 1990 was nonintervention in the regional affairs of the turbulent Middle East region. Turkish policymakers departed from this pattern of behavior during the Persian Gulf War, however, by aligning Turkey closely with the United States-led coalition against the Iraqi invasion of Kuwait. Turkey's shutting off of the Iraqi oil pipeline contributed to the success of the United Nations' sanctions on Iraq, and its actions in the Gulf War made Turkey a central player in Middle Eastern affairs. Furthermore, although Turkey had attempted to balance its relations with the Arabs and the Israelis during much of the cold war period, it formed a close strategic relationship with Jerusalem in the mid-1990s. This relationship encompassed the military, political, and economic arenas. Israel agreed, for example, to modernize and upgrade Turkish weapons technologies and the two countries engaged in joint military exercises. Military maneuvers carried out in January 1998 (to increase the efficiency of search-and-rescue operations) constituted the first joint exercise between the Israeli and Turkish navies and the American Sixth Fleet. Despite the heavy criticisms by the Syrians and Egyptians, Operation Reliant Mermaid showed that the Turkish-Israeli military alliance was real and would likely be enhanced in the future. The security relationship between Ankara and Jerusalem was augmented by growing economic ties: the two countries signed a free-trade agreement in March 1996, and hundreds of thousands of Israeli tourists poured hard currency into the Turkish economy every year.

Although Turkish foreign policy was directed almost exclusively at the Western world during the cold war period, the changes in the structure of the international system in the post–cold war period prompted Turkish policymakers to pursue a more balanced foreign policy during this time. Without a looming Soviet threat, they were able to forge relations with the Soviet successor states, especially in Central Asia and the Caucasus. The Black Sea Economic Cooperation zone—a Turkish initiative for enhanced regional cooperation—promised to increase trade with countries surrounding the Black Sea, and for the first time in decades, Turkey could count as allies countries with which it shared ethnic, linguistic, and religious ties. Furthermore, Ankara became actively involved in the Middle East region (from which it had kept its distance since the 1950s) by assuming an important role in the Persian Gulf War. The military alliance formed with Israel connected it even further to the region. As such, Turkey's foreign policy arena had many more partners in the post–cold war period than it had during the previous fifty years. Despite the development of close relations with regional foreign policy partners, however, Ankara's foreign policy orientation was strictly Western: the United States was its most important ally and the relationships with regional partners were valued not only for themselves but also for their ability to enhance Turkish-American ties.

The way states behave toward other states—the decisions they make and the actions they take—results from a plethora of factors. Despite the multiplicity and complexity of factors that contribute to foreign policy decision-making, most of the literature on foreign policy analysis has focused on two major approaches: the psychological-perceptual school of thought and the bureaucratic-organizational one. The psychological-perceptual approach (developed by Snyder, Bruck, and Sapin and adopted by many others) defines the state as the decision-makers and characterizes foreign policy decisions as these actors' responses to their perceptions of reality.[17] Overemphasizing the psychological environment to the exclusion of the operational one, this perspective leaves many questions unanswered (such as why a change in leadership does not always lead to a change in behavior). Meanwhile, the bureaucratic-organizational approach characterizes the state as a cluster of organizations and asserts that foreign policy decisions arise after multiple actors with different objectives engage in a process of extensive bargaining.[18] This perspective, however, is only applicable to industrialized countries.

Consequently, neither of these approaches seems sufficient to explain foreign policy decision-making in the current international system in which the global environment is a crucial component of foreign policy decision-making. As James Rosenau pointed out in his critique of the state of foreign policy analysis, these prominent approaches in the field do not take into account the changing realities of the world today: enhanced interdependence among actors, increased relevance of economics to foreign policy, and the erosion of the distinction between domestic and external issues.[19] This examination of Turkish foreign policy thus focused on an international political economy perspective that recognizes that the global environment, consisting of core, periphery, and semi-periphery production and exchange relations as well as a structure of polarity and military power, is one factor that shapes the character and behavior of states.[20] The external environment, however, is not the only determinant of foreign policy. Rather, domestic social, political, and economic structures also contribute to determining a state's foreign policies.

Perhaps the most striking conclusion is that despite significant changes in the international system as well as in the internal environment (i.e., shifts in political institutions and decision-making structures as well as economic capabilities), Turkish foreign policy maintained a great degree of continuity in the cold war and post–cold war periods. The pro-Western policies instituted in the aftermath of World War II were still valued, and the United States was still Turkey's most important ally. The post–cold war period, however, also brought a new element to Turkish foreign policy—an element of uncertainty. Although Ankara remained staunchly pro-Western in its foreign policy orientation, there were many questions regarding the direction of Turkish foreign policy in the future. In the post–cold war period, there was a higher degree of dissent among foreign policy elites about Turkey's role in the world as well as disagreement as to how the country's political institutions would evolve in coming years. Furthermore, the most important cleavage concerned the secular or the Islamic character of the Turkish state.

Thus, finally, a number of questions remain to be answered in the future. Will an Islamist party rise from the ashes of the Welfare Party to lead the country, thereby shifting its foreign policy toward one that emphasizes Turkey's relations with Islamic countries? Will the military establishment—the ultimate arbiters of Turkey's foreign policy orientation—maintain its prominent position in the state apparatus? Will succeeding generations of military leaders continue the tradition of promoting a pro-Western, secular Turkey or will the alterations in society be reflected in the armed forces? How will Turkish-European relations evolve in the current atmosphere of hostility and mistrust? Will the former Soviet republics in Central Asia and the Caucasus replace Western European countries as Turkey's most important trading partners?

NOTES

1. See, for example, Dankwart A. Rustow, *Turkey: America's Forgotten Ally* (New York: Council on Foreign Relations Press, 1987) or Udo Steinbach, "The European Community, the United States, the Middle East, and Turkey," *Politics in the Third Turkish Republic* (Boulder, Colo.: Westview Press, 1994).

2. James A. Caporaso, Charles F. Hermann, Charles W. Kegley, Jr., James N. Rosenau, and Dina A. Zinnes, "The Comparative Study of Foreign Policy: Perspectives on the Future," *International Studies Notes of the International Studies Association* 13.2 (Spring 1987): 33.

3. Kenneth Waltz, "The Emerging Structure of International Politics," *International Security* 18 (Fall 1993): 44–79.

4. Ian O. Lesser, "Bridge of Barrier? Turkey and the West After the Cold War," *Turkey's New Geopolitics*, eds. Graham E. Fuller and Ian O. Lesser with Paul B. Henze and J. F. Brown (Boulder, Colo.: Westview Press, 1993), 125.

5. Sabri Sayari, "Turkey: The Changing European Security Environment and the Gulf Crisis," *Middle East Journal* 46.1 (Winter 1992): 19.

6. Canan Balkir, "Turkey and the European Community: Foreign Trade and Direct Foreign Investment in the 1980s," *Turkey and Europe*, eds. Canan Balkir and Allan M. Williams (London: Pinter Publishers, 1993), 137 (Statistical Appendix, Table G).

7. Meltem Müftüler, "Turkish Economic Liberalization and European Integration," *Middle Eastern Studies* 31.1 (January 1995): 89.

8. Balkir, "Turkey and the European Community," 125.

9. Edward Mortimer, "The Black Sheep," *Financial Times* (11 November 1997).

10. Stephen Kinzer, "Europeans Shut the Door on Turkey's Membership in Union," *New York Times* (27 March 1997): A13.

11. Stephen Kinzer, "Turkey, Rejected, Will Freeze Ties to European Union," *New York Times* (15 December 1997): A3.

12. Kinzer, "Turkey, Rejected, Will Freeze Ties to European Union," A3.

13. Stephen Kinzer, "Islamic Premier Steps Down in Turkey Under Army Pressure," *New York Times* (19 June 1997): A1.

14. Kinzer, "Islamic Premier Steps Down in Turkey Under Army Pressure," A1.

15. Stephen Kinzer, "Turkey's Prime Minister, About to Step Down, Defends Record," *New York Times* (17 June 1997): A6.

16. Kinzer, "Turkey, Rejected, Will Freeze Ties to European Union," A3.

17. See, for example, Richard C. Snyder, et al. "The Decision-Making Approach to the Study of International Politics," *International Politics and Foreign Policy*, revised edition, ed. James N. Rosenau (New York: Free Press, 1969), 199–206.

18. See, for example, Graham T. Allison, *Essence of Decision: Explaining the Cuban Missile Crisis* (Boston: Little, Brown, 1971).

19. James N. Rosenau, "Introduction: New Directions and Recurrent Questions in the Comparative Study of Foreign Policy," *New Directions in the Study of Foreign Policy*, eds. Charles F. Hermann, Charles W. Kegley, Jr., and James N. Rosenau (Boston: Allen and Unwin, 1987), 3.

20. Bruce E. Moon, "Political Economy Approaches to the Comparative Study of Foreign Policy," *New Directions in the Study of Foreign Policy* (Boston: Allen and Unwin, 1987), 33–52.

Selected Bibliography

Abramowitz, Morton I. "Dateline Ankara: Turkey After Özal." *Foreign Policy* 91 (Summer 1993): 164–182.

Ahmad, Feroz. *The Making of Modern Turkey.* London: Routledge, 1993.

———. *The Turkish Experiment in Democracy: 1950–1975.* London: C. Hurst, 1977.

Akder, Halis. "Turkey: Country Profile," *Human Development Report 1990.* Ankara: United Nations Development Programme, 1990.

Arbatov, Alexei G. "Russian Policy Priorities for the 1990s." *Russian Security after the Cold War,* eds. T. P. Johnson and S. Miller, pp. 1–41. Washington, D.C.: Brasseys, 1994.

Art, Robert J. "A Defensible Defense: America's Grand Strategy after the Cold War." *International Security* 15.4 (Spring 1992): 5–53.

Avcioğlu, Doğan. *Turklerin Tarihi: Birinci Kitap, Ikinci Kitap.* Istanbul: Tekin Yayin Dagitim San. ve Tic. Ltd. Sti., 1995.

Balkir, Canan, and Allan M. Williams, eds. *Turkey and Europe.* London: Pinter Publishers, 1993.

Ball, George W. *The Past Has Another Pattern: Memoirs.* New York: W.W. Norton and Co., 1982.

Banks, Arthur S., Alan J. Day, and Thomas C. Muller, eds. *Political Handbook of the World: 1995–1996.* Binghamton, N.Y.: CSA Publications, 1997.

Barkey, Henri J., ed. *The Politics of Economic Reform in the Middle East.* New York: St. Martin's Press, 1992.

———, ed. *Reluctant Neighbor: Turkey's Role in the Middle East.* Washington, D.C.: U.S. Institute of Peace Press, 1996.

Bilge, A. Suat. *"Birinci Kibris Uyusmazliği ve Turkiye-Sovyetler Birliği Munasebetleri" Olaylarla Turkiye Dis Politikasi.* Ankara: Siyasal Kitapevi, 1993.

Birand, Mehmet Ali. *Turkiye'nin Ortak Pazar Macerasi, 1959–85.* Istanbul: Milliyet Yayinlari, 1985.

Bohlen, Celestine. "In a Search for 'Turkishness,' Turks Reveal Their Diversity." *New York Times* (18 May 1996): A1.

———. "Islamic Party Walking a Tightrope in Turkey." *New York Times* (12 July 1996): A8.

Bölükbaşi, Süha. "Ankara's Baku-Centered Transcaucasia Policy: Has It Failed?" *Middle East Journal* 51.1 (Winter 1997): 80–94.

Bozer, Ali. "Turkish Foreign Policy in the Changing World." *Mediterranean Quarterly* (Summer 1990): 15–25.

Caporaso, James A., Charles F. Hermann, Charles W. Kegley, Jr., James N. Rosenau, and Dina A. Zinnes. "The Comparative Study of Foreign Policy: Perspectives on the Future." *International Studies Notes of the International Studies Association* 13.2 (Spring 1987): 32–46.

"Commission Opinion on the Application by the Republic of Cyprus for Membership" (Brussels: Commission of the European Communities, June 1993).

"Commission Opinion on Turkey's Request for Accession to the Community" (Brussels: Commission of the European Communities, December 1989).

Coşkun, Süleyman. *Turkiyede Politika: 1920–1995.* Istanbul: CemYayinevi, 1995.

Deringil, Selim. *Turkish Foreign Policy During the Second World War: An "Active" Neutrality.* Cambridge: Cambridge University Press, 1989.

Dessouki, Ali E. Hillal, and Bahgat Korany. *The Foreign Policies of Arab States,* 2nd ed. Boulder, Colo.: Westview Press, 1991.

Dmytryshyn, Basil, and Frederick Cox. *The Soviet Union and the Middle East—A Documentary Record of Afghanistan, Iran and Turkey 1917–1985.* Princeton, N.J.: Kingston Press, 1987.

Dodd, C. H. *The Crisis of Turkish Democracy.* Huntingdon, United Kingdom: Eothen Press, 1983.

———, ed. *Turkish Foreign Policy: New Prospects.* Huntingdon, United Kingdom: Eothen Press, 1992.

Dowden, Richard. "A Disaster That Hasn't Quite Happened." *The Economist* (8 June 1996): survey 8.

"The Elusive Golden Apple: The War That Cannot Speak Its Name." *The Economist* (8 June 1996): 3–18.

Eralp, Atila, Muharrem Tunay, and Birol A. Yeşilada, eds. *The Political and Socioeconomic Transformation of Turkey.* Westport, Conn.: Praeger, 1993.

Erlanger, Steven. "New Turkish Chief's Muslim Tour Stirs U.S. Worry." *New York Times* (10 August 1996): A2.

Fuller, Graham E., and Ian O. Lesser with Paul B. Henze and J. F. Brown, eds. *Turkey's New Geopolitics.* Boulder, Colo.: Westview Press, 1993.

Geyikdaği, Mehmet Yasar. *Political Parties in Turkey: The Role of Islam.* New York: Praeger, 1984.

Gilpin, Robert. *The Political Economy of International Relations.* Princeton, N.J.: Princeton University Press, 1987.

Goldgeier, James M., and Michael McFaul. "A Tale of Two Worlds: Core and Periphery in the Post–Cold War Era." *International Organization* 46.2 (Spring 1992): 467–491.

Gruen, George E. "Turkey's Emerging Regional Role." *American Foreign Policy Interests* 17.2 (April 1995): 13–24.

Gunter, Michael M. *The Kurds in Turkey: A Political Dilemma*. Boulder, Colo.: Westview Press, 1990.

Hale, William. *The Political and Economic Development of Modern Turkey*. New York: St. Martin's Press, 1981.

Harris, George S. *Turkey: Coping with Crisis*. Boulder, Colo.: Westview Press, 1985.

Henze, Paul B. *Turkey: Toward the Twenty-First Century*. Santa Monica: RAND Publications, 1992.

Heper, Metin. *Historical Dictionary of Turkey*. Metuchen, N.J.: Scarecrow Press, 1994.

———, ed. *Politics in the Third Turkish Republic*. Boulder, Colo.: Westview Press, 1994.

Hershlag, Z. Y. *Turkey: The Challenge of Growth*. Leiden: E. J. Brill, 1968.

Holsti, K. J. *International Politics: A Framework for Analysis*. 3d ed. Englewood Cliffs, N.J.: Prentice-Hall, 1977.

———. *International Politics: A Framework for Analysis*. 6th ed. Englewood Cliffs, N.J.: Prentice-Hall, 1992.

Hyman, Anthony. "Moving Out of Moscow's Orbit: The Outlook for Central Asia." *International Affairs* 69 (April 1993): 288–304.

Jensen, Lloyd. *Explaining Foreign Policy*. Englewood Cliffs, N.J.: Prentice-Hall, 1982.

Karpat, Kemal. *Turkey's Foreign Policy in Transition: 1950–1974*. Leiden: E. J. Brill, 1975.

Kazgan, Gülten. *Ekonomide Dışa Açık Büyüme*. Istanbul: Altin Kitaplar Yayinevi, 1988.

Keohane, Robert O, and Joseph S. Nye. *Power and Interdependence*, 2nd ed. Glenview, Ill.: Scott, Foresman and Company, 1989.

Kiliç, Altemur, *Turkey and the World*. Washington, D.C.: World Affairs Press, 1959.

Kiliçbay, Ahmet. *Türk Ekonomisinin Son 10 Yili*. Istanbul: Milliyet Yayinlari, 1991.

———. "Meeting U.S. Envoy, Turkish Premier Takes Pro-Arab Stance." *New York Times* (3 July 1996): A13.

Kinzer, Stephen. "Europeans Shut the Door on Turkey's Membership in Union." *New York Times* (27 March 1997): A13.

———. "In Defense of Secularism, Turkish Army Warns Rulers." *New York Times* (2 March 1997): A10.

———. "Islamic Premier Steps Down in Turkey Under Army Pressure." *New York Times* (19 June 1997): A1.

———. "The Islamist Who Runs Turkey, Delicately." *New York Times Magazine* (23 February 1997): 30.

———. "Turkey Finds European Union Door Slow to Open." *New York Times* (23 February 1997): A3.

———. "Turkey, Rejected, Will Freeze Ties to European Union." *New York Times* (15 December 1997): A3.

———. "Turkey's Prime Minister, About to Step Down, Defends Record." *New York Times* (17 June 1997): A6.

———. "Turks, Opposing U.S., Urge Iraq to Take Control of Kurdish Area." *New York Times* (21 September 1997): A1.

———. "Turks Reinvent Their World." *New York Times* (28 December 1997): sec. 4, 6.

Lebow, Richard Ned, and Janice Gross Stein. *We All Lost the Cold War.* Princeton, N.J.: Princeton University Press, 1994.

Mango, Andrew. *Turkey: Challenge of a New Role.* Westport, Conn.: Praeger (with The Center for Strategic and International Studies), 1994.

Manisali, Erol, ed. *Turkey's Place in the Middle East.* Istanbul: Middle East Business and Banking Publications, 1989.

Mastny, Vojtech, and R. Craig Nation, eds. *Turkey Between East and West: New Challenges for a Rising Regional Power.* Boulder, Colo.: Westview Press, 1996.

McCoy, Donald R. *The Presidency of Harry S. Truman.* Lawrence: University Press of Kansas, 1984.

Moon, Bruce E. "Political Economy Approaches to the Comparative Study of Foreign Policy." *New Directions in the Study of Foreign Policy,* eds. Charles F. Hermann, Charles W. Kegley, Jr., and James N. Rosenau, pp. 33–52. Boston: Allen and Unwin, 1987.

Mortimer, Edward. "The Black Sheep," *Financial Times* (11 November 1997).

Müftüler, Meltem. "Turkish Economic Liberalization and European Integration." *Middle Eastern Studies* 31.1 (January 1995): 85–98.

Okcun, A. Gündüz. "Turkiye Iktisat Kongresi, 1923-Izmir." Ph.D. diss., Ankara University: Political Science, 1968.

Öniş, Ziya. "Turkey in the Post–Cold War Era: In Search of Identity." *Middle East Journal* 49.1 (Winter 1995): 48–68.

Oye, Kenneth A., Robert J. Lieber, and Donald Rothchild, eds. *Eagle Resurgent? The Reagan Era in American Foreign Policy.* Boston: Little, Brown and Company Limited, 1987.

Pipes, Daniel. "A New Axis: The Emerging Turkish-Israeli Entente." *Turkish Times* (1 February 1998): 4.

Pomfret, Richard. "The Economic Cooperation Organization: Current Status and Future Prospects." *Europe-Asia Studies* 49.4 (1997): 657–667.

Pope, Hugh. "Turkey's Military Orders Erbakan to Curb Islamists." *Wall Street Journal* (3 March 1997): A1.

Powell, Robert. "Guns, Butter and Anarchy." *American Political Science Review* 87.1 (March 1993): 115–127.

Robins, Philip. "Between Sentiment and Self-interest: Turkey's Policy Towards Azerbaijan and the Central Asian States." *Middle East Journal* 47.4 (Autumn 1993): 593–610.

———. "The Overlord State: Turkish Policy and the Kurdish Issue." *International Affairs* 69.4 (1993): 657–676.

————. *Turkey and the Middle East.* New York: Council on Foreign Relations Press, 1991.

Rosenau, James N. "Introduction: New Directions and Recurrent Questions in the Comparative Study of Foreign Policy." *New Directions in the Study of Foreign Policy,* eds., Charles F. Hermann, Charles W. Kegley, Jr., and James N. Rosenau, 1–12. Boston: Allen and Unwin, 1987.

Rothstein, Robert L. *The Weak in the World of the Strong: The Developing Countries in the International System.* New York: Columbia University Press, 1977.

Rouleau, Eric. "The Challenges to Turkey." *Foreign Affairs* 72 (November/December 1993): 110–126.

————. "Turkey: Beyond Atatürk." *Foreign Policy* (Summer 1996): 70–87.

Rustow, Dankwart A. *Turkey: America's Forgotten Ally.* New York: Council on Foreign Relations Press, 1987.

Safire, William. "The Second Front." *New York Times* (1 November 1990): A29.

Sander, Oral. "Turkey and the Turkic World." *Central Asian Survey* 13.1 (1994): 37–44.

Sayari, Sabri. "Turkey: The Changing European Security Environment and the Gulf Crisis." *Middle East Journal* 46.1 (Winter 1992): 9–21.

Schemann, Serge. "Unusual Naval Alliance Shows Off, and Arabs Glare." *New York Times* (8 January 1998): A1.

Schick, Irvin C., and Ertuğrul Ahmet Tonak, eds. *Turkey in Transition: New Perspectives.* New York: Oxford University Press, 1987.

Sezer, Duygu Bazoğlu. "Turkey's Grand Strategy Facing a Dilemma." *International Spectator* 27 (January-March 1992): 17–32.

————. "View from Turkey: Turkey's New Security Environment, Nuclear Weapons and Proliferation." *Comparative Strategy* 14 (1995): 149–172.

Statement by His Excellency Ismail Cem, Minister of Foreign Affairs of the Republic of Turkey at the 52nd Session of the General Assembly. New York: Permanent Mission of Turkey to the United Nations, 26 September 1997.

Talbott, Strobe. *Khruschev Remembers: The Last Testament.* Boston: Little, Brown, 1974.

"Tomorrow's Empires." *The Economist* (21 September 1991): 15–16.

"Turkey." *Trends in Developing Economies 1995.* New York: Oxford University Press, 1995.

"Turkey Declines U.S. Economic Assistance." Press Release of the Turkish Embassy, Washington, D.C., 6 June 1996.

"Turkish Parliament Passes Sweeping Democratic Reforms." Press Release of the Turkish Embassy, Washington, D.C., 24 July 1995.

Vali, Ferenc A. *Bridge Across the Bosphorus: The Foreign Policy of Turkey.* Baltimore: Johns Hopkins University Press, 1971.

Waltz, Kenneth. "The Emerging Structure of International Politics." *International Security* 18 (Fall 1993): 44–79.

————. *Foreign Policy and Democratic Politics.* Boston: Little, Brown, 1967.

Wilkens, Katherine A. "Turkey: Emerging Regional Power or State in Crisis?" *Great Decisions 1998*, pp. 75–85. New York: Foreign Policy Association, 1998.

Winrow, Gareth. *Turkey in Post-Soviet Central Asia.* London: Royal Institute of International Affairs, 1995.

Zurcher, Erik J. *Turkey: A Modern History.* London: I. B. Tauris, 1993.

Index

About the Author

YASEMIN ÇELIK is Adjunct Professor in the Department of Social Science, Fashion Institute of Technology, State University of New York, New York City, where she teaches comparative politics.

ISBN 0-275-96590-2

90000>

EAN

9 780275 965907

HARDCOVER BAR CODE